The Ultimate Slow Cooker Cookbook

800 Easy and Healthy Slow Cooker Recipes for Beginners and Advanced Users

Marta Lenius

Dr Janda Hunde

© Copyright 2020 Marta Lenius and Dr Janda Hunde- All Rights Reserved.

In no way is it legal to reproduce, duplicate, or transmit any part of this document by either electronic means or in printed format. Recording of this publication is strictly prohibited, and any storage of this material is not allowed unless with written permission from the publisher. All rights reserved.

The information provided herein is stated to be truthful and consistent, in that any liability, regarding inattention or otherwise, by any usage or abuse of any policies, processes, or directions contained within is the solitary and complete responsibility of the recipient reader. Under no circumstances will any legal liability or blame be held against the publisher for any reparation, damages, or monetary loss due to the information herein, either directly or indirectly.

Respective authors own all copyrights not held by the publisher.

Legal Notice:

This book is copyright protected. This is only for personal use. You cannot amend, distribute, sell, use, quote or paraphrase any part of the content within this book without the consent of the author or copyright owner. Legal action will be pursued if this is breached.

Disclaimer Notice:

Please note the information contained within this document is for educational and entertainment purposes only. Every attempt has been made to provide accurate, up-to-date and reliable, complete information. No warranties of any kind are expressed or implied. Readers acknowledge that the author is not engaging in the rendering of legal, financial, medical or professional advice.

By reading this document, the reader agrees that under no circumstances are we responsible for any losses, direct or indirect, which are incurred as a result of the use of information contained within this document, including, but not limited to, errors, omissions, or inaccuracies.

Table of Contents

Introduction	8
Chapter 1: Breakfast & Brunch	**9**
Perfect Cranberry Eggnog Oatmeal	9
Cinnamon Apple Rice	9
Broccoli Ham Casserole	9
Easy Brown Sugar Oatmeal	10
Spinach Cheese Frittata	10
Healthy Strawberry Oatmeal	10
Perfect Breakfast Potatoes	11
Delicious Breakfast Burrito	11
Pumpkin Pie Oatmeal	11
Apple Cranberry Oatmeal	12
Cinnamon Roll Casserole	12
Apple Cinnamon Steel Cut Oatmeal	12
Cranberry Apple French Toast	12
Hearty Pumpkin Spice Oatmeal	13
Hash Brown Breakfast Casserole	13
Healthy Banana Nut Oatmeal	14
Steel Cut Peach Oatmeal	14
Healthy Apple Pie Amaranth Porridge	14
Peanut Butter Banana Oatmeal	15
Breakfast Tater Tot Egg Bake	15
Cauliflower Hash Browns Casserole	15
Carrot Cake Oatmeal	16
Peach Breakfast Oatmeal	16
Cheesy Potatoes	16
Apple Pie Oatmeal	17
Cheesy Grits	17
Breakfast Bread Pudding	17
Rice Raisins Pudding	18
Healthy Whole Grain Porridge	18
Sweet Berry Oatmeal	18
Flavorful Millet Porridge	19
Cinnamon Apple Barley	19
Maple Blueberry Oats	19
Cinnamon Pumpkin Oatmeal	20
Feta Spinach Quiche	20
Healthy Breakfast Casserole	20
Spinach Pepper Omelet	21
Cinnamon Carrot Oatmeal	21
Easy Breakfast Apples	21
Mixed Berry Oatmeal	22
Breakfast Oatmeal Cake	22
Baked Oatmeal	22
Almond Butter Oatmeal	23
Mushroom Cheese Frittata	23
Cheese Herb Frittata	23
Cauliflower Mash	24
Ham Cheese Omelet	24
Veggie Omelet	24
Healthy Veggie Frittata	25
Cheesy Spinach Frittata	25
Chapter 2: Vegetarian & Vegan	**27**
Flavorful Ranch Carrots	27
Delicious Thai Pineapple Curry	27
Asian Vegetarian Tikka Masala	27
Healthy Split Pea Curry	28
Lentil Chickpea Pumpkin Curry	28
Easy Vegan Gumbo	28
Easy Corn Pudding	29
Quinoa Coconut Curry	29
Cauliflower Lentil Sweet Potato Curry	29
Balsamic Brussels Sprouts	30
Broccoli Rice Casserole	30
Rich & Creamy Mac and Cheese	30
Lemon Butter Carrots	31
Creamy Corn	31
Slow Cook Potatoes	31
Vegetable Farro	32
Creamy Cauliflower Mash	32
Cheesy Squash	33
Cheesy Cauliflower Casserole	33
Simple Balsamic Mushrooms	33
Healthy Green Beans	33
Herbed Mushrooms & Onions	34
Honey Milk Corn on the Cob	34
Vegetable Fajita	34
Rosemary Beets	35
Spicy Eggplant Curry	35
Delicious Mediterranean Eggplant	35
Tasty Cheesy Potatoes	36
Creamy Scalloped Potatoes	36
Chickpea Curry	36
Garlic Cauliflower Grits	37
Cheesy Cauliflower Casserole	37
Sweet Potatoes with Pineapple	38
Pecan Cheese Brussels Sprouts	38
Delicious Okra with Tomato	38
Sweet Potatoes Mash	38
Cauliflower Lentil Curry	39
Healthy Tofu Curry	39
Slow Cook Green Beans	39
Butter Ranch Mushrooms	40
Curried Spinach Lentils	40
Parmesan Zucchini	40
Parmesan Squash Casserole	41

Parmesan Potatoes 41
Creamy Potato Corn Chowder 41
Baba Ganoush 42
Bean & Mushrooms 42
Beans & Potatoes 42
Coconut Squash Lentil Curry 43
Coconut Lentil Vegetable Curry 43

Chapter 3: Beans & Grains 44
Baked Beans 44
BBQ Beans 44
Sweet & Tangy Cowboy Beans 44
BBQ Lima Beans 45
Jalapeno Pinto Beans 45
Delicious Hawaiian Beans 45
Healthy Wild Rice 46
Flavorful Herbed Brown Rice 46
Red Beans & Rice 47
Healthy Pumpkin Risotto 47
Tasty Butternut Squash Risotto 47
Parmesan Risotto 48
Mexican Rice 48
Delicious Mexican Quinoa 48
Apple Cinnamon Quinoa 49
Spinach Barley Risotto 49
Cuban Black Beans 49
Tasty Black-Eyed Peas 50
Delicious Refried Beans 50
Apple Cinnamon Buckwheat 50
Vegetarian Burritos 51
Old Fashioned Lima Beans 51
Corn & Lima Beans 51
Classic Saffron Rice 52
Simple Brown Rice 52
Curried Lentil Rice 52
Perfect Spanish Rice 53
Flavors Salsa Rice 53
Vegan Red Bean Rice 53
Basil Chicken Rice 54
Coconut Beans Rice 54
Mix Bean Chili 54
Healthy Walnut Barley 55
Barley Bean Risotto 55
Spinach Risotto 55
Jerk Seasoned Black Beans 56
Italian Rice 56
Herb Lentil Rice Casserole 56
Tasty & Healthy Quinoa 57
Asparagus Barley Risotto 57
Cajun Bean Rice 58
Delicious Shrimp Rice 58

Green Chili Beans 58
Bacon Bean Chowder 59
Delicious Chili Pepper Pinto Beans ... 59
Tasty Peas Rice 59
Slow Cook Black Eyed Peas 60
Parmesan Risotto 60
Quinoa & Oats 60
Curried Lentil Rice 60

Chapter 4: Soup & Stews 62
Flavorful White Chicken Chili 62
Delicious Chicken Noodle Soup 62
Veggie Bean Soup 62
Mexican Chicken Soup 63
Thai Chicken Soup 63
Easy Pumpkin Chili 63
Curried Tomato Soup 64
Curried Coconut Sweet Potato Soup .. 64
Buffalo Chicken Chili 64
Cauliflower Broccoli Cheese Soup 65
Flavors Stuffed Cabbage Soup 65
Cheesy Broccoli Soup 66
Ginger Carrot Soup 66
Hearty Beef Stew 66
Moroccan Chickpea Stew 67
Chicken Veggie Stew 67
Healthy Mushroom Barley Soup 68
Chickpea Stew 68
Flavorful Pork Stew 68
Vegetable Pork Stew 69
Coconut Tomato Carrot Soup 69
Simple Pumpkin Soup 69
Delicious Seafood Stew 70
Tomato Spinach Bean Soup 70
Curried Coconut Pumpkin Soup 70
Spinach Chicken Stew 71
Tasty Chicken Fajita Soup 71
Vegetable Pork Stew 71
Chili Chicken Soup 72
Curried Chicken Soup 72
Zucchini Carrot Chicken Soup 72
Split Pea Soup 73
Italian Tomato Soup 73
Turkey Kale Bean Soup 73
Healthy Tomato Spinach Soup 74
Veggie Red Lentil Soup 74
Creamy Asparagus Soup 74
Broccoli Spinach Soup 75
Sweet Potato Carrot Soup 75
Coconut Carrot Soup 75
Coconut Salmon Stew 76

Sweet Potato Soup 76
Coconut Asparagus Soup 76
Healthy & Creamy Asparagus Soup 77
Ginger Broccoli Soup 77
Easy Cauliflower Leek Soup 77
Creamy Mushroom Soup 78
Squash Apple Soup 78
Delicious Lamb Stew 78
Mushroom Beef Stew 79

Chapter 5: Poultry 80
Delicious Southwest Chicken 80
Flavors Peanut Butter Chicken 80
Easy Salsa Chicken 80
Greek Lemon Chicken 81
Easy Chicken Noodles 81
Orange Chicken 81
Delicious BBQ Chicken 82
Parmesan Chicken Rice 82
Queso Chicken Tacos 82
Easy Mexican Chicken 83
Mustard Mushroom Chicken 83
Herb Chicken Breasts 83
Balsamic Chicken 84
Creamy Chicken Penne 84
Tasty Chicken Fajita Pasta 84
Moist & Juicy Chicken Breast 85
Asian Chicken 85
Flavorful Chicken Casserole 86
Chicken Orzo 86
Garlic Herb Roasted Pepper Chicken . 86
Slow Cook Turkey Breast 87
Simple Chicken & Mushrooms 87
Lemon Herb Chicken 87
Creamy Chicken Curry 88
Taco Chicken 88
Butter Chicken 88
Spicy Chili Chicken 89
Pesto Chicken 89
Rosemary Turkey Breast 89
Garlic Olive Chicken 90
Delicious Chickpea Chicken 90
Balsamic Chicken Breasts 90
Mediterranean Chicken 91
Buffalo Chicken Drumsticks 91
Caribbean Chicken 91
Caesar Chicken 92
Onion Chicken 92
Lemon Pepper Chicken 92
Shredded Chicken 93
Delicious Greek Chicken 93

Chicken Cacciatore 93
Ginger Garlic Broccoli Chicken 94
Tasty Chicken Chili 94
Balsamic Spinach Chicken 94
Curried Chicken Thighs 95
Healthy Cauliflower Chicken 95
Tomatillo Chicken 95
Mexican Chicken Thighs 96
Honey Dijon Mustard Chicken 96
Thai Chicken Wings 96

Chapter 6: Beef, Pork & Lamb 98
Delicious Beef Bean Sloppy Joes 98
Tasty Sriracha Pork Tenderloin 98
Mediterranean Pork Chops 98
Creamy Pork Chops 99
Onion Pork Chops 99
Delicious Sweet Pork Roast 99
Asian Pork Chops 100
Sweet Applesauce Pork Chops 100
Pork Chops with Potatoes 100
Zesty Pulled Pork 101
Delicious Beef Fajitas 101
BBQ Beef Ribs 101
Italian Beef Roast 102
Flavorful Sausage Casserole 102
Beef Noodles 103
Shredded Asian Beef 103
Garlic Beef Shanks 103
Teriyaki Steak 103
Delicious Beef Curry 104
Mushroom Beef Tips 104
Asian Lamb 105
Moroccan Lamb 105
Garlic & Rosemary Lamb 105
Moroccan Lamb Stew 106
Salsa Pork Chops 106
Curried Pork Chops 106
Mexican Flank Steak 107
Braised Beef 107
Artichoke Pepper Beef 107
Italian Beef Roast 108
Olive Feta Beef 108
Olive Artichokes Beef 108
Sriracha Beef 109
Pork with Couscous 109
Spicy Pork 109
Easy Pork Carnitas 110
Orange Pork Carnitas 110
Grapefruit Pork Roast 110
Garlic Tomatoes Chuck Roast 111

Stuffed Bell Peppers	111
Butter Beef	112
Poultry Seasoned Pork Chops	112
Herb Lamb Chops	112
Delicious Beef Stroganoff	113
Taco Beef	113
Salsa Beef	113
Beef Ribs with Sauce	113
Cheesy Taco Casserole	114
Shredded Chili Beef	114
Garlic Chili Lime Shredded Beef	114
Salsa Ground Beef	115
Pulled Beef	115
Asian Sirloin Steak	115
Beef Bean Casserole	116
Butter Steak Bites	116
Sweet & Sour Pork Tenderloin	116
Orange Pork Roast	117
Hawaiian Pork	117
Beef Heart	117
Jalapeno Beef	118
Spicy Green Chili Beef	118
Slow Cook Beef Brisket	119
Balsamic Lamb Chops	119
Apple Butter Pork	119
Creamy Mushroom Pork Chops	120
Thyme Garlic Lamb Chops	120
Apple Pork Loin	120
Spicy Pork Chops	121
Adobo Pulled Pork	121
Delicious Curried Pork	121
Chili Cumin Pork	122
Orange Jalapeno Pork	122
Beef Stew	122
Asian Lamb Stew	123
Pork Chili	123
Beef Ragu	124

Chapter 7: Fish & Seafood 125

Thai Shrimp Rice	125
Caribbean Shrimp	125
Herb Lemon Cod	125
White Fish Fillet with Tomatoes	126
Coconut Fish Curry	126
Louisiana Shrimp	126
Cajun Corn Shrimp	127
BBQ Shrimp	127
Delicious Shrimp Fajitas	127
Spicy Shrimp	128
Healthy Lime Salmon	128
Shrimp Pasta	128

Shrimp Scampi	129
Tasty Shrimp Curry	129
Shrimp Fajita Soup	129
Capers Salmon	129
Easy Cilantro Lime Salmon	130
Creamy Curried Shrimp	130
Herb Flounder Fillet	130
Onion White Fish Fillet	131
Lemon Halibut	131
Garlicky Shrimp	131
Hot Shrimp	132
Easy Lemon Dill Salmon	132
Lemon Garlic Shrimp Curry	132
Shrimp Scallop Stew	133
Salmon Curry	133
Sweet & Spicy Pineapple Tuna	133
Shrimp Chicken Casserole	134
Shrimp Chicken Mushroom Casserole	134
Healthy Seafood Pasta	134
Lemon White Fish Fillet	135
Clam Chowder	135
Salmon Vegetable Chowder	135
Cod Curry	136
Shrimp Curry	136
Delicious Fish Tacos	136
Lime Salmon	137
Delicious Fish Gratin	137
Mango Shrimp Rice	137
Lemon Orange White Fish Fillets	138
Garlic Butter Salmon	138
Tasty Seafood Fondue	138
Lemon Dill White Fish Fillet	139
Marinara Shrimp	139
Shrimp Casserole	139
Asian Salmon	140
BBQ Shrimp	140
Shrimp Grits	140
Honey Salmon	141

Chapter 8: Snacks & Appetizers 142

Chili Cheese Dip	142
Perfect Hamburger Dip	142
Easy Queso Dip	142
Spicy Chili Queso Dip	143
Creamy Corn Dip	143
Flavorful Pizza Dip	143
Mexican Quinoa Dip	143
Buffalo Chicken Dip	144
Perfect Sausage Dip	144
Crab Dip	144

Cheesy Artichoke Dip 145
Artichoke Crab Dip 145
Corn Jalapeno Popper Dip 145
Southwest Spicy Artichoke Dip 146
Slow Cook Salsa 146
Baked Jalapeno Poppers.................. 146
Delicious Bean Dip 147
Perfect Cheesy Bean Dip.................. 147
Salsa Queso Dip 148
Pinto Bean Dip 148
Broccoli Dip 148
Texas Dip..................................... 148
Nacho Dip 149
Cheesy Onion Dip 149
Italian Tomato Dip 149
Crab Shrimp Dip 150
Walnut Crab Dip 150
Navy Bean Dip 150
Classic Salsa................................. 151
Mexican Dip 151

Chapter 9: Desserts.......................... 152
Delicious Apple Crisp 152
Easy Peach Cobbler Cake 152
Strawberry Dump Cake.................... 152
Baked Apples 153
Baked Peaches 153
Delicious Peach Crisp 153
Gingerbread Pudding Cake 153
Healthy Blueberry Cobbler 154
Easy Peach Cobbler 154
Peach Compote 154
Cinnamon Apples 155

Choco Rice Pudding 155
Chocolate Fudge 155
Chocolate Brownies 156
Tasty Cherry Cobbler...................... 156
Pineapple Cherry Dump Cake........... 156
White Chocolate Fudge 157
Applesauce 157
Delicious Bread Pudding 157
Rice Pudding 158
Tapioca Pudding 158
Pecan Caramel Rice Pudding............ 158
Pineapple Tapioca 159
Brown Rice Pudding 159
Coconut Rice Pudding..................... 159
Chia Strawberry Jam 160
Maple Pears 160
Cinnamon Coconut Rice Pudding..... 160
Fruit Compote 160
Pumpkin Pie Pudding 161
Chocolate Almond Fudge................. 161
Delicious Chocolate Cake 161
Fudge Brownies 162
Hot Chocolate 162
Apple Walnut Cake 162
Walnut Peanut Butter Cake 163
Butter Cake 163
Cocoa Almond Butter Brownies 163
Banana Brownies........................... 164
Moist Yogurt Cake 164

Chapter 10: 30-Day Meal Plan 165
Conclusion 167

Introduction

Advanced technology makes your daily cooking easy and healthy. Most people want to cook healthy and delicious dishes at home. Due to the busy schedule of our lifestyle, it is not possible to give much time for daily cooking. If you are also one of them then instant pot slow cooker is one of the best choices for you. You just need to add all the essential ingredients and set your instant pot on slow cook mode. Do your daily job, when you come home after 7 to 8 hours your food is ready to eat.

In this cookbook, we have used one of the advanced cooking appliances known as Instant pot Aura multi-cooker. It runs on advanced microprocessor technology. It is one of the smart cooking appliances full fill your daily cooking needs. Instant pot Aura is not a pressure cooker it uses as a slow cooker and also used as a multi-cooker. It performs different appliance operations in a single pot like it bakes your favourite cake and cookies, roast your favourite chicken, steam rice and multigrain, sauté food, make yogurt, and reheat your food. Slow cooking is one of the healthiest methods of cooking delicious and tasty food. A slow cooker is easy to use and doesn't require special skills to operate them. The cleaning process is also easy you never need to spend your day for the cleaning process.

The book contains healthy and delicious recipes from breakfast to desserts. All the recipes are done into instant pot Aura 10-in-1 multi slow cooker. The recipes written in this book are simple and easily understandable form with their exact preparation and cooking time. All the recipes written in this book come with their nutritional values which will help you tom keep track of how much calories you have eaten daily.

My goal here is to introduce you with an advanced cooking technique with instant pot Aura multi-cooker with its benefits. Various books are available in the market on this topic thanks for choosing my book. I hope the book helps and guides you to make healthy, tasty, and delicious dishes at your home using the slow cooking method.

Chapter 1: Breakfast & Brunch

Perfect Cranberry Eggnog Oatmeal

Preparation Time: 10 minutes; Cooking Time: 4 hours; Serve: 6
Ingredients:
- 1 cup cranberries
- 4 cups of water
- 4 cups eggnog
- 2 cups steel-cut oats

Directions:
1. Add all ingredients into the cooking pot and stir well.
2. Cover instant pot aura with lid.
3. Select slow cook mode and cook on LOW for 4 hours.
4. Stir well and serve.

Nutritional Value (Amount per Serving):
Calories 342; Fat 14.5 g; Carbohydrates 43.1 g; Sugar 15.2 g; Protein 10 g; Cholesterol 100 mg

Cinnamon Apple Rice

Preparation Time: 10 minutes; Cooking Time: 3 hours; Serve: 8
Ingredients:
- 4 apples, peel, cored, & diced
- 1 1/2 cups brown rice, uncooked
- 3 tbsp butter
- 1 tsp vanilla extract
- 1/2 tsp allspice
- 1 tsp ground cinnamon
- 4 cups apple juice

Directions:
1. Add all ingredients except butter into the cooking pot.
2. Add butter on top of rice.
3. Cover instant pot aura with lid.
4. Select slow cook mode and cook on HIGH for 3 hours.
5. Stir well. Top with chopped nuts and serve.

Nutritional Value (Amount per Serving):
Calories 284; Fat 5.6 g; Carbohydrates 56.9 g; Sugar 23.7 g; Protein 3.1 g; Cholesterol 11 mg

Broccoli Ham Casserole

Preparation Time: 10 minutes; Cooking Time: 3 hours; Serve: 8
Ingredients:
- 2 eggs
- 6 egg whites
- 1/4 cup chives, chopped
- 1 1/2 cups ham, cubed
- 10 oz frozen broccoli florets, chopped
- 3 cups whole grain bread, cubed
- 6 oz cheddar cheese, shredded
- 1 cup milk
- 1/4 tsp pepper
- 1/4 tsp salt

Directions:
1. In a bowl, whisk together eggs, egg whites, and milk and pour into the cooking pot.
2. Stir in 4 oz cheddar cheese, pepper, and salt.
3. Add chives, ham, broccoli, and bread and stir well.
4. Sprinkle remaining cheese on top.
5. Cover instant pot aura with lid.
6. Select slow cook mode and cook on LOW for 2 1/2 hours.
7. Serve and enjoy.

Nutritional Value (Amount per Serving):
Calories 233; Fat 11.7 g; Carbohydrates 14.2 g; Sugar 4.1 g; Protein 17.3 g; Cholesterol 80 mg

Easy Brown Sugar Oatmeal

Preparation Time: 10 minutes; Cooking Time: 8 hours; Serve: 4
Ingredients:
- 1 cup steel-cut oats, uncooked
- 1 1/2 tbsp vanilla
- 1/2 cup brown sugar
- 4 1/2 cups milk

Directions:
1. Add all ingredients into the cooking pot and stir well.
2. Cover instant pot aura with lid.
3. Select slow cook mode and cook on LOW for 8 hours.
4. Stir well. Top with the desired topping & serve.

Nutritional Value (Amount per Serving):
Calories 298; Fat 7 g; Carbohydrates 45.7 g; Sugar 30.8 g; Protein 11.7 g; Cholesterol 23 mg

Spinach Cheese Frittata

Preparation Time: 10 minutes; Cooking Time: 1 hour 30 minutes; Serve: 6
Ingredients:
- 3 eggs
- 3 egg whites
- 1 tomato, diced
- 1 cup baby spinach, chopped
- 1/4 tsp black pepper
- 2 tbsp milk
- 1 cup mozzarella cheese, shredded
- 1/2 cup onion, diced
- 1 tbsp olive oil
- Salt

Directions:
1. Add oil into the cooking pot and set instant pot aura on saute mode.
2. Add onion into the cooking pot and saute until onion is softened.
3. In a large bowl, whisk together eggs, egg whites, 1/4 cup mozzarella cheese, milk, pepper, spinach, tomato, and salt.
4. Pour egg mixture into the cooking pot and top with remaining cheese.
5. Cover instant pot aura with lid.
6. Select slow cook mode and cook on LOW for 1 1/2 hours.
7. Serve and enjoy.

Nutritional Value (Amount per Serving):
Calories 83; Fat 5.5 g; Carbohydrates 2.2 g; Sugar 1.2 g; Protein 6.4 g; Cholesterol 85 mg

Healthy Strawberry Oatmeal

Preparation Time: 10 minutes; Cooking Time: 6 hours; Serve: 8
Ingredients:
- 2 cups steel-cut oats
- 2 cups strawberries, sliced
- 1 tsp vanilla
- 1 tsp cinnamon
- 1 cup plain Greek yogurt
- 3 cups of milk
- 4 cups of water
- Pinch of sea salt

Directions:
1. Add oats, 1 1/2 cups strawberries, vanilla, cinnamon, yogurt, milk, water, and salt into the cooking pot and stir well.
2. Cover instant pot aura with lid.
3. Select slow cook mode and cook on LOW for 6 hours.
4. Top with remaining strawberries and serve.

Nutritional Value (Amount per Serving):
Calories 165; Fat 5.1 g; Carbohydrates 23.3 g; Sugar 8 g; Protein 7.1 g; Cholesterol 14 mg

Perfect Breakfast Potatoes

Preparation Time: 10 minutes; Cooking Time: 4 hours; Serve: 8

Ingredients:
- 3 lb baby potatoes, quartered
- 2 tbsp olive oil
- 2 tbsp butter, diced
- 2 tsp paprika
- 2 tsp seasoned salt
- 3 garlic cloves, minced
- 1/2 medium onion, diced
- 2 bell pepper, diced
- Pepper
- Salt

Directions:
1. Add all ingredients into the cooking pot and stir well.
2. Cover instant pot aura with lid.
3. Select slow cook mode and cook on LOW for 4 hours.
4. Stir well and serve hot.

Nutritional Value (Amount per Serving):
Calories 170; Fat 6.7 g; Carbohydrates 24.7 g; Sugar 1.9 g; Protein 4.9 g; Cholesterol 8 mg

Delicious Breakfast Burrito

Preparation Time: 10 minutes; Cooking Time: 6 hours; Serve: 8

Ingredients:
- 12 eggs
- 2 lbs breakfast sausage
- 1 cup milk
- 2 1/2 cup cheddar cheese, shredded
- 10 oz frozen hash browns
- Salt

Directions:
1. Add sausage into the cooking pot and set instant pot aura on sauté mode.
2. Cook sausage until brown. Remove sausage from the cooking pot.
3. Spread hash browns in the cooking pot.
4. Add sausage and cheese and stir to mix.
5. In a bowl, whisk eggs with milk and salt. Pour egg mixture over hash brown mixture.
6. Cover instant pot aura with lid.
7. Select slow cook mode and cook on LOW for 6 hours.
8. Serve and enjoy.

Nutritional Value (Amount per Serving):
Calories 730; Fat 55.5 g; Carbohydrates 14.9 g; Sugar 2.6 g; Protein 41.2 g; Cholesterol 380 mg

Pumpkin Pie Oatmeal

Preparation Time: 10 minutes; Cooking Time: 6 hours; Serve: 4

Ingredients:
- 1 cup steel-cut oats
- 1/2 tsp cinnamon
- 1 tsp pumpkin pie spiced
- 1 tsp vanilla
- 3 tbsp maple syrup
- 1 cup pumpkin puree
- 1 1/2 cups unsweetened almond milk
- 2 1/2 cups water
- 1/4 tsp salt

Directions:
1. Add all ingredients into the cooking pot and stir well.
2. Cover instant pot aura with lid.
3. Select slow cook mode and cook on LOW for 6 hours.
4. Stir well and serve.

Nutritional Value (Amount per Serving):
Calories 158; Fat 2.9 g; Carbohydrates 30.3 g; Sugar 11.3 g; Protein 3.8 g; Cholesterol 0 mg

Apple Cranberry Oatmeal

Preparation Time: 10 minutes; Cooking Time: 6 hours; Serve: 8
Ingredients:
- 3 cups old-fashioned oats
- 1/2 tsp ground cinnamon
- 2 tbsp butter
- 1/2 cup dried cranberries
- 2 apples, peel, cored & chopped
- 6 cups of water
- 1/4 tsp salt

Directions:
1. Add all ingredients into the cooking pot and stir well.
2. Cover instant pot aura with lid.
3. Select slow cook mode and cook on LOW for 6 hours.
4. Stir well and serve with milk.

Nutritional Value (Amount per Serving):
Calories 171; Fat 5.2 g; Carbohydrates 28.7 g; Sugar 6.8 g; Protein 3.9 g; Cholesterol 8 mg

Cinnamon Roll Casserole

Preparation Time: 10 minutes; Cooking Time: 3 hours; Serve: 10
Ingredients:
- 4 eggs, lightly beaten
- 12 oz cinnamon roll tubes, refrigerated & cut into quarters
- 1 tsp ground cinnamon
- 1 1/2 tsp vanilla
- 3 tbsp maple syrup
- 1/2 cup heavy whipping cream

Directions:
1. Add half of the cinnamon roll pieces in the cooking pot.
2. In a bowl, whisk together eggs, cinnamon, vanilla, maple syrup, and heavy cream.
3. Pour egg mixture over cinnamon rolls then spread remaining rolls over the top.
4. Cover instant pot aura with lid.
5. Select slow cook mode and cook on LOW for 3 hours.
6. Serve and enjoy.

Nutritional Value (Amount per Serving):
Calories 176; Fat 7.8 g; Carbohydrates 22.4 g; Sugar 11.5 g; Protein 3.9 g; Cholesterol 74 mg

Apple Cinnamon Steel Cut Oatmeal

Preparation Time: 10 minutes; Cooking Time: 8 hours; Serve: 6
Ingredients:
- 1 cup steel-cut oats
- 1 tsp vanilla
- 2 tsp ground cinnamon
- 1/2 cup walnuts, chopped
- 1/3 cup raisins
- 1 apple, peel, cored & chopped
- 1/4 cup maple syrup
- 1 cup of coconut milk
- 4 cups of water
- 1/4 tsp kosher salt

Directions:
1. Add all ingredients into the cooking pot and stir well.
2. Cover instant pot aura with lid.
3. Select slow cook mode and cook on LOW for 8 hours.
4. Stir well. Top with nuts and milk and serve.

Nutritional Value (Amount per Serving):
Calories 290; Fat 16.7 g; Carbohydrates 33.5 g; Sugar 18.2 g; Protein 5.6 g; Cholesterol 0 mg

Cranberry Apple French Toast

Preparation Time: 10 minutes; Cooking Time: 5 hours; Serve: 4

Ingredients:
- 6 eggs
- 1/2 cup dried cranberries
- 2 apples, core & diced
- 1/4 cup sugar
- 2 tbsp maple syrup
- 1/2 tsp cinnamon
- 1 tbsp vanilla
- 1 cup half and half
- 1 1/2 cups almond milk
- 1 1/2 lbs french bread, cut into 1-inch cubes

Directions:
1. Add bread cubes into the cooking pot.
2. Add cranberries and apples and mix slightly.
3. In a bowl, whisk together eggs, milk, sugar, maple syrup, cinnamon, vanilla, and a half and half.
4. Pour egg mixture over bread cubes in the cooking pot.
5. Cover instant pot aura with lid.
6. Select slow cook mode and cook on LOW for 5 hours.
7. Serve and enjoy.

Nutritional Value (Amount per Serving):
Calories 856; Fat 37.3 g; Carbohydrates 108.6 g; Sugar 37.5 g; Protein 25.8 g; Cholesterol 268 mg

Hearty Pumpkin Spice Oatmeal

Preparation Time: 10 minutes; Cooking Time: 4 hours; Serve: 4

Ingredients:
- 1 cup steel-cut oats
- 1 tsp vanilla
- 1/2 cup applesauce
- 1 1/2 tbsp pumpkin pie spice
- 3/4 cup pumpkin puree
- 1/4 cup maple syrup
- 1 1/2 cups water
- 1 3/4 cups milk
- 1/4 tsp salt

Directions:
1. Add all ingredients into the cooking pot and stir well.
2. Cover instant pot aura with lid.
3. Select slow cook mode and cook on LOW for 4 hours.
4. Stir well. Top with pecans and serve.

Nutritional Value (Amount per Serving):
Calories 221; Fat 4 g; Carbohydrates 41 g; Sugar 21.6 g; Protein 6.9 g; Cholesterol 9 mg

Hash Brown Breakfast Casserole

Preparation Time: 10 minutes; Cooking Time: 8 hours; Serve: 12

Ingredients:
- 12 eggs
- 30 oz frozen hash browns
- 1/2 cup milk
- 5 green onions, sliced
- 8 oz mozzarella cheese, shredded
- 8 oz cheddar cheese, shredded
- 1 lb sausage, browned & drained
- 1/2 tsp salt

Directions:
1. Add half hash browns into the cooking pot then layer in half sausage, half cheeses, half green onions, then repeat layers.
2. In a large bowl, whisk eggs with milk and salt.
3. Pour egg mixture over the hash brown mixture.
4. Cover instant pot aura with lid.
5. Select slow cook mode and cook on LOW for 8 hours.
6. Serve and enjoy.

Nutritional Value (Amount per Serving):
Calories 515; Fat 33.8 g; Carbohydrates 27.1 g; Sugar 2.1 g; Protein 25.5 g; Cholesterol 226 mg

Healthy Banana Nut Oatmeal

Preparation Time: 10 minutes; Cooking Time: 8 hours; Serve: 4

Ingredients:
- 1 cup steel-cut oats
- 1/2 tsp nutmeg
- 1 tsp vanilla
- 2 tsp cinnamon
- 2 tbsp flaxseed meal
- 2 cup of water
- 2 cups almond milk
- 1/4 cup walnuts, chopped
- 1 banana, mashed
- 1/2 tsp salt

Directions:
1. Add all ingredients into the cooking pot and stir well.
2. Cover instant pot aura with lid.
3. Select slow cook mode and cook on LOW for 8 hours.
4. Stir well. Top with nuts and serve.

Nutritional Value (Amount per Serving):
Calories 443; Fat 35.8 g; Carbohydrates 26.5 g; Sugar 6.8 g; Protein 8.5 g; Cholesterol 0 mg

Steel Cut Peach Oatmeal

Preparation Time: 10 minutes; Cooking Time: 8 hours; Serve: 4

Ingredients:
- 1 cup steel-cut oats
- 4 tbsp graham cracker crumbs
- 2 fresh peaches, sliced then quartered
- 1 tsp butter
- 1/2 tsp cinnamon
- 1/4 cup brown sugar
- 1/2 cup buttermilk
- 3 cups of milk

Directions:
1. Add oats, cinnamon, brown sugar, buttermilk, milk, peaches, and butter into the cooking pot.
2. Cover instant pot aura with lid.
3. Select slow cook mode and cook on LOW for 8 hours.
4. Top with graham cracker crumbs and serve.

Nutritional Value (Amount per Serving):
Calories 278; Fat 7 g; Carbohydrates 44.8 g; Sugar 26.7 g; Protein 10.8 g; Cholesterol 19 mg

Healthy Apple Pie Amaranth Porridge

Preparation Time: 10 minutes; Cooking Time: 8 hours; Serve: 8

Ingredients:
- 2 cups amaranth
- 2 1/2 cups water
- 1 cup of coconut milk
- 1/4 cup orange juice
- 1 tbsp vanilla
- 1/2 tsp ground nutmeg
- 1 tbsp ground cinnamon
- 10 dates, pitted
- 4 large apples, core & cut into 1-inch cubes

Directions:
1. Add all ingredients into the cooking pot and stir well.
2. Cover instant pot aura with lid.
3. Select slow cook mode and cook on LOW for 8 hours.
4. Stir well. Top with nuts and serve.

Nutritional Value (Amount per Serving):
Calories 350; Fat 10.6 g; Carbohydrates 58.9 g; Sugar 20.9 g; Protein 8.4 g; Cholesterol 0 mg

Peanut Butter Banana Oatmeal

Preparation Time: 10 minutes; Cooking Time: 7 hours; Serve: 6
Ingredients:
- 2 ripe bananas, mashed
- 1 cup steel-cut oatmeal
- 2 tbsp flax seed
- 1 tsp vanilla
- 1 tsp cinnamon
- 3 tbsp brown sugar
- 3 cups of milk
- 1/4 cup peanut butter

Directions:
1. In a medium bowl, whisk together peanut butter and mashed bananas until well combined.
2. Add flaxseed, vanilla, cinnamon, brown sugar, and milk. Stir in oatmeal.
3. Pour oatmeal mixture into the cooking pot.
4. Cover instant pot aura with lid.
5. Select slow cook mode and cook on LOW for 7 hours.
6. Stir well and serve.

Nutritional Value (Amount per Serving):
Calories 217; Fat 9.3 g; Carbohydrates 27.1 g; Sugar 15.8 g; Protein 8.4 g; Cholesterol 10 mg

Breakfast Tater Tot Egg Bake

Preparation Time: 10 minutes; Cooking Time: 8 hours; Serve: 8
Ingredients:
- 12 eggs
- 1 cup milk
- 30 oz tater tots
- 1/4 cup all-purpose flour
- 1/4 cup parmesan cheese, grated
- 2 cups cheddar cheese, shredded
- 2 onions, chopped
- 6 oz ham, diced
- 1/2 tsp pepper
- 1 tsp salt

Directions:
1. Add 1/3 tater tots, ham, onions, and cheeses in the cooking pot. Repeat layer twice.
2. In a bowl, whisk together eggs, milk, flour, pepper, and salt and pour over tater tot mixture.
3. Cover instant pot aura with lid.
4. Select slow cook mode and cook on LOW for 8 hours.
5. Serve and enjoy.

Nutritional Value (Amount per Serving):
Calories 509; Fat 29.2 g; Carbohydrates 38.6 g; Sugar 3.5 g; Protein 25.1 g; Cholesterol 295 mg

Cauliflower Hash Browns Casserole

Preparation Time: 10 minutes; Cooking Time: 7 hours; Serve: 8
Ingredients:
- 12 eggs
- 8 oz cheddar cheese, shredded
- 1 lb breakfast sausage, cooked & crumbled
- 1 cauliflower head, shredded
- 1/2 tsp dry mustard
- 1/2 cup milk
- 1/2 tsp pepper
- 1 tsp kosher salt

Directions:
1. In a bowl, whisk eggs with mustard, milk, pepper, and salt.
2. Add third shredded cauliflower in a cooking pot, and top with a third of the onion. Season with pepper and salt.
3. Top with third sausage and third cheese. Repeat the layers two times.
4. Pour egg mixture over the cauliflower mixture.

5. Cover instant pot aura with lid.
6. Select slow cook mode and cook on LOW for 7 hours.
7. Serve and enjoy.

Nutritional Value (Amount per Serving):
Calories 418; Fat 32.4 g; Carbohydrates 3.5 g; Sugar 2.2 g; Protein 27.6 g; Cholesterol 324 mg

Carrot Cake Oatmeal

Preparation Time: 10 minutes; Cooking Time: 8 hours; Serve: 12

Ingredients:
- 2 cups steel-cut oats
- 1 tsp ground nutmeg
- 1 tbsp ground cinnamon
- 2 cups of milk
- 8 cups of water
- 1 cup unsweetened shredded coconut
- 1 cup raisins
- 1 cup carrots, diced in small pieces
- 1 cup shredded carrots
- 1/4 tsp salt

Directions:
1. Add all ingredients into the cooking pot and stir well.
2. Cover instant pot aura with lid.
3. Select slow cook mode and cook on LOW for 8 hours.
4. Stir well and serve.

Nutritional Value (Amount per Serving):
Calories 179; Fat 7.2 g; Carbohydrates 25.2 g; Sugar 11 g; Protein 4.4 g; Cholesterol 3 mg

Peach Breakfast Oatmeal

Preparation Time: 10 minutes; Cooking Time: 4 hours; Serve: 4

Ingredients:
- 1 cup old-fashioned oats
- 2 cups of milk
- 1/2 tsp cinnamon
- 1/2 cup walnuts, chopped
- 2 tbsp honey
- 1 tbsp butter
- 2 tbsp brown sugar
- 1 cup can peach, diced
- 1/4 tsp salt

Directions:
1. Add all ingredients into the cooking pot and stir well.
2. Cover instant pot aura with lid.
3. Select slow cook mode and cook on LOW for 4 hours.
4. Stir well and serve.

Nutritional Value (Amount per Serving):
Calories 328; Fat 15.9 g; Carbohydrates 39.3 g; Sugar 23.6 g; Protein 10.5 g; Cholesterol 18 mg

Cheesy Potatoes

Preparation Time: 10 minutes; Cooking Time: 3 hours; Serve: 10

Ingredients:
- 32 oz hash browns, defrosted
- 1 cup milk
- 10.5 oz cream of chicken soup
- 2.5 cheddar cheese, shredded
- 1 onion, diced
- 14 oz sausage, cut into bite-size pieces

Directions:
1. Add hash browns, onion, sausage, and 2 cups of cheese into the cooking pot. Mix well.
2. In a bowl, whisk together milk and cream of chicken soup and pour over hash browns.
3. Sprinkle remaining cheese on top of the hash brown mixture.
4. Cover instant pot aura with lid.
5. Select slow cook mode and cook on HIGH for 3 hours.

6. Serve and enjoy.

Nutritional Value (Amount per Serving):
   Calories 438; Fat 26.4 g; Carbohydrates 36.5 g; Sugar 3.1 g; Protein 13.8 g; Cholesterol 36.5 mg

Apple Pie Oatmeal

Preparation Time: 10 minutes; Cooking Time: 6 hours; Serve: 8

Ingredients:
- 2 cups steel-cut oatmeal
- 1/4 tsp ground nutmeg
- 1/4 tsp ground ginger
- 1/2 tsp ground cinnamon
- 3/4 tsp vanilla
- 2 apples, peel, core, & chopped
- 7 cups of water

Directions:
1. Add all ingredients into the cooking pot and stir well.
2. Cover instant pot aura with lid.
3. Select slow cook mode and cook on LOW for 6 hours.
4. Stir well and serve.

Nutritional Value (Amount per Serving):
   Calories 69; Fat 0.9 g; Carbohydrates 14.7 g; Sugar 5.9 g; Protein 1.4 g; Cholesterol 0 mg

Cheesy Grits

Preparation Time: 10 minutes; Cooking Time: 6 hours; Serve: 10

Ingredients:
- 2 cups yellow stone-ground grits
- 2 tbsp butter
- 2 1/2 cups cheddar cheese, shredded
- 8 oz cream cheese, softened
- 2 cups heavy whipping cream
- 32 oz chicken broth
- 1/2 tsp pepper
- 2 tsp garlic salt

Directions:
1. In a bowl, whisk together broth, cream cheese, cream, pepper, and garlic salt. Add 2 cups cheese and grits and mix well.
2. Pour mixture into the cooking pot.
3. Cover instant pot aura with lid.
4. Select slow cook mode and cook on LOW for 6 hours.
5. Add butter and stir until butter is melted. Top with remaining cheese. Cover and let sit for 10 minutes.
6. Serve and enjoy.

Nutritional Value (Amount per Serving):
   Calories 441; Fat 30.5 g; Carbohydrates 30.1 g; Sugar 0.6 g; Protein 14.4 g; Cholesterol 94 mg

Breakfast Bread Pudding

Preparation Time: 10 minutes; Cooking Time: 3 hours; Serve: 8

Ingredients:
- 4 eggs
- 8 cups of bread cubes
- 1/4 cup sugar
- 1 tsp vanilla
- 1 tsp nutmeg
- 1 tbsp cinnamon
- 1/4 cup butter, melted
- 2 cups heavy cream

Directions:
1. Add bread cubes into the cooking pot.
2. In a mixing bowl, mix together the remaining ingredients and pour over bread cubes in the cooking pot.
3. Cover instant pot aura with lid.

4. Select slow cook mode and cook on LOW for 3 hours.
5. Serve warm and enjoy.

Nutritional Value (Amount per Serving):
Calories 314; Fat 19.2 g; Carbohydrates 28.2 g; Sugar 6.6 g; Protein 3.5 g; Cholesterol 138 mg

Rice Raisins Pudding

Preparation Time: 10 minutes; Cooking Time: 4 hours; Serve: 4

Ingredients:
- 1 cup of brown rice
- 1 tbsp coconut sugar
- 1 tsp cinnamon
- 2 tsp vanilla
- 2 tbsp ground flaxseed meal
- 1/2 cup raisins
- 1 cup of coconut milk
- 1 cup almond milk
- 2 cups of water
- 1/2 tsp salt

Directions:
1. Add all ingredients into the cooking pot and stir well.
2. Cover instant pot aura with lid.
3. Select slow cook mode and cook on LOW for 4 hours.
4. Stir well and serve.

Nutritional Value (Amount per Serving):
Calories 548; Fat 30.8 g; Carbohydrates 63.9 g; Sugar 15 g; Protein 7.9 g; Cholesterol 0 mg

Healthy Whole Grain Porridge

Preparation Time: 10 minutes; Cooking Time: 8 hours; Serve: 8

Ingredients:
- 1/2 cup quinoa
- 1/2 cup wild rice
- 1/2 cup steel-cut oats
- 4 cups almond milk
- 1 cup walnuts, chopped
- 6 cups of water
- 1/4 cup dried cranberries
- 1/4 cup dried apricots, chopped
- 2 tbsp honey
- 1 cinnamon stick
- 3/4 cup dry pearl barley
- 1/2 tsp sea salt

Directions:
1. Add all ingredients into the cooking pot and stir well.
2. Cover instant pot aura with lid.
3. Select slow cook mode and cook on LOW for 8 hours.
4. Discard cinnamon stick.
5. Stir well and serve.

Nutritional Value (Amount per Serving):
Calories 554; Fat 39.2 g; Carbohydrates 45.9 g; Sugar 9.5 g; Protein 12.1 g; Cholesterol 0 mg

Sweet Berry Oatmeal

Preparation Time: 10 minutes; Cooking Time: 7 hours; Serve: 8

Ingredients:
- 2 cups steel-cut oats
- 1/4 cup maple syrup
- 1 cup dried cranberries
- 1/2 cup dried blueberries
- 8 cups of water
- 1/2 tsp salt

Directions:
1. Add oats, water, blueberries, and salt into the cooking pot and stir well.
2. Cover instant pot aura with lid.
3. Select slow cook mode and cook on LOW for 7 hours.
4. Stir in maple syrup and cranberries.

5. Serve and enjoy.

Nutritional Value (Amount per Serving):
Calories 116; Fat 1.4 g; Carbohydrates 23 g; Sugar 7.5 g; Protein 2.8 g; Cholesterol 0 mg

Flavorful Millet Porridge

Preparation Time: 10 minutes; Cooking Time: 8 hours; Serve: 6

Ingredients:
- 1 1/4 cup millet
- 1/2 tsp nutmeg
- 1 tsp cinnamon
- 3 cups of water
- 2 1/2 cups milk
- 2 dates, pitted & chopped
- 1/2 tsp almond extract
- 1 1/2 tsp vanilla
- 1/2 tsp cardamom
- Pinch of salt

Directions:
1. Grind 1 cup millet in grinder until broken down and transfer into the cooking pot along with remaining ingredients. Stir well.
2. Cover instant pot aura with lid.
3. Select slow cook mode and cook on LOW for 8 hours.
4. Stir well and serve.

Nutritional Value (Amount per Serving):
Calories 223; Fat 3.9 g; Carbohydrates 38.1 g; Sugar 6.6 g; Protein 8 g; Cholesterol 8 mg

Cinnamon Apple Barley

Preparation Time: 10 minutes; Cooking Time: 8 hours; Serve: 4

Ingredients:
- 2 apples cored, peeled, and chopped
- 1/2 cup barley
- 1 tsp cinnamon
- 1/8 cup brown sugar
- 3 cups of water
- 1/8 tsp cardamom
- 1/4 tsp clove
- 1/4 tsp nutmeg

Directions:
1. Add all ingredients into the cooking pot and stir well.
2. Cover instant pot aura with lid.
3. Select slow cook mode and cook on LOW for 8 hours.
4. Stir well and serve.

Nutritional Value (Amount per Serving):
Calories 176; Fat 0.9 g; Carbohydrates 23 g; Sugar 5.1 g; Protein 20.4 g; Cholesterol 5 mg

Maple Blueberry Oats

Preparation Time: 10 minutes; Cooking Time: 7 hours; Serve: 6

Ingredients:
- 1 cup steel-cut oats
- 1 tbsp lemon zest
- 1 tsp vanilla
- 5 cups of water
- 1/2 cup quinoa, rinsed
- 1 cup blueberries
- 2 tbsp maple syrup
- 1 tbsp butter, melted
- 1/4 tsp salt

Directions:
1. Add all ingredients into the cooking pot and stir well.
2. Cover instant pot aura with lid.
3. Select slow cook mode and cook on LOW for 7 hours.
4. Stir well and serve.

Nutritional Value (Amount per Serving):

Calories 131; Fat 3.5 g; Carbohydrates 22 g; Sugar 6.6 g; Protein 3.2 g; Cholesterol 5 mg

Cinnamon Pumpkin Oatmeal

Preparation Time: 10 minutes; Cooking Time: 8 hours; Serve: 6

Ingredients:
- 1 cup steel-cut oats
- 1 cup pumpkin puree
- 2 tsp ground cinnamon
- 2 tsp pumpkin pie spice
- 2 tbsp chia seeds
- 2 cups of milk
- 2 1/2 cups water
- 1/4 cup maple syrup

Directions:
1. Add all ingredients into the cooking pot and stir well.
2. Cover instant pot aura with lid.
3. Select slow cook mode and cook on LOW for 8 hours.
4. Stir well and serve.

Nutritional Value (Amount per Serving):
Calories 132; Fat 3.2 g; Carbohydrates 22.8 g; Sugar 13 g; Protein 4.6 g; Cholesterol 7 mg

Feta Spinach Quiche

Preparation Time: 10 minutes; Cooking Time: 4 hours; Serve: 4

Ingredients:
- 4 eggs
- 4 oz feta cheese
- 2 cups of milk
- 10 oz frozen spinach, chopped and thawed
- Pepper
- Salt

Directions:
1. Whisk all ingredients in the large bowl.
2. Pour egg mixture into the cooking pot.
3. Cover instant pot aura with lid.
4. Select slow cook mode and cook on LOW for 4 hours.
5. Serve and enjoy.

Nutritional Value (Amount per Serving):
Calories 215; Fat 13.2 g; Carbohydrates 10.1 g; Sugar 7.3 g; Protein 15.6 g; Cholesterol 199 mg

Healthy Breakfast Casserole

Preparation Time: 10 minutes; Cooking Time: 5 hours; Serve: 10

Ingredients:
- 10 eggs
- 1/2 tsp coriander
- 1/2 tsp garlic powder
- 12 oz pork sausage rolls
- 1 cup pepper jack cheese
- 1 cup milk
- 1 cup of salsa
- 1 tsp chili powder
- 1 tsp cumin
- 1/4 tsp pepper
- 1/4 tsp salt

Directions:
1. Add sausage into the cooking pot and set instant pot aura on saute mode and saute sausage until no longer pink.
2. Add salsa and seasoning. Stir well.
3. In a bowl, whisk eggs with milk.
4. Pour egg mixture over sausage then add cheese and stir well.
5. Cover instant pot aura with lid.
6. Select slow cook mode and cook on LOW for 5 hours.

7. Serve and enjoy.

Nutritional Value (Amount per Serving):
Calories 247; Fat 21.1 g; Carbohydrates 4.1 g; Sugar 2.9 g; Protein 12.4 g; Cholesterol 205 mg

Spinach Pepper Omelet

Preparation Time: 10 minutes; Cooking Time: 1 hour 30 minutes; Serve: 4

Ingredients:
- 6 eggs
- 4 egg whites
- 1 tsp dried parsley
- 1 tsp garlic powder
- 1 cup bell peppers, sliced
- 1/2 cup onion, sliced
- 1 cup spinach
- 1/2 cup milk
- Pepper
- Salt

Directions:
1. In a large bowl, whisk together eggs, pepper, parsley, garlic powder, milk, egg whites, and salt.
2. Add spinach, bell peppers, and onion and stir well.
3. Pour egg mixture into the cooking pot.
4. Cover instant pot aura with lid.
5. Select slow cook mode and cook on LOW for 1 1/2 hours.
6. Serve and enjoy.

Nutritional Value (Amount per Serving):
Calories 146; Fat 7.4 g; Carbohydrates 6.7 g; Sugar 4.4 g; Protein 13.7 g; Cholesterol 248 mg

Cinnamon Carrot Oatmeal

Preparation Time: 10 minutes; Cooking Time: 6 hours; Serve: 2

Ingredients:
- 1/2 cup steel-cut oats
- 1 small carrot, grated
- 1/4 cup pecans, chopped
- 2 tbsp brown sugar
- 1/2 tsp cinnamon
- 1/8 tsp ground cloves
- 1/8 tsp nutmeg
- 1/4 small zucchini, peeled and grated
- 1 tsp vanilla
- 1 1/2 cups milk
- 1/8 Tsp salt

Directions:
1. Add all ingredients except pecans into the cooking pot and stir well.
2. Cover instant pot aura with lid.
3. Select slow cook mode and cook on LOW for 6 hours.
4. Stir well, top with pecans and serve.

Nutritional Value (Amount per Serving):
Calories 329; Fat 15.9 g; Carbohydrates 37.7 g; Sugar 19.5 g; Protein 10.7 g; Cholesterol 15 mg

Easy Breakfast Apples

Preparation Time: 10 minutes; Cooking Time: 3 hours; Serve: 10

Ingredients:
- 9 cups apple, diced
- 2 tsp ground cinnamon
- 1 1/2 cups water
- 2 tbsp fresh lemon juice
- 1/2 tsp nutmeg

Directions:
1. Add all ingredients into the cooking pot and stir well.
2. Cover instant pot aura with lid.
3. Select slow cook mode and cook on HIGH for 3 hours.

4. Stir and serve.

Nutritional Value (Amount per Serving):
Calories 107; Fat 0.4 g; Carbohydrates 28.2 g; Sugar 21 g; Protein 0.6 g; Cholesterol 0 mg

Mixed Berry Oatmeal

Preparation Time: 5 minutes; Cooking Time: 20 minutes; Serve: 4

Ingredients:
- 1 egg
- 2 cups old fashioned oats
- 1 cup blueberries
- 1/2 cup blackberries
- 1/2 cup strawberries, sliced
- 1/4 cup maple syrup
- 1 1/2 cups milk
- 1 1/2 tsp baking powder
- 1/2 tsp salt

Directions:
1. In a bowl, mix together oats, salt, and baking powder.
2. Add vanilla, egg, maple syrup, and milk and stir well. Add berries and stir well.
3. Pour mixture into the cooking pot.
4. Cover instant pot aura with lid.
5. Select bake mode then set the temperature to 375 F and timer for 20 minutes.
6. Serve and enjoy.

Nutritional Value (Amount per Serving):
Calories 461; Fat 8.4 g; Carbohydrates 80.7 g; Sugar 23.4 g; Protein 15 g; Cholesterol 48 mg

Breakfast Oatmeal Cake

Preparation Time: 5 minutes; Cooking Time: 25 minutes; Serve: 8

Ingredients:
- 2 eggs
- 1 cup oats
- 3 tbsp yogurt
- 1/2 tsp baking powder
- 1/2 tsp baking soda
- 1 tsp cinnamon
- 1 tsp vanilla
- 3 tbsps honey
- 1 apple, peeled & chopped
- 1 tbsp butter

Directions:
1. Add 3/4 cup oats and remaining ingredients into the blender and blend until smooth.
2. Add remaining oats and stir well.
3. Line instant pot aura cooking pot with parchment paper.
4. Pour batter into the cooking pot.
5. Cover instant pot aura with lid.
6. Select bake mode then set the temperature to 350 F and timer for 25 minutes.
7. Slice and serve.

Nutritional Value (Amount per Serving):
Calories 112; Fat 3.3 g; Carbohydrates 18.2 g; Sugar 10 g; Protein 3.2 g; Cholesterol 45 mg

Baked Oatmeal

Preparation Time: 5 minutes; Cooking Time: 25 minutes; Serve: 6

Ingredients:
- 2 eggs, lightly beaten
- 3 cups quick oats
- 1 tsp ground cinnamon
- 1 tsp vanilla
- 1 tbsp baking powder
- 1 1/4 cup milk
- 1/2 cup butter, melted
- 1 cup brown sugar

Directions:

1. In a bowl, whisk sugar, vanilla, cinnamon, baking powder, eggs, milk, and butter until well mixed. Add oats and stir well.
2. Pour mixture into the cooking pot.
3. Cover instant pot aura with lid.
4. Select bake mode then set the temperature to 350 F and timer for 25 minutes.
5. Serve and enjoy.

Nutritional Value (Amount per Serving):
Calories 434; Fat 20.5 g; Carbohydrates 55.6 g; Sugar 26.4 g; Protein 9.1 g; Cholesterol 99 mg

Almond Butter Oatmeal

Preparation Time: 5 minutes; Cooking Time: 35 minutes; Serve: 2
Ingredients:
- 2 cups old fashioned oats
- 1/2 cup almond butter
- 1/4 cup maple syrup
- 1 3/4 cup milk
- 2 tsp vanilla
- 1/4 tsp salt

Directions:
1. In a bowl, whisk together milk, vanilla, maple syrup, almond butter, and salt. Add oats and stir well.
2. Pour mixture into the cooking pot.
3. Cover instant pot aura with lid.
4. Select bake mode then set the temperature to 375 F and timer for 35 minutes.
5. Serve and enjoy.

Nutritional Value (Amount per Serving):
Calories 870; Fat 17 g; Carbohydrates 145.6 g; Sugar 38 g; Protein 27.9 g; Cholesterol 18 mg

Mushroom Cheese Frittata

Preparation Time: 10 minutes; Cooking Time: 4 hours; Serve: 4
Ingredients:
- 6 eggs
- 4 oz mushrooms, sliced
- 2 tsp Italian seasoning
- 1/2 cup cheddar cheese, shredded
- 1/4 cup cherry tomatoes, sliced
- 1 tbsp olive oil
- Pepper
- Salt

Directions:
1. Add oil, mushrooms, and cherry tomatoes into the cooking pot and set instant pot aura on saute mode and cook until mushrooms are softened.
2. In a bowl, whisk together eggs, cheese, pepper, and salt.
3. Pour egg mixture in the cooking pot.
4. Cover instant pot aura with lid.
5. Select slow cook mode and cook on LOW for 4 hours.
6. Slice and serve.

Nutritional Value (Amount per Serving):
Calories 197; Fat 15.5 g; Carbohydrates 2.3 g; Sugar 1.6 g; Protein 12.8 g; Cholesterol 262 mg

Cheese Herb Frittata

Preparation Time: 10 minutes; Cooking Time: 3 hours; Serve: 6
Ingredients:
- 8 eggs
- 1 tsp oregano, dried
- 3/4 cup goat cheese, crumbled
- 1/2 cup onion, sliced
- 1 1/2 cups red peppers, roasted and chopped
- 4 cups baby arugula
- 1/3 cup milk

- Pepper
- Salt

Directions:
1. In a bowl, whisk together eggs, oregano, and milk. Season with pepper and salt.
2. Arrange red peppers, onion, arugula, and cheese into the cooking pot.
3. Pour egg mixture over the vegetables.
4. Cover instant pot aura with lid.
5. Select slow cook mode and cook on LOW for 3 hours.
6. Serve and enjoy.

Nutritional Value (Amount per Serving):
Calories 246; Fat 16.9 g; Carbohydrates 6.6 g; Sugar 4.4 g; Protein 18 g; Cholesterol 250 mg

Cauliflower Mash

Preparation Time: 10 minutes; Cooking Time: 6 hours; Serve: 4

Ingredients:
- 1 medium cauliflower head, cut into florets
- 1 1/2 cups vegetable stock
- 1 tbsp garlic, minced
- Pepper
- Salt

Directions:
1. Add cauliflower florets, garlic, and stock in the cooking pot.
2. Cover instant pot aura with lid.
3. Select slow cook mode and cook on LOW for 6 hours.
4. Drain cauliflower well and transfer into the large bowl.
5. Mash cauliflower until smooth. Season with pepper and salt.
6. Stir well and serve.

Nutritional Value (Amount per Serving):
Calories 41; Fat 0.2 g; Carbohydrates 8.7 g; Sugar 3.7 g; Protein 3.1 g; Cholesterol 0 mg

Ham Cheese Omelet

Preparation Time: 10 minutes; Cooking Time: 2 hours 30 minutes; Serve: 4

Ingredients:
- 6 eggs
- 1 garlic clove, minced
- 1 cup mozzarella cheese, shredded
- 3/4 cup ham, chopped
- 1/2 cup milk
- 1 small onion, chopped
- 1 red bell pepper, sliced
- Pepper
- Salt

Directions:
1. In a bowl, whisk eggs with garlic, pepper, salt, and milk.
2. Pour egg mixture in the cooking pot.
3. Add ham, onions, and bell peppers to the cooking pot.
4. Cover instant pot aura with lid.
5. Select slow cook mode and cook on HIGH for 2 1/2 hours.
6. Top with cheese, cover and let sit for 10 minutes.
7. Serve and enjoy.

Nutritional Value (Amount per Serving):
Calories 189; Fat 10.7 g; Carbohydrates 7.4 g; Sugar 4.1 g; Protein 16 g; Cholesterol 266 mg

Veggie Omelet

Preparation Time: 10 minutes; Cooking Time: 1 hour 30 minutes; Serve: 4

Ingredients:
- 6 eggs
- 4 egg whites

- 1/2 cup onion, sliced
- 1 cup spinach
- 1 mushroom, sliced
- 1/2 cup milk
- 1 tsp parsley, dried
- 1 tsp garlic powder
- 1 bell pepper, diced
- Pepper
- Salt

Directions:
1. In a large bowl, whisk together egg whites, eggs, parsley, garlic powder, almond milk, pepper, and salt.
2. Stir in mushroom, bell peppers, spinach, and onion.
3. Pour egg mixture in the cooking pot.
4. Cover instant pot aura with lid.
5. Select slow cook mode and cook on HIGH for 1 1/2 hours.
6. Slices and serve.

Nutritional Value (Amount per Serving):
Calories 147; Fat 7.4 g; Carbohydrates 6.8 g; Sugar 4.5 g; Protein 13.8 g; Cholesterol 248 mg

Healthy Veggie Frittata

Preparation Time: 10 minutes; Cooking Time: 3 hours; Serve: 4

Ingredients:
- 10 eggs
- 2 tbsp pesto
- 1 cup broccoli, chopped
- 1 cup zucchini, shredded
- 1/4 tsp red pepper flakes
- 1 tsp dried oregano
- 1 tsp garlic powder
- 1/2 cup feta cheese
- 2 tbsp fresh basil, chopped
- 2 cups kale, chopped
- 1/2 cup fennel, chopped
- 1 cup red pepper, chopped
- 1/4 cup milk
- 1/2 tsp black pepper
- 1/2 tsp salt

Directions:
1. In a large bowl, whisk eggs, feta cheese, milk, and spices.
2. Pour egg mixture in the cooking pot.
3. Add chopped vegetables and stir well.
4. Sprinkle fresh herbs on top. Top with pesto.
5. Cover instant pot aura with lid.
6. Select slow cook mode and cook on LOW for 3 hours.
7. Serve and enjoy.

Nutritional Value (Amount per Serving):
Calories 295; Fat 18.8 g; Carbohydrates 12.9 g; Sugar 5.4 g; Protein 20.4 g; Cholesterol 429 mg

Cheesy Spinach Frittata

Preparation Time: 10 minutes; Cooking Time: 1 hour 30 minutes; Serve: 6

Ingredients:
- 3 eggs
- 3 egg whites
- 1 cup mozzarella cheese, shredded
- 1 garlic clove, minced
- 1/2 cup onion, diced
- 1 tomato, diced
- 1 cup spinach, chopped
- 2 tbsp milk
- 1 tbsp olive oil
- 1/4 tsp pepper
- Salt

Directions:
1. Add oil and onion into the cooking pot and set instant pot aura on saute mode and saute onion until softened.

2. In a bowl, whisk 3/4 cup mozzarella cheese, and remaining ingredients and pour in the cooking pot.
3. Top with remaining cheese.
4. Cover instant pot aura with lid.
5. Select slow cook mode and cook on LOW for 1 1/2 hour.
6. Serve and enjoy.

Nutritional Value (Amount per Serving):
Calories 84; Fat 5.5 g; Carbohydrates 2.4 g; Sugar 1.2 g; Protein 6.5 g; Cholesterol 85 mg

Chapter 2: Vegetarian & Vegan

Flavorful Ranch Carrots

Preparation Time: 10 minutes; Cooking Time: 5 hours; Serve: 6
Ingredients:
- 1 lb baby carrots
- 2 cups vegetable broth
- 2 tbsp dry ranch mix

Directions:
1. Add baby carrot and broth into the cooking pot.
2. Add ranch seasoning and stir well.
3. Cover instant pot aura with lid.
4. Select slow cook mode and cook on HIGH for 5 hours.
5. Stir well and serve warm.

Nutritional Value (Amount per Serving):
Calories 41; Fat 0.6 g; Carbohydrates 6.9 g; Sugar 3.8 g; Protein 2.1 g; Cholesterol 0 mg

Delicious Thai Pineapple Curry

Preparation Time: 10 minutes; Cooking Time: 6 hours; Serve: 4
Ingredients:
- 1 fresh pineapple, cut into 1-inch pieces
- 3 cups garbanzo beans, soaked overnight in water & drained
- 2 onions, cut into 1-inch pieces
- 2 green bell pepper, cut into 1-inch pieces
- 1 lb sweet potatoes, peel & cut into 1-inch pieces
- 1 1/2 tsp granulated garlic
- 1 tsp crushed red pepper
- 3 tbsp curry powder
- 14.5 oz can coconut milk
- 1 1/2 tsp salt

Directions:
1. Add coconut milk, curry powder, crushed red pepper, garlic, and salt into the cooking pot and stir well.
2. Add remaining ingredients and stir well.
3. Cover instant pot aura with lid.
4. Select slow cook mode and cook on LOW for 6 hours.
5. Stir well and serve.

Nutritional Value (Amount per Serving):
Calories 613; Fat 24.6 g; Carbohydrates 84.8 g; Sugar 10.4 g; Protein 16.6 g; Cholesterol 0 mg

Asian Vegetarian Tikka Masala

Preparation Time: 10 minutes; Cooking Time: 8 hours; Serve: 6
Ingredients:
- 4 cups cauliflower florets
- 1 cup of coconut milk
- 3/4 cup green peas
- 3/4 tsp ground ginger
- 1 tsp paprika
- 2 tbsp garam masala
- 3 tbsp tomato paste
- 15 oz can tomato, crushed
- 3 cups vegetable broth
- 1 tbsp garlic, minced
- 1/2 onion, diced
- 2 carrots, peeled and cut into 1-inch pieces
- 3 cups potatoes, peeled and cubed
- 1 tsp kosher salt

Directions:
1. Add all ingredients except green peas and coconut milk into the cooking pot and stir well.
2. Cover instant pot aura with lid.

3. Select slow cook mode and cook on LOW for 8 hours.
4. Stir in green peas and coconut milk and let sit for 5 minutes.
5. Stir well and serve.

Nutritional Value (Amount per Serving):
Calories 230; Fat 10.9 g; Carbohydrates 29.5 g; Sugar 10 g; Protein 8.3 g; Cholesterol 0 mg

Healthy Split Pea Curry

Preparation Time: 10 minutes; Cooking Time: 8 hours; Serve: 6

Ingredients:
- 28 oz can tomatoes, crushed
- 1 cup heavy cream
- 1/2 tsp ground ginger
- 2 tsp curry powder
- 1 tbsp turmeric
- 1 tbsp green curry paste
- 3 garlic cloves, minced
- 1/2 cup onion, diced
- 15 oz can coconut milk
- 1 1/2 cup dry split peas
- 1/2 tsp salt

Directions:
1. Add all ingredients except heavy cream into the cooking pot and stir well.
2. Cover instant pot aura with lid.
3. Select slow cook mode and cook on LOW for 8 hours.
4. Stir in heavy cream and let sit for 5 minutes.
5. Stir well and serve over rice.

Nutritional Value (Amount per Serving):
Calories 425; Fat 23.8 g; Carbohydrates 42.4 g; Sugar 9 g; Protein 15.5 g; Cholesterol 27 mg

Lentil Chickpea Pumpkin Curry

Preparation Time: 10 minutes; Cooking Time: 8 hours 30 minutes; Serve: 6

Ingredients:
- 30 oz can chickpeas, drained
- 15 oz can coconut milk
- 1/4 tsp cayenne pepper
- 1 tbsp curry powder
- 1 cup pumpkin puree
- 1 cup split red lentils, rinsed
- 2 cups vegetable broth
- 2 garlic cloves, minced
- 1 onion, diced
- 1 tsp kosher salt

Directions:
1. Add all ingredients except coconut milk into the cooking pot and stir well.
2. Cover instant pot aura with lid.
3. Select slow cook mode and cook on LOW for 8 hours.
4. Stir in coconut milk and cook on low for 30 minutes more.
5. Stir well and serve.

Nutritional Value (Amount per Serving):
Calories 460; Fat 17.8 g; Carbohydrates 59.6 g; Sugar 3.1 g; Protein 19.2 g; Cholesterol 0 mg

Easy Vegan Gumbo

Preparation Time: 10 minutes; Cooking Time: 8 hours; Serve: 6

Ingredients:
- 2 large carrots, peeled & chopped
- 2 celery stalks, chopped
- 1 green bell pepper, chopped
- 1 small onion, chopped
- 1/4 cup fresh parsley, chopped
- 2 tbsp tomato paste
- 1/2 tsp dried thyme
- 2 tbsp cajun seasoning
- 2 tbsp soy sauce
- 1 1/2 cups mushrooms, cut into quarters
- 1 1/2 cups asparagus, chopped

- 30 oz can kidney beans, rinsed & drained
- 30 oz can tomato, diced
- 3 cups vegetable broth
- 1 tbsp garlic, minced
- 1/4 tsp kosher salt

Directions:
1. Add all ingredients except parsley into the cooking pot and stir well.
2. Cover instant pot aura with lid.
3. Select slow cook mode and cook on LOW for 8 hours.
4. Garnish with parsley and serve.

Nutritional Value (Amount per Serving):
Calories 211; Fat 1.4 g; Carbohydrates 38.8 g; Sugar 12.3 g; Protein 13.8 g; Cholesterol 0 mg

Easy Corn Pudding

Preparation Time: 10 minutes; Cooking Time: 2 hours; Serve: 8
Ingredients:
- 3 eggs
- 2 cups corn kernels, chopped 1/2 cup corn
- 1/2 cup milk
- 1 tbsp butter, melted
- 2 tbsp sugar
- Pinch of salt

Directions:
1. Add corn into the cooking pot.
2. In a bowl, whisk eggs with milk, butter, sugar, and salt and pour over corn in the cooking pot.
3. Cover instant pot aura with lid.
4. Select slow cook mode and cook on LOW for 2 hours.
5. Stir and serve.

Nutritional Value (Amount per Serving):
Calories 88; Fat 3.8 g; Carbohydrates 11.1 g; Sugar 5.1 g; Protein 3.9 g; Cholesterol 66 mg

Quinoa Coconut Curry

Preparation Time: 10 minutes; Cooking Time: 4 hours; Serve: 8
Ingredients:
- 1/4 cup quinoa
- 29 oz can coconut milk
- 28 oz can tomato, diced
- 15 oz can chickpeas, drained & rinsed
- 1/2 onion, diced
- 2 cups broccoli florets
- 3 cups sweet potatoes, peel & chopped
- 1 tsp miso
- 2 tsp tamari sauce
- 1 tsp turmeric
- 1 tbsp fresh ginger, grated
- 2 garlic cloves, minced
- 1/2 tsp chili flakes

Directions:
1. Add all ingredients into the cooking pot and stir well.
2. Cover instant pot aura with lid.
3. Select slow cook mode and cook on HIGH for 4 hours.
4. Stir well and serve.

Nutritional Value (Amount per Serving):
Calories 390; Fat 23.2 g; Carbohydrates 42.5 g; Sugar 4.4 g; Protein 8.3 g; Cholesterol 0 mg

Cauliflower Lentil Sweet Potato Curry

Preparation Time: 10 minutes; Cooking Time: 7 hours; Serve: 8
Ingredients:
- 3 cups cauliflower florets
- 4 green onions, sliced

- 1/2 cup cilantro, chopped
- 1 cup of coconut milk
- 6 oz can tomato paste
- 1 cinnamon stick
- 2 tsp fresh ginger, grated
- 1 1/2 tsp turmeric
- 2 tsp ground cumin
- 1 1/2 tsp ground coriander
- 3 garlic cloves, minced
- 3 tbsp red curry paste
- 3 cups vegetable broth
- 2 cups dried red lentils, rinsed
- 2 1/2 cups water
- 1 onion, chopped
- 4 1/2 cups sweet potato, peel & cubed
- 1 tsp kosher salt

Directions:
1. Add all ingredients except coconut milk into the cooking pot and stir well.
2. Cover instant pot aura with lid.
3. Select slow cook mode and cook on LOW for 7 hours.
4. Discard cinnamon stick.
5. Stir in coconut milk.
6. Stir well and serve over rice.

Nutritional Value (Amount per Serving):
Calories 419; Fat 10.4 g; Carbohydrates 64.6 g; Sugar 13.8 g; Protein 19.4 g; Cholesterol 0 mg

Balsamic Brussels Sprouts

Preparation Time: 10 minutes; Cooking Time: 4 hours; Serve: 6

Ingredients:
- 2 lbs brussels sprouts, rinsed & halved
- 2 tbsp olive oil
- 1 tbsp brown sugar
- 1/2 cup balsamic vinegar
- Pepper
- salt

Directions:
1. Add brussels sprouts, oil, pepper, and salt into the cooking pot and stir well.
2. Cover instant pot aura with lid.
3. Select slow cook mode and cook on LOW for 4 hours.
4. Mix together vinegar and brown sugar and pour over brussels sprouts and mix well.
5. Serve and enjoy.

Nutritional Value (Amount per Serving):
Calories 115; Fat 5.2 g; Carbohydrates 15.4 g; Sugar 4.8 g; Protein 5.2 g; Cholesterol 0 mg

Broccoli Rice Casserole

Preparation Time: 10 minutes; Cooking Time: 4 hours; Serve: 6

Ingredients:
- 2 lbs frozen broccoli florets
- 2 cans condensed cream of mushroom soup
- 1 onion, chopped
- 8 oz jar cheez whiz
- 1 cup minute rice, uncooked
- Pepper
- salt

Directions:
1. Add all ingredients into the cooking pot and stir well.
2. Cover instant pot aura with lid.
3. Select slow cook mode and cook on HIGH for 4 hours.
4. Stir well and serve.

Nutritional Value (Amount per Serving):
Calories 364; Fat 14.2 g; Carbohydrates 43.8 g; Sugar 8.4 g; Protein 10.4 g; Cholesterol 28 mg

Rich & Creamy Mac and Cheese

Preparation Time: 10 minutes; Cooking Time: 3 hours; Serve: 6

Ingredients:
- 1 lb elbow macaroni pasta
- 1/2 tsp garlic powder
- 1/2 tsp onion powder
- 1 tsp paprika
- 16 oz cheddar cheese, shredded
- 1/4 cup butter, melted
- 12 oz can evaporate milk
- 3 cups of milk
- 1 tsp kosher salt

Directions:
1. Add all ingredients into the cooking pot and stir well.
2. Cover instant pot aura with lid.
3. Select slow cook mode and cook on LOW for 3 hours.
4. Stir well and serve.

Nutritional Value (Amount per Serving):
Calories 795; Fat 40.9 g; Carbohydrates 68.6 g; Sugar 8.8 g; Protein 36.3 g; Cholesterol 126 mg

Lemon Butter Carrots

Preparation Time: 10 minutes; Cooking Time: 3 hours; Serve: 4

Ingredients:
- 2 lbs carrots, cut into matchsticks
- 1 tbsp lemon zest
- 1/4 cup fresh lemon juice
- 1 tbsp fresh thyme, chopped
- 1/4 cup butter
- 1 onion, diced
- Pepper
- Salt

Directions:
1. Add all ingredients into the cooking pot and stir well.
2. Cover instant pot aura with lid.
3. Select slow cook mode and cook on HIGH for 3 hours.
4. Stir well and serve.

Nutritional Value (Amount per Serving):
Calories 212; Fat 11.7 g; Carbohydrates 26 g; Sugar 12.7 g; Protein 2.5 g; Cholesterol 31 mg

Creamy Corn

Preparation Time: 10 minutes; Cooking Time: 4 hours; Serve: 8

Ingredients:
- 32 oz frozen corn
- 1/2 cup parmesan cheese, grated
- 1 tbsp sugar
- 1/2 cup milk
- 1/2 tsp garlic powder
- 4 oz cream cheese, softened
- 1/2 cup butter, melted
- 1/4 tsp pepper
- 1/2 tsp salt

Directions:
1. Add all ingredients except parmesan cheese into the cooking pot and stir well.
2. Cover instant pot aura with lid.
3. Select slow cook mode and cook on LOW for 4 hours.
4. Add parmesan cheese 30 minutes before serving.
5. Stir well and serve.

Nutritional Value (Amount per Serving):
Calories 740; Fat 27.1 g; Carbohydrates 119.3 g; Sugar 22.3 g; Protein 26.4 g; Cholesterol 58 mg

Slow Cook Potatoes

Preparation Time: 10 minutes; Cooking Time: 8 hours; Serve: 6

Ingredients:
- 3 lbs potatoes, halved
- 1/8 tsp cayenne pepper

- 1/4 tsp garlic powder
- 1 1/4 tsp dried oregano
- 1 1/4 tsp paprika
- 1/4 cup butter, melted
- 1 onion, halved
- Pepper
- Salt

Directions:
1. Add all ingredients into the cooking pot and stir well.
2. Cover instant pot aura with lid.
3. Select slow cook mode and cook on LOW for 8 hours.
4. Stir well and serve.

Nutritional Value (Amount per Serving):
Calories 234; Fat 8 g; Carbohydrates 37.9 g; Sugar 3.5 g; Protein 4.2 g; Cholesterol 20 mg

Vegetable Farro

Preparation Time: 10 minutes; Cooking Time: 2 hours 30 minutes; Serve: 8
Ingredients:
- 2 cups pearled faro
- 1/2 cup fresh basil, chopped
- 1/2 cup parmesan cheese, grated
- 2 tbsp olive oil
- 4 cups of water
- 2 cups cherry tomatoes, halved
- 1 cup onion, chopped
- 1/4 tsp pepper
- 1 1/2 tsp salt

Directions:
1. Add oil into the cooking pot and set instant pot aura on saute mode.
2. Add onion and saute until onion is softened.
3. Add all ingredients except parmesan cheese and basil into the cooking pot.
4. Cover instant pot aura with lid.
5. Select slow cook mode and cook on HIGH for 2 1/2 hours.
6. Stir in parmesan cheese and basil.
7. Stir well and serve.

Nutritional Value (Amount per Serving):
Calories 231; Fat 6.7 g; Carbohydrates 33.7 g; Sugar 1.8 g; Protein 11.3 g; Cholesterol 10 mg

Creamy Cauliflower Mash

Preparation Time: 10 minutes; Cooking Time: 6 hours; Serve: 6
Ingredients:
- 1 large cauliflower head, cut into florets
- 3 tbsp butter
- 4 cups of water
- 1 cup vegetable broth
- 4 tbsp fresh herbs, chopped
- 4 garlic cloves, minced
- Pepper
- Salt

Directions:
1. Add cauliflower florets, water, broth, garlic, pepper, and salt into the cooking pot and stir well.
2. Cover instant pot aura with lid.
3. Select slow cook mode and cook on LOW for 6 hours.
4. Add butter and mash cauliflower mixture using an immersion blender until smooth.
5. Add fresh herbs, pepper, and salt and mix well.
6. Serve and enjoy.

Nutritional Value (Amount per Serving):
Calories 97; Fat 6.2 g; Carbohydrates 8.7 g; Sugar 3.5 g; Protein 3.9 g; Cholesterol 15 mg

Cheesy Squash

Preparation Time: 10 minutes; Cooking Time: 1 hour 30 minutes; Serve: 8
Ingredients:
- 4 medium yellow squash, cut into half-moon shapes
- 6 oz Velveeta cheese, cubed
- 4 tbsp butter, cubed
- 1 small onion, sliced
- Pepper
- salt

Directions:
1. Add squash and onion into the cooking pot. Season with pepper and salt.
2. Add cheese and butter on top of the squash and onion mixture.
3. Cover instant pot aura with lid.
4. Select slow cook mode and cook on LOW for 1 1/2 hours.
5. Serve and enjoy.

Nutritional Value (Amount per Serving):
Calories 131; Fat 10.5 g; Carbohydrates 6.4 g; Sugar 3.6 g; Protein 5.2 g; Cholesterol 30 mg

Cheesy Cauliflower Casserole

Preparation Time: 10 minutes; Cooking Time: 4 hours; Serve: 8
Ingredients:
- 2 cauliflower heads, cut into florets
- 1/4 cup parmesan cheese, shredded
- 1/2 cup cheddar cheese, shredded
- 3 cans cream of celery soup
- 1 onion, diced
- 1 cup celery, chopped
- 1/2 cup water

Directions:
1. Add cauliflower, celery, and onion into the cooking pot.
2. Pour remaining ingredients over cauliflower mixture in the cooking pot.
3. Cover instant pot aura with lid.
4. Select slow cook mode and cook on LOW for 4 hours.
5. Serve and enjoy.

Nutritional Value (Amount per Serving):
Calories 158; Fat 9.1 g; Carbohydrates 13.6 g; Sugar 3.9 g; Protein 7.2 g; Cholesterol 25 mg

Simple Balsamic Mushrooms

Preparation Time: 10 minutes; Cooking Time: 2 hours; Serve: 4
Ingredients:
- 2 lbs mushrooms, cut off the tip of the stem
- 2 tbsp maple syrup
- 1 tbsp tamari
- 2 tbsp balsamic vinegar
- 1 tbsp garlic, diced
- 1/4 cup olive oil
- 1/4 tsp pepper
- 1/2 tsp sea salt

Directions:
1. Add all ingredients into the cooking pot and stir well.
2. Cover instant pot aura with lid.
3. Select slow cook mode and cook on HIGH for 2 hours.
4. Stir well and serve.

Nutritional Value (Amount per Serving):
Calories 190; Fat 13.3 g; Carbohydrates 15.3 g; Sugar 10 g; Protein 7.7 g; Cholesterol 0 mg

Healthy Green Beans

Preparation Time: 10 minutes; Cooking Time: 4 hours; Serve: 6

Ingredients:
- 2 lbs fresh green beans, washed & trimmed
- 14.5 oz vegetable broth
- 1 tbsp butter
- 2 garlic cloves, minced
- 1 onion, diced

Directions:
1. Add butter into the cooking pot and set instant pot aura on saute mode.
2. Add onion and saute until onion is softened.
3. Add remaining ingredients into the cooking pot and stir well.
4. Cover instant pot aura with lid.
5. Select slow cook mode and cook on LOW for 4 hours.
6. Stir well and serve.

Nutritional Value (Amount per Serving):
Calories 84; Fat 2.5 g; Carbohydrates 13.1 g; Sugar 3.1 g; Protein 4.4 g; Cholesterol 5 mg

Herbed Mushrooms & Onions

Preparation Time: 10 minutes; Cooking Time: 4 hours; Serve: 10

Ingredients:
- 4 cups mushrooms, sliced
- 4 cups onions, sliced
- 2 garlic cloves, minced
- 1/2 tsp black pepper
- 1/2 tsp dried thyme
- 1/2 tsp dried oregano
- 1/2 cup butter, sliced
- 1/2 tsp sea salt

Directions:
1. Add all ingredients into the cooking pot and stir well.
2. Cover instant pot aura with lid.
3. Select slow cook mode and cook on HIGH for 4 hours.
4. Stir well and serve.

Nutritional Value (Amount per Serving):
Calories 107; Fat 9.4 g; Carbohydrates 5.6 g; Sugar 2.5 g; Protein 1.6 g; Cholesterol 24 mg

Honey Milk Corn on the Cob

Preparation Time: 10 minutes; Cooking Time: 3 hours; Serve: 6

Ingredients:
- 3 ears of corn, cut in half
- 1/4 cup butter
- 1 tbsp honey
- 7 oz can coconut milk

Directions:
1. Add corn into the cooking pot.
2. Add butter, honey, and coconut milk on top of corn in the cooking pot.
3. Cover instant pot aura with lid.
4. Select slow cook mode and cook on HIGH for 3 hours.
5. Stir and serve.

Nutritional Value (Amount per Serving):
Calories 210; Fat 15.6 g; Carbohydrates 18.3 g; Sugar 5.4 g; Protein 3.3 g; Cholesterol 20 mg

Vegetable Fajita

Preparation Time: 10 minutes; Cooking Time: 4 hours; Serve: 10

Ingredients:
- 4 red bell peppers, seeded & sliced
- 4 green bell peppers, seeded & sliced
- 6 tomatoes, diced
- 3 medium onions, sliced
- 4 oz can green chili peppers, diced
- 2 tsp chili powder
- 2 tsp ground cumin
- 1 1/2 tbsp vegetable oil

- 2 garlic cloves, minced
- 1/2 tsp dried oregano
- Pepper
- Salt

Directions:
1. Add all ingredients into the cooking pot and stir well.
2. Cover instant pot aura with lid.
3. Select slow cook mode and cook on LOW for 4 hours.
4. Stir well and serve.

Nutritional Value (Amount per Serving):
Calories 82; Fat 2.7 g; Carbohydrates 14.4 g; Sugar 8.2 g; Protein 2.2 g; Cholesterol 0 mg

Rosemary Beets

Preparation Time: 10 minutes; Cooking Time: 3 hours; Serve: 4
Ingredients:
- 6 beets, trimmed, peeled, & sliced
- 2 tbsp fresh rosemary, chopped
- 2 tbsp apple cider vinegar
- 2 tbsp honey
- 3 tbsp olive oil
- 1/2 tsp sea salt

Directions:
1. Add beets into the cooking pot.
2. Mix together honey, oil, vinegar, rosemary, and salt and pour over beets in the cooking pot.
3. Cover instant pot aura with lid.
4. Select slow cook mode and cook on HIGH for 3 hours.
5. Stir well and serve.

Nutritional Value (Amount per Serving):
Calories 195; Fat 11 g; Carbohydrates 24.7 g; Sugar 20.6 g; Protein 2.6 g; Cholesterol 0 mg

Spicy Eggplant Curry

Preparation Time: 10 minutes; Cooking Time: 5 hours; Serve: 6
Ingredients:
- 1 large eggplant, cubed
- 1/2 cup vegetable broth
- 14 oz can coconut milk
- 3/4 cup tomato paste
- 1/4 tsp cayenne pepper
- 1 tbsp garam masala
- 1/4 tsp cumin
- 1 tbsp curry powder
- 1 cup can chickpeas, rinsed & drained
- 1 cup carrot, chopped
- 1 cup zucchini, chopped
- 1 tbsp garlic, minced
- 1 onion, chopped
- 1 tsp sea salt

Directions:
1. Add all ingredients into the cooking pot and stir well.
2. Cover instant pot aura with lid.
3. Select slow cook mode and cook on LOW for 5 hours.
4. Stir well and serve over rice.

Nutritional Value (Amount per Serving):
Calories 251; Fat 15.2 g; Carbohydrates 27 g; Sugar 8.4 g; Protein 6.7 g; Cholesterol 0 mg

Delicious Mediterranean Eggplant

Preparation Time: 10 minutes; Cooking Time: 5 hours; Serve: 4
Ingredients:
- 1 lb eggplant, peel & cut into 1-inch cubes
- 4 oz feta cheese, crumbled
- 2 tsp dried basil
- 1 tbsp garlic, minced
- 1 large zucchini, chopped

- 4 tomatoes, diced
- 1 onion, diced
- 1 bell pepper, chopped
- 1 tbsp olive oil
- Pepper
- Salt

Directions:
1. Add all ingredients except feta cheese into the cooking pot and stir well.
2. Cover instant pot aura with lid.
3. Select slow cook mode and cook on LOW for 5 hours.
4. Top with feta cheese and serve.

Nutritional Value (Amount per Serving):
Calories 192; Fat 10.3 g; Carbohydrates 20.9 g; Sugar 11.9 g; Protein 7.9 g; Cholesterol 25 mg

Tasty Cheesy Potatoes

Preparation Time: 10 minutes; Cooking Time: 6 hours; Serve: 10

Ingredients:
- 30 oz shredded hash browns, frozen
- 2 cups cheddar cheese, shredded
- 10.75 oz cream of onion soup
- 2 cups sour cream
- Pepper
- Salt

Directions:
1. Add all ingredients into the cooking pot and stir well.
2. Cover instant pot aura with lid.
3. Select slow cook mode and cook on LOW for 6 hours.
4. Serve and enjoy.

Nutritional Value (Amount per Serving):
Calories 440; Fat 29.3 g; Carbohydrates 34.6 g; Sugar 24 g; Protein 9.9 g; Cholesterol 45 mg

Creamy Scalloped Potatoes

Preparation Time: 10 minutes; Cooking Time: 6 hours; Serve: 8

Ingredients:
- 3 lbs potatoes, wash, peel & thinly sliced
- 1/2 cup parmesan cheese, shredded
- 2 cups mozzarella cheese, shredded
- 1/4 tsp dried thyme
- 1/4 tsp black pepper
- 1 tsp dried parsley
- 1 tsp garlic, minced
- 1 tbsp cornstarch
- 1/2 cup vegetable broth
- 2 cups heavy whipping cream
- 2 tsp salt

Directions:
1. In a measuring cup, stir together broth, parsley, garlic, cornstarch, cream, pepper, thyme, and salt.
2. Place 1/3 of sliced potatoes in the bottom of the cooking pot then drizzle with 1/3 cup of the broth mixture and top with 1/3 of the cheese. Repeat layers 3 times.
3. Cover instant pot aura with lid.
4. Select slow cook mode and cook on LOW for 6 hours.
5. Serve and enjoy.

Nutritional Value (Amount per Serving):
Calories 295; Fat 15.7 g; Carbohydrates 29.5 g; Sugar 2 g; Protein 10.5 g; Cholesterol 55 mg

Chickpea Curry

Preparation Time: 10 minutes; Cooking Time: 8 hours; Serve: 6

Ingredients:
- 16 oz chickpeas, soaked in water for overnight & drained
- 3 cups of water
- 1/4 tsp baking soda

- 1/2 tsp ground cinnamon
- 1 1/2 tsp turmeric
- 2 tsp cayenne pepper
- 1 tbsp garam masala
- 2 tbsp cumin
- 2 cups tomatoes, diced
- 1/4 cup tomato paste
- 1 tbsp garlic, chopped
- 1 1/2 cup onion, diced
- 1 tbsp olive oil
- Pepper
- Salt

Directions:
1. Add oil into the cooking pot and set instant pot aura on saute mode.
2. Add onion into the cooking pot and saute until softened. Add garlic and saute for 2 minutes.
3. Add remaining ingredients into the cooking pot and stir well.
4. Cover instant pot aura with lid.
5. Select slow cook mode and cook on LOW for 8 hours.
6. Stir well and serve.

Nutritional Value (Amount per Serving):
Calories 340; Fat 7.7 g; Carbohydrates 55.1 g; Sugar 12.4 g; Protein 16.5 g; Cholesterol 0 mg

Garlic Cauliflower Grits

Preparation Time: 10 minutes; Cooking Time: 2 hours; Serve: 8
Ingredients:
- 6 cups cauliflower rice
- 1/2 cup vegetable stock
- 1/4 tsp onion powder
- 1/4 tsp garlic powder
- 1 cup cream cheese
- 1/2 tsp pepper
- 1 tsp salt

Directions:
1. Add all ingredients into the cooking pot and stir well.
2. Cover instant pot aura with lid.
3. Select slow cook mode and cook on LOW for 2 hours.
4. Stir well and serve.

Nutritional Value (Amount per Serving):
Calories 145; Fat 11.5 g; Carbohydrates 6.1 g; Sugar 3.2 g; Protein 5.2 g; Cholesterol 32 mg

Cheesy Cauliflower Casserole

Preparation Time: 10 minutes; Cooking Time: 6 hours; Serve: 8
Ingredients:
- 12 eggs
- 1 cauliflower head, shredded
- 2 cups cheddar cheese, shredded
- 1/2 cup milk
- 1 lb sausage, cooked and crumbled
- Pepper
- Salt

Directions:
1. In a bowl, whisk the egg with milk, pepper, and salt.
2. Add about third shredded cauliflower into the cooking pot. Season with pepper and salt.
3. Top with about third sausage and third cheese. Repeat layers twice.
4. Pour egg mixture into the cooking pot.
5. Cover instant pot aura with lid.
6. Select slow cook mode and cook on LOW for 6 hours.
7. Serve and enjoy.

Nutritional Value (Amount per Serving):
Calories 416; Fat 32.3 g; Carbohydrates 3.4 g; Sugar 2.2 g; Protein 27.5 g; Cholesterol 324 mg

Sweet Potatoes with Pineapple

Preparation Time: 10 minutes; Cooking Time: 2 hours; Serve: 5
Ingredients:
- 20 oz can yams, drained
- 5 oz can pineapple, crushed and drained
- 1 tbsp brown sugar

Directions:
1. Add all ingredients into the cooking pot and stir well.
2. Cover instant pot aura with lid.
3. Select slow cook mode and cook on LOW for 2 hours.
4. Stir well and serve.

Nutritional Value (Amount per Serving):
Calories 155; Fat 0.2 g; Carbohydrates 37.4 g; Sugar 6.4 g; Protein 11.8 g; Cholesterol 0 mg

Pecan Cheese Brussels Sprouts

Preparation Time: 10 minutes; Cooking Time: 1 hour 30 minutes; Serve: 2
Ingredients:
- 1 1/2 lbs Brussels sprouts, trimmed and halved
- 1/4 cup pecans, chopped
- 1 tbsp olive oil
- 1 1/2 tbsp maple syrup
- 2 tbsp balsamic vinegar
- 2 tbsp parmesan cheese, grated
- 1/8 tsp black pepper
- 1/4 tsp sea salt

Directions:
1. Add all ingredients into the cooking pot and stir well.
2. Cover instant pot aura with lid.
3. Select slow cook mode and cook on LOW for 1 1/2 hour.
4. Stir and serve.

Nutritional Value (Amount per Serving):
Calories 381; Fat 20.7 g; Carbohydrates 43.7 g; Sugar 16.9 g; Protein 16 g; Cholesterol 6 mg

Delicious Okra with Tomato

Preparation Time: 10 minutes; Cooking Time: 2 hours; Serve: 4
Ingredients:
- 1 1/2 cups okra, diced
- 2 large tomatoes, diced
- 1 tsp hot sauce
- 1/2 tbsp garlic, minced
- 1 small onion, diced

Directions:
1. Add all ingredients into the cooking pot and stir well.
2. Cover instant pot aura with lid.
3. Select slow cook mode and cook on LOW for 2 hours.
4. Stir and serve.

Nutritional Value (Amount per Serving):
Calories 40; Fat 0.3 g; Carbohydrates 8.3 g; Sugar 3.7 g; Protein 1.8 g; Cholesterol 0 mg

Sweet Potatoes Mash

Preparation Time: 10 minutes; Cooking Time: 3 hours; Serve: 4
Ingredients:
- 3 lbs sweet potatoes, peel and diced
- 1/8 tsp cinnamon
- 1 tbsp butter
- 3/4 cup water
- Pepper
- Salt

Directions:
1. Add all ingredients into the cooking pot and stir well.
2. Cover instant pot aura with lid.
3. Select slow cook mode and cook on HIGH for 3 hours.
4. Mash the potatoes until smooth.
5. Add butter and stir well and serve.

Nutritional Value (Amount per Serving):
Calories 427; Fat 3.5 g; Carbohydrates 94.9 g; Sugar 1.7 g; Protein 5.2 g; Cholesterol 8 mg

Cauliflower Lentil Curry

Preparation Time: 10 minutes; Cooking Time: 6 hours; Serve: 2

Ingredients:
- 1/2 cauliflower head, cut into florets
- 1 carrot, chopped
- 1 cup brown lentils, rinsed
- 12 oz water
- 12 oz tomato sauce
- 1 1/2 tbsp curry powder
- 1/2 tbsp ginger, grated
- 1 garlic clove, minced
- 1/2 onion, diced
- Pepper
- Salt

Directions:
1. Add all ingredients into the cooking pot and stir well.
2. Cover instant pot aura with lid.
3. Select slow cook mode and cook on LOW for 6 hours.
4. Stir well and serve over rice.

Nutritional Value (Amount per Serving):
Calories 159; Fat 1.5 g; Carbohydrates 32.4 g; Sugar 13.6 g; Protein 8.1 g; Cholesterol 0 mg

Healthy Tofu Curry

Preparation Time: 10 minutes; Cooking Time: 2 hours; Serve: 2

Ingredients:
- 1/2 cup tofu, diced
- 1 cup bell pepper, diced
- 1/2 tbsp garam masala
- 1 tbsp peanut butter
- 1/2 tbsp curry powder
- 5 oz coconut milk
- 1 tsp garlic, minced
- 1/2 cup onion, chopped
- 4 oz tomato paste
- 3/4 tsp salt

Directions:
1. Add all ingredients except tofu into the blender and blend until smooth.
2. Add blended mixture and tofu into the cooking pot and stir well.
3. Cover instant pot aura with lid.
4. Select slow cook mode and cook on LOW for 2 hours.
5. Stir and serve.

Nutritional Value (Amount per Serving):
Calories 338; Fat 24.2 g; Carbohydrates 25.9 g; Sugar 14.7 g; Protein 12.5 g; Cholesterol 0 mg

Slow Cook Green Beans

Preparation Time: 10 minutes; Cooking Time: 1 hour 30 minutes; Serve: 6

Ingredients:
- 1 lb green beans
- 2 tbsp water
- 1 tbsp rosemary, minced
- 2 tbsp fresh lemon juice
- 1 tsp fresh thyme, minced

Directions:

1. Add all ingredients into the cooking pot and stir well.
2. Cover instant pot aura with lid.
3. Select slow cook mode and cook on LOW for 1 1/2 hour.
4. Stir well and serve.

Nutritional Value (Amount per Serving):
Calories 27; Fat 0.2 g; Carbohydrates 6 g; Sugar 1.2 g; Protein 1.5 g; Cholesterol 0 mg

Butter Ranch Mushrooms

Preparation Time: 10 minutes; Cooking Time: 3 Hours; Serve: 6
Ingredients:
- 2 lbs mushrooms, rinsed and pat dry
- 3/4 cup butter, melted
- 2 packets ranch dressing mix

Directions:
1. Add all ingredients into the cooking pot and stir well.
2. Cover instant pot aura with lid.
3. Select slow cook mode and cook on LOW for 3 hours.
4. Stir well and serve.

Nutritional Value (Amount per Serving):
Calories 239; Fat 23.5 g; Carbohydrates 5.5 g; Sugar 2.9 g; Protein 5.1 g; Cholesterol 61 mg

Curried Spinach Lentils

Preparation Time: 10 minutes; Cooking Time: 2 hours; Serve: 10
Ingredients:
- 1 cup fresh spinach
- 2 tbsp green curry paste
- 3/4 cup green lentils, rinsed
- 1 sweet potato, cut into chunks
- 1/2 onion, diced
- 2 cups vegetable broth
- Salt

Directions:
1. Add all ingredients except spinach into the cooking pot and stir well.
2. Cover instant pot aura with lid.
3. Select slow cook mode and cook on HIGH for 2 hours.
4. Add spinach and stir until spinach is wilted.
5. Stir well and serve.

Nutritional Value (Amount per Serving):
Calories 77; Fat 1.1 g; Carbohydrates 12 g; Sugar 0.7 g; Protein 4.9 g; Cholesterol 0 mg

Parmesan Zucchini

Preparation Time: 10 minutes; Cooking Time: 3 hours; Serve: 3
Ingredients:
- 2 zucchini, cut into half-moons
- 1/4 cup parmesan cheese, grated
- 1/2 tsp Italian seasoning
- 1 tbsp olive oil
- 1 tbsp butter
- 1 tbsp garlic, minced
- 1 onion, sliced
- 2 tomatoes, diced
- 1/2 tsp pepper
- 1/4 tsp salt

Directions:
1. Add all ingredients except cheese into the cooking pot and stir well.
2. Cover instant pot aura with lid.
3. Select slow cook mode and cook on LOW for 3 hours.
4. Top with cheese and serve.

Nutritional Value (Amount per Serving):

Calories 194; Fat 13.3 g; Carbohydrates 12.9 g; Sugar 6.1 g; Protein 9.2 g; Cholesterol 25 mg

Parmesan Squash Casserole

Preparation Time: 10 minutes; Cooking Time: 6 hours; Serve: 6

Ingredients:
- 2 cups yellow squash, quartered and sliced
- 2 cups zucchini, quartered and sliced
- 1 tsp garlic powder
- 1 tsp Italian seasoning
- 1/4 cup parmesan cheese, grated
- 1/4 cup butter, cut into pieces
- 1/4 tsp pepper
- 1/2 tsp sea salt

Directions:
1. Add sliced yellow squash and zucchini into the cooking pot.
2. Sprinkle with garlic powder, Italian seasoning, pepper, and salt.
3. Top with cheese and butter.
4. Cover instant pot aura with lid.
5. Select slow cook mode and cook on LOW for 6 hours.
6. Serve and enjoy.

Nutritional Value (Amount per Serving):
Calories 115; Fat 10.1 g; Carbohydrates 3.4 g; Sugar 1.5 g; Protein 4.2 g; Cholesterol 28 mg

Parmesan Potatoes

Preparation Time: 10 minutes; Cooking Time: 4 hours; Serve: 6

Ingredients:
- 3 lbs baby potatoes, cut in half
- 1 tsp dried rosemary
- 4 garlic cloves, minced
- 1/4 tsp black pepper
- 2 tbsp parmesan cheese, grated
- 2 fresh thyme sprigs
- 1 tsp dried oregano
- 4 tbsp olive oil
- 1 tsp sea salt

Directions:
1. In a bowl, add all ingredients and mix well. Pour into the cooking pot.
2. Cover instant pot aura with lid.
3. Select slow cook mode and cook on LOW for 4 hours.
4. Serve and enjoy.

Nutritional Value (Amount per Serving):
Calories 229; Fat 10.4 g; Carbohydrates 30.2 g; Sugar 0.1 g; Protein 7.1 g; Cholesterol 2 mg

Creamy Potato Corn Chowder

Preparation Time: 10 minutes; Cooking Time: 8 hours; Serve: 8

Ingredients:
- 16 oz frozen corn
- 24 oz potato, diced
- 1/2 tsp garlic powder
- 1 tsp dried oregano
- 1 tsp dried thyme
- 6 cups chicken stock
- 3 tbsp flour
- 1/4 cup heavy cream
- 2 tbsp butter
- 1/2 tsp onion powder
- Pepper
- Salt

Directions:
1. Add all ingredients except butter and heavy cream into the cooking pot and stir well.
2. Cover instant pot aura with lid.
3. Select slow cook mode and cook on LOW for 8 hours.
4. Stir in heavy cream and butter.

5. Stir well and serve.

Nutritional Value (Amount per Serving):
Calories 388; Fat 8.4 g; Carbohydrates 76.2 g; Sugar 11.3 g; Protein 12.7 g; Cholesterol 13 mg

Baba Ganoush

Preparation Time: 10 minutes; Cooking Time: 1 hour; Serve: 6

Ingredients:
- 1 medium eggplant, peel and diced
- 3 tbsp lemon juice
- 1 tbsp tahini
- 1/4 cup fresh parsley, chopped
- 1/2 tsp olive oil
- 1/4 tsp liquid smoke
- 1 garlic clove, minced
- Pepper
- Salt

Directions:
1. Add all ingredients into the cooking pot and stir well.
2. Cover instant pot aura with lid.
3. Select slow cook mode and cook on HIGH for 1 hour.
4. Mash eggplant mixture until get the desired consistency.
5. Serve and enjoy.

Nutritional Value (Amount per Serving):
Calories 41; Fat 2 g; Carbohydrates 5.5 g; Sugar 2.5 g; Protein 1.3 g; Cholesterol 0 mg

Bean & Mushrooms

Preparation Time: 10 minutes; Cooking Time: 2 hours 30 minutes; Serve: 8

Ingredients:
- 1 1/2 cups mushrooms, sliced
- 4 cups green beans, trimmed
- 1/4 cup water
- 2 tbsp bacon drippings
- 2 garlic cloves, minced
- 1/4 cup leeks, sliced
- 5 bacon slices, cooked and sliced
- Pepper
- Salt

Directions:
1. Add all ingredients into the cooking pot and stir well.
2. Cover instant pot aura with lid.
3. Select slow cook mode and cook on LOW for 2 1/2 hours.
4. Serve and enjoy.

Nutritional Value (Amount per Serving):
Calories 113; Fat 7.1 g; Carbohydrates 5.2 g; Sugar 1.1 g; Protein 7.7 g; Cholesterol 18 mg

Beans & Potatoes

Preparation Time: 10 minutes; Cooking Time: 4 hours; Serve: 6

Ingredients:
- 1 lb green beans, trimmed and cut
- 1 lb potatoes, sliced in half
- 2 shallots, sliced
- 1 tbsp red wine vinegar
- 4 tbsp butter
- 2 cups vegetable broth
- 2 cups of water
- Pepper
- Salt

Directions:
1. Add all ingredients into the cooking pot and stir well.
2. Cover instant pot aura with lid.
3. Select slow cook mode and cook on HIGH for 4 hours.
4. Serve and enjoy.

Nutritional Value (Amount per Serving):
Calories 159; Fat 8.3 g; Carbohydrates 18.2 g; Sugar 2.2 g; Protein 4.4 g; Cholesterol 20 mg

Coconut Squash Lentil Curry

Preparation Time: 10 minutes; Cooking Time: 8 hours; Serve: 8

Ingredients:
- 4 cups butternut squash, peeled and cubed
- 2 cups red lentils
- 1 tsp ground cumin
- 1 tsp turmeric
- 1 tsp garam masala
- 1 tsp ground coriander
- 1 1/2 tsp curry powder
- 2 tbsp ginger, minced
- 3 cups vegetable stock
- 19 oz can tomato, diced
- 14 oz can coconut milk
- 1 onion, minced
- 1/2 tsp salt

Directions:
1. Add all ingredients into the cooking pot and stir well.
2. Cover instant pot aura with lid.
3. Select slow cook mode and cook on LOW for 8 hours.
4. Stir well and serve.

Nutritional Value (Amount per Serving):
Calories 329; Fat 11.4 g; Carbohydrates 44.9 g; Sugar 5.7 g; Protein 15.2 g; Cholesterol 0 mg

Coconut Lentil Vegetable Curry

Preparation Time: 10 minutes; Cooking Time: 8 hours; Serve: 10

Ingredients:
- 2 cups brown lentils
- 15 oz can tomato sauce
- 15 oz can tomato, diced
- 2 carrots, peel and diced
- 1 sweet potato, peel and diced
- 2 garlic cloves, minced
- 1 onion, diced
- 14 oz can coconut milk
- 3 cups vegetable broth
- 1/4 tsp ground cloves
- 3 tbsp curry powder

Directions:
1. Add all ingredients except milk into the cooking pot and stir well.
2. Cover instant pot aura with lid.
3. Select slow cook mode and cook on LOW for 8 hours.
4. Stir in coconut milk and serve.

Nutritional Value (Amount per Serving):
Calories 106; Fat 3.2 g; Carbohydrates 15.3 g; Sugar 6.8 g; Protein 5.1 g; Cholesterol 0 mg

Chapter 3: Beans & Grains

Baked Beans

Preparation Time: 10 minutes; Cooking Time: 8 hours; Serve: 10
Ingredients:
- 3 cups dried navy beans, soaked in water for overnight & drained
- 4 cups chicken broth
- 1/4 cup molasses
- 3/4 cup brown sugar
- 15 oz can tomato sauce
- 1/4 tsp cayenne pepper
- 1 tsp black pepper
- 1 tbsp ground mustard
- 1 bell pepper, diced
- 1 onion, diced
- 1 lb bacon, cut into 1-inch pieces
- 1 tbsp kosher salt

Directions:
1. Add bacon, bell pepper, and onion into the cooking pot and set instant pot aura on saute mode.
2. Saute until onion softens.
3. Add remaining ingredients into the cooking pot and stir well.
4. Cover instant pot aura with lid.
5. Select slow cook mode and cook on LOW for 8 hours.
6. Stir and serve.

Nutritional Value (Amount per Serving):
Calories 561; Fat 20.9 g; Carbohydrates 60.5 g; Sugar 20.8 g; Protein 33.8 g; Cholesterol 50 mg

BBQ Beans

Preparation Time: 10 minutes; Cooking Time: 6 hours; Serve: 16
Ingredients:
- 15 oz can kidney beans, drained & rinsed
- 30 oz can great northern beans, drained & rinsed
- 30 oz can black beans, drained & rinsed
- 2 lbs kielbasa, cut into bite-size pieces
- 1/2 lb bacon, cooked & chopped
- 14 oz chicken broth
- 1/4 cup molasses
- 1/2 cup maple syrup
- 1 tbsp apple cider vinegar
- 1 tsp chili powder
- 1 tbsp mustard
- 1 tbsp Worcestershire sauce
- 3/4 cup ketchup
- 1/2 cup BBQ sauce
- 1 onion, diced

Directions:
1. Add all ingredients except kielbasa into the cooking pot and stir well.
2. Top with kielbasa and stir gently.
3. Cover instant pot aura with lid.
4. Select slow cook mode and cook on LOW for 6 hours.
5. Stir and serve.

Nutritional Value (Amount per Serving):
Calories 412; Fat 16.9 g; Carbohydrates 44.5 g; Sugar 14.8 g; Protein 21.8 g; Cholesterol 55 mg

Sweet & Tangy Cowboy Beans

Preparation Time: 10 minutes; Cooking Time: 4 hours; Serve: 20
Ingredients:
- 1 lb ground beef
- 15 oz can pork and beans
- 15 oz can white beans
- 15 oz can kidney beans
- 2 tbsp bacon drippings
- 1 lb bacon, cooked and chopped

- 2 1/2 tbsp yellow mustard
- 1/4 cup molasses
- 1 cup ketchup
- 3/4 cup brown sugar
- 1 large onion, diced

Directions:
1. Add ground beef and onion into the cooking pot and set instant pot aura on sauté mode.
2. Sauté until meat is no longer pink.
3. Add remaining ingredients into the cooking pot and stir well.
4. Cover instant pot aura with lid.
5. Select slow cook mode and cook on HIGH for 4 hours.
6. Stir and serve.

Nutritional Value (Amount per Serving):
Calories 279; Fat 11.8 g; Carbohydrates 24.6 g; Sugar 11.1 g; Protein 19.7 g; Cholesterol 48 mg

BBQ Lima Beans

Preparation Time: 10 minutes; Cooking Time: 6 hours; Serve: 20
Ingredients:
- 1 1/2 lbs dried lima beans, soak in water for overnight & drain
- 1/4 lb bacon, diced
- 1/2 cup corn syrup
- 10 drops Tabasco sauce
- 1 1/2 cup ketchup
- 1/2 cup brown sugar
- 2 1/4 cups onions, chopped
- 6 cups of water
- 1 tsp salt

Directions:
1. Add all ingredients into the cooking pot and stir well.
2. Cover instant pot aura with lid.
3. Select slow cook mode and cook on HIGH for 6 hours.
4. Stir and serve.

Nutritional Value (Amount per Serving):
Calories 129; Fat 2.8 g; Carbohydrates 22.1 g; Sugar 10.7 g; Protein 4.9 g; Cholesterol 6 mg

Jalapeno Pinto Beans

Preparation Time: 10 minutes; Cooking Time: 8 hours; Serve: 6
Ingredients:
- 1 lb pinto beans, soak in water for overnight & drain
- 14 oz beef broth
- 32 oz vegetable broth
- 6 bacon sliced, cooked & chopped
- 2 jalapeno peppers, seeded & chopped
- 15 oz can tomato, diced & drained
- 1 tsp garlic powder
- 1 tsp cumin
- 1 tsp black pepper
- 1 tbsp garlic, minced
- 1 onion, sliced

Directions:
1. Add all ingredients into the cooking pot and stir well.
2. Cover instant pot aura with lid.
3. Select slow cook mode and cook on HIGH for 8 hours.
4. Stir and serve.

Nutritional Value (Amount per Serving):
Calories 441; Fat 5.4 g; Carbohydrates 55 g; Sugar 5.7 g; Protein 30.8 g; Cholesterol 50 mg

Delicious Hawaiian Beans

Preparation Time: 10 minutes; Cooking Time: 8 hours; Serve: 12
Ingredients:

- 15 oz can kidney beans, rinsed & drained
- 15 oz can white beans, rinsed & drained
- 28 oz can pinto beans, rinsed & drained
- 1 tbsp cajun seasoning
- 6 oz can pineapple juice
- 1 tbsp Worcestershire sauce
- 2 tbsp Dijon mustard
- 2 tbsp vinegar
- 1/3 cup molasses
- 1/3 cup brown sugar
- 1/2 cup ketchup
- 1 tbsp garlic, minced
- 1/2 onion, diced

Directions:
1. Add all ingredients into the cooking pot and stir well.
2. Cover instant pot aura with lid.
3. Select slow cook mode and cook on LOW for 8 hours.
4. Stir and serve.

Nutritional Value (Amount per Serving):
Calories 187; Fat 0.9 g; Carbohydrates 39.1 g; Sugar 14.3 g; Protein 8.2 g; Cholesterol 0 mg

Healthy Wild Rice

Preparation Time: 10 minutes; Cooking Time: 6 hours; Serve: 4
Ingredients:
- 12 oz wild rice
- 8 oz mushrooms, sliced
- 21 oz vegetable broth
- 1/4 cup pecans, chopped
- 1/8 tsp black pepper
- 1/2 tsp dried tarragon
- 1/2 tsp dried marjoram
- 1/3 cup onion, diced
- 3 tbsp soy sauce
- 1 tbsp butter
- 1/2 cup carrot, chopped
- 1 tsp sea salt

Directions:
1. Add all ingredients except pecans into the cooking pot and stir well.
2. Cover instant pot aura with lid.
3. Select slow cook mode and cook on LOW for 6 hours.
4. Add pecans and stir well and let it sit for 10 minutes.
5. Stir and serve.

Nutritional Value (Amount per Serving):
Calories 434; Fat 10.2 g; Carbohydrates 70.5 g; Sugar 5.1 g; Protein 19.2 g; Cholesterol 8 mg

Flavorful Herbed Brown Rice

Preparation Time: 10 minutes; Cooking Time: 3 hours; Serve: 4
Ingredients:
- 2 cups brown rice
- 1/2 tsp dried oregano
- 1/2 tsp dried thyme
- 4 cups chicken broth
- 8 oz mushrooms, sliced
- 2 tbsp butter
- Pepper
- salt

Directions:
1. Add butter into the cooking pot and set instant pot aura on sauté mode.
2. Once butter is melted then add brown rice into the cooking pot and sauté for 2-4 minutes.
3. Add remaining ingredients into the cooking pot and stir well.
4. Cover instant pot aura with lid.
5. Select slow cook mode and cook on HIGH for 3 hours.
6. Stir well and serve.

Nutritional Value (Amount per Serving):

Calories 446; Fat 9.9 g; Carbohydrates 75.4 g; Sugar 1.7 g; Protein 13.9 g; Cholesterol 15 mg

Red Beans & Rice

Preparation Time: 10 minutes; Cooking Time: 8 hours; Serve: 6
Ingredients:
- 2 cups dried red beans, soak in water for overnight & drained
- 4 cups of water
- 1/2 lb smoked sausage, cut into small pieces
- 2 garlic cloves, minced
- 1/2 cup onion, chopped
- Pepper
- Salt

Directions:
1. Add all ingredients into the cooking pot and stir well.
2. Cover instant pot aura with lid.
3. Select slow cook mode and cook on LOW for 7 1/2 hours.
4. Remove 1/4 cup beans from the cooking pot and mash well. Return mashed beans into the cooking pot and cook for 30 minutes more.
5. Stir and serve.

Nutritional Value (Amount per Serving):
Calories 340; Fat 11.4 g; Carbohydrates 38.8 g; Sugar 1.7 g; Protein 21.3 g; Cholesterol 32 mg

Healthy Pumpkin Risotto

Preparation Time: 10 minutes; Cooking Time: 1 hour 30 minutes; Serve: 4
Ingredients:
- 1 1/2 cup Arborio rice
- 2 cups roasted pumpkin
- 1 tsp black pepper
- 4 cups vegetable broth
- 1/2 cup onion, chopped
- 1 tbsp garlic, crushed
- 2 tsp dried sage
- 2 tbsp olive oil
- 2 tsp salt

Directions:
1. Add oil into the cooking pot and set instant pot aura on sauté mode.
2. Add onion, garlic, and sage into the cooking pot and sauté until onion is softened.
3. Add remaining ingredients into the cooking pot and stir well.
4. Cover instant pot aura with lid.
5. Select slow cook mode and cook on HIGH for 1 1/2 hours.
6. Stir well and serve.

Nutritional Value (Amount per Serving):
Calories 509; Fat 15 g; Carbohydrates 77.4 g; Sugar 1.3 g; Protein 15.9 g; Cholesterol 0 mg

Tasty Butternut Squash Risotto

Preparation Time: 10 minutes; Cooking Time: 4 hours; Serve: 8
Ingredients:
- 1 1/4 cups Arborio rice
- 1/4 cup parmesan cheese, grated
- 1 tsp dried sage
- 2 garlic cloves, minced
- 1 small onion, diced
- 2 cups butternut squash, cut into small cubes
- 3 1/2 cups vegetable broth
- 2 tbsp olive oil

Directions:
1. Add all ingredients except parmesan cheese and butternut squash into the cooking pot and stir well.
2. Cover instant pot aura with lid.

3. Select slow cook mode and cook on LOW for 3 hours.
4. Add butternut squash stir well and cook for 1 hour more.
5. Add parmesan cheese and stir well.
6. Serve and enjoy.

Nutritional Value (Amount per Serving):
Calories 198; Fat 5.9 g; Carbohydrates 29.5 g; Sugar 1.5 g; Protein 6.9 g; Cholesterol 5 mg

Parmesan Risotto

Preparation Time: 10 minutes; Cooking Time: 2 hours; Serve: 6

Ingredients:
- 1 1/4 cups Arborio rice
- 3/4 cup parmesan cheese, shredded
- 1 tbsp garlic powder
- 1 tbsp dried onion flakes
- 1/4 cup white wine
- 1/4 cup olive oil
- 4 cups vegetable broth
- 1/2 tsp black pepper
- 1 tsp kosher salt

Directions:
1. Add all ingredients except parmesan cheese into the cooking pot and stir well.
2. Cover instant pot aura with lid.
3. Select slow cook mode and cook on HIGH for 2 hours.
4. Add parmesan cheese and stir well.
5. Serve and enjoy.

Nutritional Value (Amount per Serving):
Calories 351; Fat 15.8 g; Carbohydrates 35.2 g; Sugar 1.2 g; Protein 15.6 g; Cholesterol 21 mg

Mexican Rice

Preparation Time: 10 minutes; Cooking Time: 5 hours; Serve: 4

Ingredients:
- 1 cup white rice
- 1/2 tsp dried oregano
- 1/2 tsp chili powder
- 1 tsp cumin
- 1/4 tsp black pepper
- 1/2 jalapeno, chopped
- 4 oz can green chilies, diced
- 1/2 cup can tomato, diced
- 1 cup tomato sauce
- 1 cup chicken stock
- 1/2 tsp salt

Directions:
1. Add all ingredients into the cooking pot and stir well.
2. Cover instant pot aura with lid.
3. Select slow cook mode and cook on LOW for 5 hours.
4. Stir well and serve.

Nutritional Value (Amount per Serving):
Calories 203; Fat 0.9 g; Carbohydrates 44 g; Sugar 3.9 g; Protein 4.9 g; Cholesterol 0 mg

Delicious Mexican Quinoa

Preparation Time: 10 minutes; Cooking Time: 2 hours; Serve: 6

Ingredients:
- 3/4 cup quinoa, rinsed
- 14 oz can black beans, rinsed and drained
- 1/2 tsp garlic, minced
- 1 tsp cumin
- 1 bay leaf
- 3/4 cup salsa
- 1 1/2 cups water
- 1 tsp salt

Directions:

1. Add all ingredients into the cooking pot and stir well.
2. Cover instant pot aura with lid.
3. Select slow cook mode and cook on HIGH for 2 hours.
4. Fluff quinoa with fork and discard bay leaf.
5. Stir well and serve.

Nutritional Value (Amount per Serving):
Calories 150; Fat 1.7 g; Carbohydrates 27.7 g; Sugar 1.5 g; Protein 7.1 g; Cholesterol 0 mg

Apple Cinnamon Quinoa

Preparation Time: 10 minutes; Cooking Time: 2 hours; Serve: 5

Ingredients:
- 1 cup quinoa, rinsed
- 1 tsp vanilla
- 1/4 tsp nutmeg
- 2 tsp cinnamon
- 1 apple, peel & dice
- 1/4 cup pepitas
- 4 dates, chopped
- 3 cups almond milk
- 1/4 tsp salt

Directions:
1. Add all ingredients into the cooking pot and stir well.
2. Cover instant pot aura with lid.
3. Select slow cook mode and cook on HIGH for 2 hours.
4. Stir well and serve.

Nutritional Value (Amount per Serving):
Calories 504; Fat 37.2 g; Carbohydrates 42.1 g; Sugar 13.8 g; Protein 8.8 g; Cholesterol 0 mg

Spinach Barley Risotto

Preparation Time: 10 minutes; Cooking Time: 6 hours; Serve: 4

Ingredients:
- 1 cup pearl barley
- 1/2 cup halloumi, cut into small pieces
- 2 1/2 cups fresh spinach, chopped
- 2 1/2 cups vegetable stock
- 2 garlic cloves, chopped
- 1 onion, chopped

Directions:
1. Add barley, stock, garlic, and onion into the cooking pot and stir well.
2. Cover instant pot aura with lid.
3. Select slow cook mode and cook on LOW for 6 hours.
4. Add spinach and stir until spinach is wilted.
5. Top with halloumi and serve.

Nutritional Value (Amount per Serving):
Calories 237; Fat 3.9 g; Carbohydrates 43.6 g; Sugar 2.1 g; Protein 8.8 g; Cholesterol 8 mg

Cuban Black Beans

Preparation Time: 10 minutes; Cooking Time: 8 hours; Serve: 8

Ingredients:
- 16 oz dry black beans, soak in water for overnight & drained
- 1 bay leaf
- 1 tomato, chopped
- 1 tsp balsamic vinegar
- 1/2 cup onion, diced
- 1/2 cup bell pepper, chopped
- 2 tbsp olive oil
- 2 garlic cloves, minced
- 1 tsp dry oregano
- 4 cups of water
- 1 tbsp salt

Directions:

1. Add oil into the cooking pot and set instant pot aura on saute mode.
2. Add onion, bell pepper, and garlic and saute until onion is softened.
3. Add remaining ingredients into the cooking pot and stir well.
4. Cover instant pot aura with lid.
5. Select slow cook mode and cook on LOW for 8 hours.
6. Stir well and serve.

Nutritional Value (Amount per Serving):
Calories 232; Fat 4.4 g; Carbohydrates 37.3 g; Sugar 2.1 g; Protein 12.6 g; Cholesterol 0 mg

Tasty Black-Eyed Peas

Preparation Time: 10 minutes; Cooking Time: 8 hours; Serve: 8

Ingredients:
- 1 lb dried black-eyed peas, soak in water for overnight & drain
- 2 tsp Cajun seasoning
- 32 oz beef broth
- 1 ham hock

Directions:
1. Add all ingredients into the cooking pot and stir well.
2. Cover instant pot aura with lid.
3. Select slow cook mode and cook on LOW for 8 hours.
4. Stir well and serve.

Nutritional Value (Amount per Serving):
Calories 183; Fat 2.2 g; Carbohydrates 35.7 g; Sugar 1.9 g; Protein 19.2 g; Cholesterol 10 mg

Delicious Refried Beans

Preparation Time: 10 minutes; Cooking Time: 8 hours; Serve: 6

Ingredients:
- 1 lb dry pinto beans, soak in water for overnight & drained
- 1 tsp cumin
- 2 tsp pepper
- 2 tbsp garlic, minced
- 1 jalapeno pepper, cut the top and quartered
- 1 onion, quartered
- 4 cups vegetable stock
- 5 cups of water
- 3 tsp salt

Directions:
1. Add all ingredients into the cooking pot and stir well.
2. Cover instant pot aura with lid.
3. Select slow cook mode and cook on HIGH for 8 hours.
4. Drain water from beans and mash the beans using an immersion blender until get desired consistency.
5. Stir well and serve.

Nutritional Value (Amount per Serving):
Calories 282; Fat 1.1 g; Carbohydrates 51.3 g; Sugar 3 g; Protein 17 g; Cholesterol 0 mg

Apple Cinnamon Buckwheat

Preparation Time: 10 minutes; Cooking Time: 4 hours; Serve: 4

Ingredients:
- 1 1/2 cups buckwheat groats
- 1 tsp vanilla
- 1 tsp pumpkin pie spice
- 2 tsp cinnamon
- 1/2 cup maple syrup
- 3 apples, core & chopped
- 1 cup almond milk
- 4 cups of water
- Pinch of salt

Directions:
1. Add all ingredients into the cooking pot and stir well.
2. Cover instant pot aura with lid.
3. Select slow cook mode and cook on HIGH for 4 hours.
4. Stir well and serve.

Nutritional Value (Amount per Serving):
Calories 486; Fat 16.1 g; Carbohydrates 86 g; Sugar 44.2 g; Protein 7.6 g; Cholesterol 0 mg

Vegetarian Burritos

Preparation Time: 10 minutes; Cooking Time: 2 hours; Serve: 4
Ingredients:
- 1 cup can black beans, drained & rinsed
- 3/4 tsp chili powder
- 1 cup of salsa
- 3/4 cup rice, rinsed
- 1 1/2 cups water
- 1 cup can sweet corn, drained
- 1/4 tsp salt

Directions:
1. Add all ingredients into the cooking pot and stir well.
2. Cover instant pot aura with lid.
3. Select slow cook mode and cook on LOW for 2 hours.
4. Stir well and serve.

Nutritional Value (Amount per Serving):
Calories 239; Fat 1 g; Carbohydrates 51.3 g; Sugar 3.8 g; Protein 8.1 g; Cholesterol 0 mg

Old Fashioned Lima Beans

Preparation Time: 10 minutes; Cooking Time: 4 hours; Serve: 10
Ingredients:
- 1 lb dried lima beans, soak in water for overnight & drained
- 4 cups chicken broth
- 1 tsp chili powder
- 1 tsp garlic, minced
- 2 onions, chopped
- 3 cups meaty ham hocks
- Pepper
- Salt

Directions:
1. Add all ingredients into the cooking pot and stir well.
2. Cover instant pot aura with lid.
3. Select slow cook mode and cook on LOW for 4 hours.
4. Stir well and serve.

Nutritional Value (Amount per Serving):
Calories 188; Fat 8.8 g; Carbohydrates 11.8 g; Sugar 1.9 g; Protein 14.6 g; Cholesterol 36 mg

Corn & Lima Beans

Preparation Time: 10 minutes; Cooking Time: 10 hours 30 minutes; Serve: 10
Ingredients:
- 1 lb dry lima beans
- 8 cup of water
- 3 celery stalks, sliced
- 1 onion, chopped
- 2 cups frozen corn

Directions:
1. Add all ingredients except corn into the cooking pot and stir well.
2. Cover instant pot aura with lid.
3. Select slow cook mode and cook on LOW for 10 hours.
4. Add corn and stir well and cook on HIGH for 30 minutes more.

5. Stir well and serve.

Nutritional Value (Amount per Serving):
Calories 83; Fat 0.8 g; Carbohydrates 16.1 g; Sugar 2.2 g; Protein 4.3 g; Cholesterol 0 mg

Classic Saffron Rice

Preparation Time: 10 minutes; Cooking Time: 3 hours; Serve: 6

Ingredients:
- 2 cups jasmine rice
- 1 small onion, diced
- 1 tsp garlic powder
- 1 tsp saffron threads
- 1 bay leaf
- 1 tbsp olive oil
- 4 cups vegetable broth
- Pepper
- salt

Directions:
1. Add all ingredients into the cooking pot and stir well.
2. Cover instant pot aura with lid.
3. Select slow cook mode and cook on HIGH for 3 hours.
4. Stir and serve.

Nutritional Value (Amount per Serving):
Calories 266; Fat 3.3 g; Carbohydrates 50.2 g; Sugar 1.1 g; Protein 7.5 g; Cholesterol 0 mg

Simple Brown Rice

Preparation Time: 10 minutes; Cooking Time: 3 hours; Serve: 6

Ingredients:
- 2 cups brown rice
- 5 cups of water
- 2 tsp salt

Directions:
1. Add all ingredients into the cooking pot and stir well.
2. Cover instant pot aura with lid.
3. Select slow cook mode and cook on HIGH for 3 hours.
4. Stir and serve.

Nutritional Value (Amount per Serving):
Calories 229; Fat 1.7 g; Carbohydrates 48.2 g; Sugar 0 g; Protein 4.8 g; Cholesterol 0 mg

Curried Lentil Rice

Preparation Time: 10 minutes; Cooking Time: 5 hours; Serve: 6

Ingredients:
- 1 cup of rice
- 1 tsp garlic powder
- 3 1/2 cups vegetable broth
- 1 vegetarian bouillon cube
- 1 tbsp curry powder
- 1/2 cup lentils
- 1 onion, diced
- 1/4 tsp pepper
- Salt

Directions:
1. Add all ingredients into the cooking pot and stir well.
2. Cover instant pot aura with lid.
3. Select slow cook mode and cook on LOW for 5 hours.
4. Stir and serve.

Nutritional Value (Amount per Serving):
Calories 205; Fat 1.4 g; Carbohydrates 37.6 g; Sugar 1.7 g; Protein 9.6 g; Cholesterol 0 mg

Perfect Spanish Rice

Preparation Time: 10 minutes; Cooking Time: 3 hours; Serve: 12
Ingredients:
- 2 cups of rice
- 2 tbsp fresh cilantro, chopped
- 1 1/2 tsp ground cumin
- 2 tsp chili powder
- 2 bell peppers, diced
- 1 1/2 tsp garlic, minced
- 14.5 oz can tomato, diced
- 2 cups tomato sauce
- 2 cups chicken broth
- 1 onion, diced
- 2 tbsp olive oil
- 1 1/2 tsp salt

Directions:
1. Add oil into the cooking pot and set instant pot aura on saute mode.
2. Add onion and rice and saute for 5 minutes.
3. Add remaining ingredients into the cooking pot and stir well.
4. Cover instant pot aura with lid.
5. Select slow cook mode and cook on HIGH for 3 hours.
6. Stir and serve.

Nutritional Value (Amount per Serving):
Calories 169; Fat 3 g; Carbohydrates 31.6 g; Sugar 4.5 g; Protein 4.3 g; Cholesterol 0 mg

Flavors Salsa Rice

Preparation Time: 10 minutes; Cooking Time: 2 hours; Serve: 6
Ingredients:
- 4 cups cooked brown rice
- 1/2 cup cheddar cheese, grated
- 4 oz can green chili peppers, diced
- 8 oz can tomato sauce
- 1 lb sausage, browned & drained
- 1 cup of salsa
- Pepper
- Salt

Directions:
1. Add all ingredients except cheese into the cooking pot and stir well. Sprinkle cheese on top.
2. Cover instant pot aura with lid.
3. Select slow cook mode and cook on HIGH for 2 hours.
4. Stir and serve.

Nutritional Value (Amount per Serving):
Calories 778; Fat 28.1 g; Carbohydrates 102.2 g; Sugar 3 g; Protein 27.9 g; Cholesterol 73 mg

Vegan Red Bean Rice

Preparation Time: 10 minutes; Cooking Time: 5 hours; Serve: 6
Ingredients:
- 30 oz can red beans, drained & rinsed
- 1 cup of rice
- 1/4 tsp cayenne pepper
- 1 tsp paprika
- 1 bay leaf
- 2 1/3 cups vegetable broth
- 1 tbsp garlic, minced
- 2 tsp dried thyme
- 1 cup celery, chopped
- 1 cup green bell pepper, chopped
- 1 cup onion, chopped
- Pepper
- Salt

Directions:
1. Add all ingredients except rice, pepper, and salt into the cooking pot and stir well.
2. Cover instant pot aura with lid.
3. Select slow cook mode and cook on LOW for 4 hours.
4. Add rice, pepper, and salt and stir well and cook on HIGH for 1 hour more.

5. Stir well and serve.

Nutritional Value (Amount per Serving):
Calories 268; Fat 1.4 g; Carbohydrates 51.8 g; Sugar 5.1 g; Protein 12.3 g; Cholesterol 0 mg

Basil Chicken Rice

Preparation Time: 10 minutes; Cooking Time: 6 hours 25 minutes; Serve: 6

Ingredients:
- 2 lbs chicken breasts, skinless & boneless
- 2 cups white minute rice
- 3 tbsp butter
- 1/2 cup leeks, diced
- 1/4 tsp black pepper
- 2 tbsp dried basil
- 15 oz chicken broth
- 1/2 tsp salt

Directions:
1. Add all ingredients except minute rice into the cooking pot and stir well.
2. Cover instant pot aura with lid.
3. Select slow cook mode and cook on LOW for 6 hours.
4. Remove chicken from the cooking pot. Add minute rice then return chicken to the cooking pot, cover and cook on LOW for 25 minutes more.
5. Stir well and serve.

Nutritional Value (Amount per Serving):
Calories 580; Fat 17.8 g; Carbohydrates 50.7 g; Sugar 0.6 g; Protein 49.8 g; Cholesterol 150 mg

Coconut Beans Rice

Preparation Time: 10 minutes; Cooking Time: 8 hours; Serve: 8

Ingredients:
- 1 cup dried red beans, soak in water for overnight & drained
- 1 1/2 cups rice, rinsed
- 2 cups of coconut milk
- 3 cups vegetable stock
- 2 garlic cloves, minced
- 1/4 tsp allspice
- 1 tsp red pepper flakes
- 1/2 tsp ground ginger
- 1/2 tsp thyme
- 1 lime juice
- 1/2 tsp salt

Directions:
1. Add all ingredients into the cooking pot and stir well.
2. Cover instant pot aura with lid.
3. Select slow cook mode and cook on LOW for 8 hours.
4. Stir well and serve.

Nutritional Value (Amount per Serving):
Calories 348; Fat 14.9 g; Carbohydrates 46.5 g; Sugar 2.9 g; Protein 9.3 g; Cholesterol 0 mg

Mix Bean Chili

Preparation Time: 10 minutes; Cooking Time: 4 hours; Serve: 6

Ingredients:
- 15 oz can pinto beans, drained
- 15 oz can black beans, drained
- 30 oz can kidney beans, drained
- 15 oz can tomato, diced
- 1 tsp cayenne pepper
- 1 1/2 cups frozen corn, defrosted
- 2 bell peppers, diced
- 1 tsp cumin
- 1 cup of salsa
- 2 1/2 cups vegetable stock
- 2 garlic cloves, minced
- 1 small onion, diced
- Pepper
- Salt

Directions:

1. Add all ingredients into the cooking pot and stir well.
2. Cover instant pot aura with lid.
3. Select slow cook mode and cook on HIGH for 4 hours.
4. Stir well and serve.

Nutritional Value (Amount per Serving):
Calories 327; Fat 2.2 g; Carbohydrates 63 g; Sugar 10.3 g; Protein 18 g; Cholesterol 0 mg

Healthy Walnut Barley

Preparation Time: 10 minutes; Cooking Time: 6 hours; Serve: 6
Ingredients:
- 2/3 cup pearl barley
- 1 apple, peeled, cored, and chopped
- 1/4 cup dates, chopped
- 1/4 cup dried apricot halves, chopped
- 1/4 cup dried cranberries
- 1 cup of orange juice
- 1 2/3 cups water
- 2 tbsp walnuts, chopped
- 1/2 tsp ground allspice

Directions:
1. Add all ingredients into the cooking pot and stir well.
2. Cover instant pot aura with lid.
3. Select slow cook mode and cook on LOW for 6 hours.
4. Stir well and serve.

Nutritional Value (Amount per Serving):
Calories 158; Fat 2 g; Carbohydrates 33.5 g; Sugar 12.8 g; Protein 3.5 g; Cholesterol 0 mg

Barley Bean Risotto

Preparation Time: 10 minutes; Cooking Time: 2 hours 30 minutes; Serve: 4
Ingredients:
- 1 1/4 cups pearl barley, rinsed
- 2 1/2 cups vegetable broth
- 15 oz can garbanzo beans, rinsed and drained
- 1/2 small onion, minced
- 1/2 cauliflower head, cut into florets
- 1 tbsp garlic, minced
- 3 carrots, peeled and chopped
- 1 1/2 tbsp olive oil
- 1/4 cup fresh parsley, chopped
- 1 1/2 tbsp fresh lemon juice
- 1 1/4 cups water
- Pepper
- Kosher salt

Directions:
1. Add oil, carrots, cauliflower, garlic, and onion into the cooking pot and set instant pot aura on saute mode and saute vegetables for 5 minutes.
2. Add barley and cook for 2 minutes.
3. Add water, broth, garbanzo beans, pepper, and salt.
4. Cover instant pot aura with lid.
5. Select slow cook mode and cook on HIGH for 2 1/2 hours.
6. Add lemon juice and parsley and stir well.
7. Stir well and serve.

Nutritional Value (Amount per Serving):
Calories 452; Fat 8.2 g; Carbohydrates 81.3 g; Sugar 4.5 g; Protein 15.9 g; Cholesterol 0 mg

Spinach Risotto

Preparation Time: 10 minutes; Cooking Time: 6 hours; Serve: 4
Ingredients:
- 1 cup pearl barley
- 2 1/2 cups fresh spinach, chopped
- 1 onion, chopped
- 2 1/2 cups vegetable stock

- 2 garlic cloves, chopped
- Pepper
- Salt

Directions:
1. Add all ingredients except spinach into the cooking pot and stir well.
2. Cover instant pot aura with lid.
3. Select slow cook mode and cook on LOW for 6 hours.
4. Add spinach and stir until spinach is wilted.
5. Serve and enjoy.

Nutritional Value (Amount per Serving):
Calories 197; Fat 0.8 g; Carbohydrates 43.2 g; Sugar 2.1 g; Protein 6.2 g; Cholesterol 0 mg

Jerk Seasoned Black Beans

Preparation Time: 10 minutes; Cooking Time: 5 hours; Serve: 6
Ingredients:
- 1 lb black beans, soak in water for overnight & drain
- 14 oz tomatoes, chopped
- 1 bay leaf
- 1 tsp jerk seasoning
- 1 red pepper, chopped
- 1 chili pepper, chopped
- 2 garlic cloves, chopped
- 5 cups vegetable broth
- 2 tbsp fresh lime juice
- 1 large onion, chopped
- 2 tbsp olive oil

Directions:
1. Add oil, onion, garlic, peppers, and seasoning into the cooking pot and set instant pot aura on saute mode and saute until onion is softened.
2. Add remaining ingredients into the cooking pot and stir well.
3. Cover instant pot aura with lid.
4. Select slow cook mode and cook on HIGH for 5 hours.
5. Stir well and serve.

Nutritional Value (Amount per Serving):
Calories 364; Fat 7.1 g; Carbohydrates 56 g; Sugar 6.3 g; Protein 21.6 g; Cholesterol 0 mg

Italian Rice

Preparation Time: 10 minutes; Cooking Time: 8 hours; Serve: 4
Ingredients:
- 1 1/2 cups brown rice, rinsed and drained
- 1 tbsp tomato paste
- 4 cups vegetable stock
- 1 tsp fresh oregano
- 1 tsp garlic, minced
- Pepper
- Salt

Directions:
1. Add all ingredients into the cooking pot and stir well.
2. Cover instant pot aura with lid.
3. Select slow cook mode and cook on LOW for 8 hours.
4. Stir well and serve.

Nutritional Value (Amount per Serving):
Calories 269; Fat 2.1 g; Carbohydrates 56.4 g; Sugar 1.2 g; Protein 6 g; Cholesterol 0 mg

Herb Lentil Rice Casserole

Preparation Time: 10 minutes; Cooking Time: 4 hours; Serve: 6
Ingredients:
- 3/4 cup dried lentils, rinsed and drained
- 3/4 cup brown rice, uncooked
- 1 cup carrots, chopped

- 1/4 tsp sage
- 1/2 tsp dried oregano
- 1/2 tsp dried basil
- 1/2 tsp dried thyme
- 1/2 cup bell pepper, chopped
- 3/4 cup cheese, shredded
- 1 cup vegetable broth
- 1 cup tomatoes, chopped
- 1/4 tsp garlic powder
- 1 onion, chopped
- 1/4 tsp salt

Directions:
1. Add all ingredients into the cooking pot and stir well.
2. Cover instant pot aura with lid.
3. Select slow cook mode and cook on HIGH for 4 hours.
4. Stir well and serve.

Nutritional Value (Amount per Serving):
Calories 259; Fat 5.9 g; Carbohydrates 38.5 g; Sugar 3.7 g; Protein 13.1 g; Cholesterol 15 mg

Tasty & Healthy Quinoa

Preparation Time: 10 minutes; Cooking Time: 2 hours; Serve: 8
Ingredients:
- 1 1/2 cups quinoa, rinsed and drained
- 3 cups vegetable stock
- 1 bell pepper, chopped
- 2 garlic cloves, minced
- 1 onion, chopped
- 2 tbsp olive oil
- 1/2 tsp chili powder
- 2 tbsp tomato paste
- 4 tbsp chicken bouillon
- 1 tsp salt

Directions:
1. Add oil, onion, bell pepper, and garlic into the cooking pot and set instant pot aura on saute mode and saute until onion is softened.
2. Add remaining ingredients and stir well.
3. Cover instant pot aura with lid.
4. Select slow cook mode and cook on HIGH for 2 hours.
5. Stir well and serve.

Nutritional Value (Amount per Serving):
Calories 165; Fat 5.6 g; Carbohydrates 24.4 g; Sugar 2.1 g; Protein 5.2 g; Cholesterol 0 mg

Asparagus Barley Risotto

Preparation Time: 10 minutes; Cooking Time: 2 hours 30 minutes; Serve: 4
Ingredients:
- 8 oz asparagus, cut into 1-inch pieces
- 1 1/2 cups pearl barley
- 1 cup peas
- 1 onion, chopped
- 1 carrot, chopped
- 2 garlic cloves, chopped
- 2 tsp vegetable bouillon paste
- 4 1/2 cups water
- 2 tsp lemon zest
- 1 cup parmesan cheese, grated
- 1/2 cup fresh mint leaves, chopped

Directions:
1. Add all ingredients except asparagus, peas, mint, lemon zest, and parmesan cheese into the cooking pot and stir well.
2. Cover instant pot aura with lid.
3. Select slow cook mode and cook on HIGH for 2 1/2 hours.
4. Add asparagus cook on HIGH for 5 minutes more.
5. Stir in peas, mint, lemon zest, and parmesan cheese.
6. Serve and enjoy.

Nutritional Value (Amount per Serving):

Calories 436; Fat 8.3 g; Carbohydrates 73.5 g; Sugar 5.7 g; Protein 20.7 g; Cholesterol 20 mg

Cajun Bean Rice

Preparation Time: 10 minutes; Cooking Time: 8 hours; Serve: 6
Ingredients:
- 2 cups dried red kidney beans, soak in water for overnight & drain
- 1 cup of brown rice
- 6 cups of water
- 1 tbsp paprika
- 2 tbsp Cajun seasoning
- 1/2 cup chives
- 6 garlic cloves, minced
- 2 celery stalk, chopped
- 1 bell pepper, chopped
- 1 onion, chopped
- 1/2 tsp salt

Directions:
1. Add all ingredients into the cooking pot and stir well.
2. Cover instant pot aura with lid.
3. Select slow cook mode and cook on LOW for 8 hours.
4. Stir well and serve.

Nutritional Value (Amount per Serving):
Calories 345; Fat 1.8 g; Carbohydrates 66.9 g; Sugar 3.4 g; Protein 17.2 g; Cholesterol 0 mg

Delicious Shrimp Rice

Preparation Time: 10 minutes; Cooking Time: 2 hours 45 minutes; Serve: 8
Ingredients:
- 2 eggs, beaten
- 2 cups shrimp, cleaned and deveined
- 3 1/2 cups chicken broth
- 2 garlic cloves, minced
- 2 tbsp soy sauce
- 1 3/4 cup rice, uncooked
- 16 oz frozen mixed vegetables, thawed and drained
- 1 bell pepper, seeded and diced

Directions:
1. Add all ingredients except eggs into the cooking pot and stir well.
2. Cover instant pot aura with lid.
3. Select slow cook mode and cook on HIGH for 2 hours.
4. Pour egg over rice and stir well, cover, and cook for 45 minutes more.
5. Stir well and serve.

Nutritional Value (Amount per Serving):
Calories 167; Fat 1.9 g; Carbohydrates 19.7 g; Sugar 3.6 g; Protein 8.6 g; Cholesterol 53 mg

Green Chili Beans

Preparation Time: 10 minutes; Cooking Time: 8 hours; Serve: 6
Ingredients:
- 3 cups dried pinto beans, rinsed and drained
- 16 oz can green chili, diced
- 8 cups of water
- 1 medium onion, diced
- 2 1/2 tbsp chicken bouillon granules

Directions:
1. Add all ingredients into the cooking pot and stir well.
2. Cover instant pot aura with lid.
3. Select slow cook mode and cook on HIGH for 8 hours.
4. Stir well and serve.

Nutritional Value (Amount per Serving):
Calories 358; Fat 1.2 g; Carbohydrates 65.2 g; Sugar 4.7 g; Protein 21.5 g; Cholesterol 0 mg

Bacon Bean Chowder

Preparation Time: 10 minutes; Cooking Time: 8 hours; Serve: 6
Ingredients:
- 1 1/2 cup dried navy beans, soak in water for overnight & drain
- 1 celery stalk, sliced
- 2 medium carrots, sliced
- 8 bacon slices, cooked and crumbled
- 1/8 tsp pepper
- 1 cup milk
- 46 oz can chicken broth
- 1 tsp Italian seasoning
- 1 medium onion, chopped

Directions:
1. Add all ingredients except milk into the cooking pot and stir well.
2. Cover instant pot aura with lid.
3. Select slow cook mode and cook on LOW for 8 hours.
4. Transfer 2 cups of beans into the blender and blend until smooth.
5. Return blended beans into the cooking pot and stir well.
6. Add milk and stir well. Cover and cook on high for 10 minutes more.
7. Stir well and serve.

Nutritional Value (Amount per Serving):
Calories 751; Fat 30.1 g; Carbohydrates 39.6 g; Sugar 5.7 g; Protein 77.7 g; Cholesterol 140 mg

Delicious Chili Pepper Pinto Beans

Preparation Time: 10 minutes; Cooking Time: 8 hours; Serve: 6
Ingredients:
- 2 cups dried pinto beans, soak in water for overnight & drain
- 2 cups of water
- 1 tsp ground cumin
- 1 tsp chili powder
- 1 tsp garlic powder
- 1 large bell pepper, diced
- 1 poblano pepper, diced
- 4 cups chicken stock
- 14 oz smoked sausage, sliced
- 2 bay leaves
- 1 medium onion, diced
- Salt

Directions:
1. Add all ingredients into the cooking pot and stir well.
2. Cover instant pot aura with lid.
3. Select slow cook mode and cook on LOW for 8 hours.
4. Stir well and serve.

Nutritional Value (Amount per Serving):
Calories 476; Fat 20.2 g; Carbohydrates 45.5 g; Sugar 4.1 g; Protein 27.9 g; Cholesterol 56 mg

Tasty Peas Rice

Preparation Time: 10 minutes; Cooking Time: 2 hours; Serve: 4
Ingredients:
- 1 cup brown rice, uncooked
- 1 cup frozen peas
- 2 tbsp green onion, sliced
- 1 bell pepper, chopped
- 2 tbsp butter
- 1 1/4 cup water
- Pepper
- Salt

Directions:
1. Add all ingredients into the cooking pot and stir well.
2. Cover instant pot aura with lid.
3. Select slow cook mode and cook on HIGH for 2 hours.
4. Stir well and serve.

Nutritional Value (Amount per Serving):

Calories 265; Fat 7.2 g; Carbohydrates 44.4 g; Sugar 3.4 g; Protein 6 g; Cholesterol 15 mg

Slow Cook Black Eyed Peas

Preparation Time: 10 minutes; Cooking Time: 6 hours; Serve: 6

Ingredients:
- 1 lb dried black-eyed peas, soak in water for overnight & drain
- 1 garlic clove, diced
- 1 small onion, diced
- 2 cups of water
- 2 cups vegetable broth
- 1/2 tsp pepper
- 1 tsp ground sage
- 1/8 tsp thyme
- 1 bay leaf
- 1 tsp sea salt

Directions:
1. Add all ingredients into the cooking pot and stir well.
2. Cover instant pot aura with lid.
3. Select slow cook mode and cook on LOW for 6 hours.
4. Stir well and serve.

Nutritional Value (Amount per Serving):
Calories 75; Fat 1.1 g; Carbohydrates 11.8 g; Sugar 0.7 g; Protein 5.5 g; Cholesterol 0 mg

Parmesan Risotto

Preparation Time: 10 minutes; Cooking Time: 2 hours; Serve: 5

Ingredients:
- 3/4 cup parmesan cheese, shredded
- 1 1/4 cups Arborio rice
- 4 tbsp white wine
- 4 tbsp olive oil
- 1 tbsp garlic powder
- 4 cups vegetable broth
- 1/2 tsp pepper
- 1/2 tsp salt

Directions:
1. Add all ingredients except cheese into the cooking pot and stir well.
2. Cover instant pot aura with lid.
3. Select slow cook mode and cook on HIGH for 2 hours.
4. Add cheese and stir until cheese is melted & serve.

Nutritional Value (Amount per Serving):
Calories 427; Fat 20.1 g; Carbohydrates 41.5 g; Sugar 1.1 g; Protein 18.7 g; Cholesterol 25 mg

Quinoa & Oats

Preparation Time: 10 minutes; Cooking Time: 7 hours; Serve: 6

Ingredients:
- 1/2 cup quinoa, rinsed and drained
- 1 1/2 cups steel-cut oats
- 1 tsp vanilla
- 2 tbsp pure maple syrup
- 4 cups almond milk
- 1/4 tsp salt

Directions:
1. Add all ingredients except cheese into the cooking pot and stir well.
2. Cover instant pot aura with lid.
3. Select slow cook mode and cook on LOW for 7 hours.
4. Stir well and serve.

Nutritional Value (Amount per Serving):
Calories 517; Fat 40.3 g; Carbohydrates 36.4 g; Sugar 9.6 g; Protein 8.4 g; Cholesterol 0 mg

Curried Lentil Rice

Preparation Time: 10 minutes; Cooking Time: 4 hours; Serve: 6

Ingredients:
- 1/2 cup lentils, rinsed and drained
- 1 cup white rice, rinsed and drained
- 1 onion, diced
- 1 tsp garlic powder
- 3 1/2 cups vegetable broth
- 1 tbsp curry powder
- 1/4 tsp pepper
- Salt

Directions:
1. Add all ingredients into the cooking pot and stir well.
2. Cover instant pot aura with lid.
3. Select slow cook mode and cook on HIGH for 4 hours.
4. Stir well and serve.

Nutritional Value (Amount per Serving):
Calories 204; Fat 1.3 g; Carbohydrates 37.5 g; Sugar 1.7 g; Protein 9.6 g; Cholesterol 0 mg

Chapter 4: Soup & Stews

Flavorful White Chicken Chili

Preparation Time: 10 minutes; Cooking Time: 8 hours; Serve: 8
Ingredients:
- 4 chicken breasts, skinless & boneless
- 1 tsp dried oregano
- 1 tsp ground cumin
- 1 tbsp chili powder
- 1 jalapeno pepper, minced
- 8 oz can green chilies, chopped
- 30 oz can great northern beans, drained & rinsed
- 2 garlic cloves, minced
- 1 small onion, chopped
- 6 cups chicken broth

Directions:
1. Add all ingredients into the cooking pot and stir well.
2. Cover instant pot aura with lid.
3. Select slow cook mode and cook on LOW for 8 hours.
4. Remove chicken from cooking pot and shred using a fork.
5. Return shredded chicken to the cooking pot and stir well.
6. Serve and enjoy.

Nutritional Value (Amount per Serving):
Calories 304; Fat 7.2 g; Carbohydrates 26.3 g; Sugar 1.1 g; Protein 33.2 g; Cholesterol 65 mg

Delicious Chicken Noodle Soup

Preparation Time: 10 minutes; Cooking Time: 4 hours 20 minutes; Serve: 4
Ingredients:
- 6 oz pasta, uncooked
- 1 lb chicken
- 1/2 tsp dried rosemary
- 1/2 tsp dried thyme
- 2 bay leaves
- 2 garlic cloves, minced
- 1 small onion, diced
- 2 carrots, chopped
- 2 celery stalks, sliced
- 3 cups of water
- 4 cups chicken broth
- 1/2 tsp pepper
- 1 tsp salt

Directions:
1. Add all ingredients except noodles into the cooking pot and stir well.
2. Cover instant pot aura with lid.
3. Select slow cook mode and cook on HIGH for 4 hours.
4. Remove chicken from cooking pot and shred using a fork.
5. Return shredded chicken and noodles into the cooking pot, cover, and cook on HIGH for 10-20 minutes more.
6. Discard bay leaves.
7. Stir well and serve.

Nutritional Value (Amount per Serving):
Calories 358; Fat 5.9 g; Carbohydrates 30.1 g; Sugar 3.1 g; Protein 43.2 g; Cholesterol 118 mg

Veggie Bean Soup

Preparation Time: 10 minutes; Cooking Time: 6 hours; Serve: 6
Ingredients:
- 1 lb dried great northern beans, soak in water for overnight & drained
- 2 cups of water
- 4 cups vegetable broth
- 1/2 tsp dried sage
- 1 tbsp garlic, minced
- 1 onion, diced
- 2 celery stalks, diced

- 3 carrots, diced
- Pepper
- salt

Directions:
1. Add all ingredients into the cooking pot and stir well.
2. Cover instant pot aura with lid.
3. Select slow cook mode and cook on HIGH for 6 hours.
4. Stir well and serve.

Nutritional Value (Amount per Serving):
Calories 305; Fat 1.8 g; Carbohydrates 53.2 g; Sugar 4.5 g; Protein 20.4 g; Cholesterol 0 mg

Mexican Chicken Soup

Preparation Time: 10 minutes; Cooking Time: 3 hours; Serve: 6
Ingredients:
- 1 1/2 lbs chicken breasts, skinless & boneless
- 12 oz frozen corn
- 15 oz can black beans, drained & rinsed
- 16 oz jar salsa
- 32 oz chicken stock
- 1 envelope taco seasoning
- 1/2 cup water
- 2 tsp olive oil

Directions:
1. Add oil into the cooking pot and set instant pot aura on saute mode.
2. Add chicken into the cooking pot and saute until chicken is no longer pink.
3. Add remaining ingredients into the cooking pot and stir well.
4. Cover instant pot aura with lid.
5. Select slow cook mode and cook on LOW for 3 hours.
6. Remove chicken from cooking pot and shred using a fork, return shredded chicken to the pot.
7. Stir well and serve.

Nutritional Value (Amount per Serving):
Calories 671; Fat 17.6 g; Carbohydrates 84.3 g; Sugar 15.4 g; Protein 52.7 g; Cholesterol 110 mg

Thai Chicken Soup

Preparation Time: 10 minutes; Cooking Time: 3 hours; Serve: 4
Ingredients:
- 1 lb cooked chicken, chopped
- 2 tbsp basil, chopped
- 1 tbsp garlic powder
- 1 tbsp ginger root
- 1 tbsp green curry paste
- 2 tsp thyme
- 4 cups chicken broth
- 14 oz coconut milk
- 1 cup jasmine rice
- Pepper
- Salt

Directions:
1. Add all ingredients into the cooking pot and stir well.
2. Cover instant pot aura with lid.
3. Select slow cook mode and cook on LOW for 3 hours.
4. Stir well and serve.

Nutritional Value (Amount per Serving):
Calories 619; Fat 29.3 g; Carbohydrates 45.6 g; Sugar 4.6 g; Protein 43.4 g; Cholesterol 87 mg

Easy Pumpkin Chili

Preparation Time: 10 minutes; Cooking Time: 3 hours; Serve: 4
Ingredients:

- 15 oz can pumpkin puree
- 1 lb ground beef
- 1 tsp dried parsley
- 1/2 tsp paprika
- 1/2 tsp chili powder
- 3 garlic cloves, minced
- 1 cup onion, diced
- 1 cup bell pepper, diced
- 28 oz can tomatoes, crushed
- 14.5 oz can tomatoes, diced
- Pepper
- Salt

Directions:
1. Add all ingredients into the cooking pot and stir well.
2. Cover instant pot aura with lid.
3. Select slow cook mode and cook on HIGH for 3 hours.
4. Stir well and serve.

Nutritional Value (Amount per Serving):
Calories 459; Fat 7.3 g; Carbohydrates 58.9 g; Sugar 28 g; Protein 41.7 g; Cholesterol 101 mg

Curried Tomato Soup

Preparation Time: 10 minutes; Cooking Time: 3 hours; Serve: 4
Ingredients:
- 28 oz fresh tomatoes, chopped
- 2 cups vegetable stock
- 2 tsp ginger garlic paste
- 1 1/2 tbsp curry powder
- 1/4 cup green onions, chopped
- 1/2 cup cauliflower florets
- Pepper
- Salt

Directions:
1. Add all ingredients into the cooking pot and stir well.
2. Cover instant pot aura with lid.
3. Select slow cook mode and cook on HIGH for 3 hours.
4. Puree the soup using an immersion blender until smooth.
5. Stir well and serve.

Nutritional Value (Amount per Serving):
Calories 64; Fat 1.3 g; Carbohydrates 12.2 g; Sugar 6.1 g; Protein 3.1 g; Cholesterol 0 mg

Curried Coconut Sweet Potato Soup

Preparation Time: 10 minutes; Cooking Time: 6 hours; Serve: 4
Ingredients:
- 2 medium sweet potatoes, peel & dice
- 30 oz can coconut milk
- 2 tbsp curry powder
- 1 red bell pepper
- 15 oz can chickpeas, rinsed & diced
- 1 medium onion, chopped
- 1 tbsp garlic, minced
- 1/8 tsp black pepper
- 1/4 tsp sea salt

Directions:
1. Add all ingredients into the cooking pot and stir well.
2. Cover instant pot aura with lid.
3. Select slow cook mode and cook on LOW for 6 hours.
4. Transfer soup into the blender and blend until smooth.
5. Stir well and serve.

Nutritional Value (Amount per Serving):
Calories 633; Fat 47.2 g; Carbohydrates 50 g; Sugar 3 g; Protein 11.4 g; Cholesterol 0 mg

Buffalo Chicken Chili

Preparation Time: 10 minutes; Cooking Time: 8 hours; Serve: 6
Ingredients:

- 1 lb ground chicken
- 8 oz cream cheese
- 1/2 tsp dried cilantro
- 1/2 tsp celery salt
- 1/2 tsp garlic powder
- 1/2 tsp onion powder
- 1 cup corn kernels
- 1 packet ranch dressing mix
- 1/2 cup buffalo wing sauce
- 2 cups chicken stock
- 14.5 oz can tomatoes, drained
- 15 oz can navy beans, drained & rinsed
- 1/4 tsp salt

Directions:
1. Add ground chicken into the cooking pot and set instant pot aura on saute mode.
2. Saute chicken until fully cooked.
3. Add remaining ingredients except for cream cheese into the cooking pot and stir well. Top with cream cheese.
4. Cover instant pot aura with lid.
5. Select slow cook mode and cook on LOW for 8 hours.
6. Stir well and serve.

Nutritional Value (Amount per Serving):
Calories 399; Fat 19.6 g; Carbohydrates 24.8 g; Sugar 4 g; Protein 31.9 g; Cholesterol 109 mg

Cauliflower Broccoli Cheese Soup

Preparation Time: 10 minutes; Cooking Time: 6 hours; Serve: 6
Ingredients:
- 2 cups cauliflower florets, chopped
- 3 cups broccoli florets, chopped
- 1 cup Greek yogurt
- 6 oz cheddar cheese, shredded
- 1 cup milk
- 3 1/2 cups chicken broth
- 1 carrot, diced
- 1/2 cup onion, diced
- 2 garlic cloves, minced
- Pepper
- Salt

Directions:
1. Add all ingredients except milk, cheese, and yogurt into the cooking pot and stir well.
2. Cover instant pot aura with lid.
3. Select slow cook mode and cook on LOW for 6 hours.
4. Transfer soup into the blender along with milk, cheese, and yogurt and blend until smooth and Creamy.
5. Stir well and serve.

Nutritional Value (Amount per Serving):
Calories 226; Fat 12.2 g; Carbohydrates 11.8 g; Sugar 6.8 g; Protein 18.2 g; Cholesterol 35 mg

Flavors Stuffed Cabbage Soup

Preparation Time: 10 minutes; Cooking Time: 4 hours; Serve: 8
Ingredients:
- 1/2 cabbage head, cut into 1-inch pieces
- 1 tsp basil
- 1 tsp oregano
- 1 tbsp garlic salt
- 1 lb ground beef
- 19 oz tomato soup
- 23 oz jar spaghetti sauce
- 1 tbsp Worcestershire sauce
- 42 oz beef broth
- 2/3 cup rice, uncooked

Directions:
1. Add ground beef and onion into the cooking pot and set instant pot aura on saute mode.
2. Saute meat until brown.
3. Add remaining ingredients into the cooking pot and stir well.

4. Cover instant pot aura with lid.
5. Select slow cook mode and cook on HIGH for 4 hours.
6. Stir well and serve.

Nutritional Value (Amount per Serving):
Calories 293; Fat 6.8 g; Carbohydrates 33.9 g; Sugar 14.9 g; Protein 24.4 g; Cholesterol 51 mg

Cheesy Broccoli Soup

Preparation Time: 10 minutes; Cooking Time: 5 hours; Serve: 6

Ingredients:
- 1 lb broccoli florets, chopped
- 4 oz parmesan cheese, grated
- 6 oz cheddar cheese, shredded
- 8 oz Colby Jack cheese, shredded
- 1/4 tsp black pepper
- 32 oz chicken broth
- 12 oz can evaporate milk
- 1/4 cup flour
- 2 garlic cloves, minced
- 1/4 cup butter
- 1 onion, diced
- 1/8 tsp salt

Directions:
1. Add butter into the cooking pot and set instant pot aura on saute mode.
2. Once butter is melted then add onion and garlic into the cooking pot and saute for 3-4 minutes.
3. Add flour and stir for 1 minute. Slowly add evaporated milk and whisk until smooth.
4. Add broth, broccoli, pepper, and salt and stir well.
5. Cover instant pot aura with lid.
6. Select slow cook mode and cook on LOW for 5 hours.
7. Add cheese into the cooking pot and stir until cheese is melted.
8. Serve and enjoy.

Nutritional Value (Amount per Serving):
Calories 541; Fat 38.8 g; Carbohydrates 18.7 g; Sugar 1.4 g; Protein 32.2 g; Cholesterol 114 mg

Ginger Carrot Soup

Preparation Time: 10 minutes; Cooking Time: 8 hours 30 minutes; Serve: 6

Ingredients:
- 2 lbs carrots, chopped
- 8 oz heavy cream
- 4 cups chicken stock
- 1 tbsp ginger, peeled & sliced
- 1 tbsp garlic, minced
- 2 onions, chopped
- Pepper
- Salt

Directions:
1. Add all ingredients except cream into the cooking pot and stir well.
2. Cover instant pot aura with lid.
3. Select slow cook mode and cook on LOW for 8 hours.
4. Puree the soup using an immersion blender until smooth.
5. Add cream and stir well, cover, and cook on HIGH for 30 minutes more.
6. Stir well and serve.

Nutritional Value (Amount per Serving):
Calories 219; Fat 14.5 g; Carbohydrates 20.9 g; Sugar 9.5 g; Protein 3 g; Cholesterol 52 mg

Hearty Beef Stew

Preparation Time: 10 minutes; Cooking Time: 8 hours; Serve: 6

Ingredients:
- 1 lb beef stew cubes
- 10 oz frozen green peas
- 8 oz can tomato sauce
- 20 oz can cream of mushroom soup

- 1 oz dry onion soup mix
- 1 bay leaf
- 4 potatoes, cubed
- 4 carrots, sliced
- Pepper
- Salt

Directions:
1. Add all ingredients into the cooking pot and stir well.
2. Cover instant pot aura with lid.
3. Select slow cook mode and cook on LOW for 8 hours.
4. Stir well and serve.

Nutritional Value (Amount per Serving):
Calories 297; Fat 6.1 g; Carbohydrates 51.1 g; Sugar 10.9 g; Protein 11 g; Cholesterol 15 mg

Moroccan Chickpea Stew

Preparation Time: 10 minutes; Cooking Time: 4 hours; Serve: 4
Ingredients:
- 2 potatoes, cubed
- 14 oz can chickpeas, drained & rinsed
- 2 tbsp maple syrup
- 1/8 tsp cayenne pepper
- 1/2 tsp turmeric
- 1/2 tsp cinnamon
- 1 tsp paprika
- 2 tsp curry powder
- 1 1/2 tsp cumin
- 1 cup vegetable broth
- 2 cups tomato sauce
- 1 tbsp garlic, chopped
- 1 onion, chopped
- 1 tbsp vegetable oil
- Pepper
- Salt

Directions:
1. Add oil into the cooking pot and set instant pot aura on sauté mode.
2. Once the oil is hot then add onion and sauté until onion is softened. Add garlic and sauté for 1 minute.
3. Add remaining ingredients into the cooking pot and stir well.
4. Cover instant pot aura with lid.
5. Select slow cook mode and cook on HIGH for 4 hours.
6. Stir well and serve.

Nutritional Value (Amount per Serving):
Calories 311; Fat 5.7 g; Carbohydrates 57.6 g; Sugar 13.9 g; Protein 10.4 g; Cholesterol 0 mg

Chicken Veggie Stew

Preparation Time: 10 minutes; Cooking Time: 4 hours; Serve: 6
Ingredients:
- 1 1/2 lbs chicken breasts, boneless & cut into chunks
- 1 cup bell pepper, diced
- 1 tsp thyme, dried
- 1 cup chicken stock
- 3 cups zucchini, diced
- 8 oz mushrooms, sliced
- 6 oz tomato paste
- 1 tbsp garlic cloves, diced
- 1 onion, diced
- 1 tsp basil, dried
- 1 tsp oregano, dried
- Salt

Directions:
1. Add all ingredients into the cooking pot and stir well.
2. Cover instant pot aura with lid.
3. Select slow cook mode and cook on LOW for 4 hours.
4. Stir well and serve.

Nutritional Value (Amount per Serving):
Calories 275; Fat 9 g; Carbohydrates 12.6 g; Sugar 17 g; Protein 36.6 g; Cholesterol 101 mg

Healthy Mushroom Barley Soup

Preparation Time: 10 minutes; Cooking Time: 8 hours; Serve: 8
Ingredients:
- 16 oz mushrooms, sliced
- 2/3 cup pearl barley
- 1 large onion, diced
- 1 1/2 tsp olive oil
- 6 cups vegetable broth
- 1 garlic clove, minced
- 1/4 tsp pepper
- 1/2 tsp salt

Directions:
1. Add oil, onion, mushrooms, and garlic into the cooking pot and set instant pot aura on sauté mode and sauté onion for 5 minutes.
2. Add remaining ingredients into the cooking pot and stir well.
3. Cover instant pot aura with lid.
4. Select slow cook mode and cook on LOW for 8 hours.
5. Stir well and serve.

Nutritional Value (Amount per Serving):
Calories 115; Fat 2.3 g; Carbohydrates 17.4 g; Sugar 2.4 g; Protein 7.3 g; Cholesterol 0 mg

Chickpea Stew

Preparation Time: 10 minutes; Cooking Time: 4 hours; Serve: 4
Ingredients:
- 16 oz can chickpeas, drained
- 1 onion, chopped
- 1/2 tsp dried rosemary, crushed
- 2 lbs stew beef, cut into cubes
- 1/2 cup chicken stock
- 10 oz can tomatoes, diced
- 1 carrot, peeled and sliced
- 1 tbsp olive oil
- Pepper
- Salt

Directions:
1. Add oil and meat into the cooking pot and set instant pot aura on sauté mode and sauté meat until brown.
2. Add remaining ingredients into the cooking pot and stir well.
3. Cover instant pot aura with lid.
4. Select slow cook mode and cook on LOW for 4 hours.
5. Stir well and serve.

Nutritional Value (Amount per Serving):
Calories 530; Fat 18.5 g; Carbohydrates 33.5 g; Sugar 4.4 g; Protein 56.7 g; Cholesterol 0 mg

Flavorful Pork Stew

Preparation Time: 10 minutes; Cooking Time: 4 hours; Serve: 6
Ingredients:
- 1 lb pork tenderloin, cut into cubes
- 14 oz can tomatoes, diced
- 1/2 tsp ground cumin
- 1/2 tsp curry powder
- 1/2 tsp cinnamon
- 2 garlic cloves, minced
- 1 cup celery, sliced
- 1 cup onion, sliced
- 1/4 cup water
- 2 tbsp cornstarch
- 1/8 tsp cayenne
- Pepper
- Salt

Directions:
1. In a small bowl, whisk together cornstarch and water and set aside.
2. Add remaining ingredients into the cooking pot and stir well.
3. Cover instant pot aura with lid.
4. Select slow cook mode and cook on HIGH for 4 hours.

5. Add cornstarch mixture into the stew and stir for 2 minutes.
6. Stir well and serve.

Nutritional Value (Amount per Serving):
Calories 146; Fat 2.8 g; Carbohydrates 8.8 g; Sugar 3.3 g; Protein 20.8 g; Cholesterol 55 mg

Vegetable Pork Stew

Preparation Time: 10 minutes; Cooking Time: 8 hours; Serve: 4

Ingredients:
- 4 pork chops, boneless
- 1/2 cup olives
- 2 yellow bell pepper, sliced
- 2 red bell peppers, sliced
- 1 onion, sliced
- 2 tsp garlic, minced
- 1 tbsp olive oil
- 2 tsp chili, diced
- 1 bay leaf
- 2 1/4 cups vegetable stock
- 14 oz can tomatoes, chopped

Directions:
1. Add oil, onion, chili, and garlic into the cooking pot and set instant pot aura on saute mode and saute until onion soften.
2. Add remaining ingredients into the cooking pot and stir well.
3. Cover instant pot aura with lid.
4. Select slow cook mode and cook on LOW for 8 hours.
5. Stir well and serve.

Nutritional Value (Amount per Serving):
Calories 384; Fat 25.7 g; Carbohydrates 19.1 g; Sugar 11 g; Protein 21 g; Cholesterol 69 mg

Coconut Tomato Carrot Soup

Preparation Time: 10 minutes; Cooking Time: 4 hours; Serve: 4

Ingredients:
- 4 medium carrots, peeled and chopped
- 1 cup of coconut milk
- 14 oz can tomatoes, diced
- 1 tsp ground cumin
- 1 tsp ground coriander
- 1 tbsp turmeric

Directions:
1. Add all ingredients into the cooking pot and stir well.
2. Cover instant pot aura with lid.
3. Select slow cook mode and cook on LOW for 4 hours.
4. Transfer soup into the blender and blend until smooth.
5. Serve and enjoy.

Nutritional Value (Amount per Serving):
Calories 192; Fat 14.6 g; Carbohydrates 15.7 g; Sugar 8.4 g; Protein 3 g; Cholesterol 0 mg

Simple Pumpkin Soup

Preparation Time: 10 minutes; Cooking Time: 8 hours; Serve: 4

Ingredients:
- 2 cups pumpkin puree
- 4 cups of water
- 1/4 tsp nutmeg
- 1 cup of coconut milk

Directions:
1. Add all ingredients into the cooking pot and stir well.
2. Cover instant pot aura with lid.
3. Select slow cook mode and cook on LOW for 8 hours.
4. Transfer soup into the blender and blend until smooth.

5. Serve and enjoy.

Nutritional Value (Amount per Serving):
Calories 180; Fat 14.7 g; Carbohydrates 13.3 g; Sugar 6.1 g; Protein 2.7 g; Cholesterol 0 mg

Delicious Seafood Stew

Preparation Time: 10 minutes; Cooking Time: 5 hours; Serve: 6

Ingredients:
- 1 lb baby potatoes, cut into pieces
- 1 tbsp garlic, minced
- 2 lbs seafood
- 4 cups vegetable broth
- 28 oz can tomatoes, crushed
- 1/4 tsp red pepper flakes
- 1/2 tsp celery salt
- 1 tsp dried cilantro
- 1 tsp dried basil
- 1 tsp dried thyme
- 1/2 onion, chopped
- 1/2 cup white wine
- Pepper
- Salt

Directions:
1. Add all ingredients except seafood into the cooking pot and stir well.
2. Cover instant pot aura with lid.
3. Select slow cook mode and cook on LOW for 4 hours.
4. Add seafood and stir well cover and cook for 1 hour more.
5. Stir well and serve.

Nutritional Value (Amount per Serving):
Calories 184; Fat 3.4 g; Carbohydrates 26.8 g; Sugar 7.7 g; Protein 9.8 g; Cholesterol 11 mg

Tomato Spinach Bean Soup

Preparation Time: 10 minutes; Cooking Time: 6 hours; Serve: 6

Ingredients:
- 14 oz can Great Northern beans, rinsed and drained
- 14 oz can tomato puree
- 8 cups fresh spinach, chopped
- 1 tsp dried basil, crushed
- 1 tsp garlic, minced
- 1/2 cup onion, chopped
- 1/2 cup of brown rice
- 5 1/2 cups vegetable broth
- 1/4 tsp pepper
- 1/4 tsp salt

Directions:
1. Add all ingredients except spinach into the cooking pot and stir well.
2. Cover instant pot aura with lid.
3. Select slow cook mode and cook on LOW for 6 hours.
4. Stir in spinach and serve.

Nutritional Value (Amount per Serving):
Calories 207; Fat 2.2 g; Carbohydrates 35.3 g; Sugar 4.4 g; Protein 12.9 g; Cholesterol 0 mg

Curried Coconut Pumpkin Soup

Preparation Time: 10 minutes; Cooking Time: 5 hours; Serve: 6

Ingredients:
- 30 oz pumpkin puree
- 4 cups vegetable broth
- 14 oz coconut milk
- 2 tbsp red curry paste

Directions:
1. Add all ingredients into the cooking pot and stir well.
2. Cover instant pot aura with lid.
3. Select slow cook mode and cook on LOW for 5 hours.
4. Stir well and serve.

Nutritional Value (Amount per Serving):
Calories 246; Fat 18.6 g; Carbohydrates 16.7 g; Sugar 7.4 g; Protein 6.3 g; Cholesterol 0 mg

Spinach Chicken Stew

Preparation Time: 10 minutes; Cooking Time: 4 hours; Serve: 4
Ingredients:
- 28 oz chicken thighs, skinless
- 2 garlic cloves, minced
- 1/2 tsp dried rosemary
- 1/2 onion, diced
- 1 cup celery, diced
- 2 carrots, peeled and diced
- 2 cups chicken stock
- 1/2 cup heavy cream
- 1 cup fresh spinach
- 1/2 tsp oregano
- 1/4 tsp dried thyme
- Pepper
- Salt

Directions:
1. Add all ingredients except spinach and heavy cream into the cooking pot and stir well.
2. Cover instant pot aura with lid.
3. Select slow cook mode and cook on LOW for 4 hours.
4. Stir spinach and heavy cream and serve.

Nutritional Value (Amount per Serving):
Calories 461; Fat 20.7 g; Carbohydrates 6.9 g; Sugar 2.9 g; Protein 59 g; Cholesterol 197 mg

Tasty Chicken Fajita Soup

Preparation Time: 10 minutes; Cooking Time: 7 hours; Serve: 8
Ingredients:
- 1 1/2 lbs chicken breast
- 1 orange pepper, diced
- 1 yellow bell pepper, diced
- 6 oz mushrooms, sliced
- 1 onion, diced
- 14 oz can tomatoes, diced
- 4 cups chicken stock
- 2 tbsp cilantro, chopped
- 4 tbsp taco seasoning
- 2 garlic cloves, minced
- 1 tsp salt

Directions:
1. Add all ingredients into the cooking pot and stir well.
2. Cover instant pot aura with lid.
3. Select slow cook mode and cook on LOW for 6 hours.
4. Remove chicken and shred using a fork, return shredded chicken to the cooking pot and cook on LOW for 1 hour more.
5. Stir well and serve.

Nutritional Value (Amount per Serving):
Calories 134; Fat 2.8 g; Carbohydrates 6.8 g; Sugar 3.7 g; Protein 20.1 g; Cholesterol 55 mg

Vegetable Pork Stew

Preparation Time: 10 minutes; Cooking Time: 8 hours; Serve: 8
Ingredients:
- 2 1/2 lbs pork chops, boneless
- 1 1/2 cups rutabaga, peeled and cubed
- 15 oz can tomatoes, diced
- 4 cups chicken broth, low-sodium
- 2 tbsp olive oil
- 1/2 tsp cumin
- 1 1/2 tsp oregano
- 1 tbsp chili powder
- 2 garlic cloves
- 1/2 cup onion, chopped
- 1/2 tsp black pepper
- 1 tsp kosher salt

Directions:

1. Add all ingredients into the cooking pot and stir well.
2. Cover instant pot aura with lid.
3. Select slow cook mode and cook on LOW for 8 hours.
4. Remove pork and shred using a fork, return shredded pork to the cooking pot.
5. Stir well and serve.

Nutritional Value (Amount per Serving):
Calories 532; Fat 39.7 g; Carbohydrates 7.1 g; Sugar 4 g; Protein 35.4 g; Cholesterol 122 mg

Chili Chicken Soup

Preparation Time: 10 minutes; Cooking Time: 8 hours; Serve: 6

Ingredients:
- 1 lb chicken breasts
- 7 oz can green chilies, diced
- 1 bell pepper, diced
- 1 onion, diced
- 2 jalapeno peppers, minced
- 1 tbsp garlic, minced
- 4 cups chicken broth
- 1/2 lime juice
- 1 tsp paprika
- 1 tsp oregano
- 1 tsp cumin
- 1 tsp salt

Directions:
1. Add all ingredients into the cooking pot and stir well.
2. Cover instant pot aura with lid.
3. Select slow cook mode and cook on LOW for 8 hours.
4. Remove chicken and shred using a fork, return shredded chicken to the cooking pot.
5. Stir well and serve.

Nutritional Value (Amount per Serving):
Calories 198; Fat 6.9 g; Carbohydrates 7 g; Sugar 2.5 g; Protein 26.1 g; Cholesterol 67 mg

Curried Chicken Soup

Preparation Time: 10 minutes; Cooking Time: 8 hours; Serve: 6

Ingredients:
- 2 lbs chicken breasts, skinless and boneless
- 2 tbsp green curry paste
- 14 oz coconut milk
- 1 carrot, diced
- 1 green pepper, cored, seeded, and diced
- 2 cups chicken broth, low-sodium
- 1 1/2 tsp fresh ginger, grated

Directions:
1. Add all ingredients into the cooking pot and stir well.
2. Cover instant pot aura with lid.
3. Select slow cook mode and cook on LOW for 8 hours.
4. Remove chicken and shred using a fork, return shredded chicken to the cooking pot.
5. Stir well and serve.

Nutritional Value (Amount per Serving):
Calories 477; Fat 28.5 g; Carbohydrates 7.7 g; Sugar 3.4 g; Protein 47.2 g; Cholesterol 135 mg

Zucchini Carrot Chicken Soup

Preparation Time: 10 minutes; Cooking Time: 7 hours; Serve: 4

Ingredients:
- 1 lb chicken breast, skinless and boneless
- 1 bay leaves
- 2 garlic cloves, minced
- 1 small zucchini, cubed
- 1 small onion, diced
- 2 celery stalks, diced
- 2 tsp Worcestershire sauce

- 5 cups chicken broth
- 1/4 tsp dried thyme leaves
- 1 medium carrot, diced
- 1/2 tsp sea salt

Directions:
1. Add all ingredients into the cooking pot and stir well.
2. Cover instant pot aura with lid.
3. Select slow cook mode and cook on LOW for 7 hours.
4. Remove chicken and shred using a fork, return shredded chicken to the cooking pot.
5. Stir well and serve.

Nutritional Value (Amount per Serving):
Calories 202; Fat 4.7 g; Carbohydrates 6.7 g; Sugar 3.5 g; Protein 31 g; Cholesterol 73 mg

Split Pea Soup

Preparation Time: 10 minutes; Cooking Time: 6 hours; Serve: 4

Ingredients:
- 1/2 lb dry split peas
- 1/2 onion, diced
- 1 cup turkey bacon, diced
- 16 oz chicken stock
- 1 bay leaf
- 1/4 tsp thyme
- 1 cup of water
- 2 garlic cloves, minced
- 1 cup carrots, chopped
- 1/2 cup celery, chopped

Directions:
1. Add all ingredients into the cooking pot and stir well.
2. Cover instant pot aura with lid.
3. Select slow cook mode and cook on LOW for 6 hours.
4. Stir well and serve.

Nutritional Value (Amount per Serving):
Calories 252; Fat 1.8 g; Carbohydrates 39.6 g; Sugar 7 g; Protein 19.7 g; Cholesterol 16 mg

Italian Tomato Soup

Preparation Time: 10 minutes; Cooking Time: 6 hours; Serve: 4

Ingredients:
- 28 oz tomatoes, chopped
- 2 garlic cloves, chopped
- 1/2 onion, chopped
- 1 tsp Italian seasoning
- 1/4 cup olive oil
- 1/2 cup heavy cream
- 1/2 cup ricotta cheese
- 1/4 cup chicken stock

Directions:
1. Add all ingredients except heavy cream and cheese into the cooking pot and stir well.
2. Cover instant pot aura with lid.
3. Select slow cook mode and cook on LOW for 6 hours.
4. Puree the soup using a blender until smooth. Return soup into the cooking pot.
5. Stir in cheese and heavy cream.
6. Stir well and serve.

Nutritional Value (Amount per Serving):
Calories 250; Fat 21.4 g; Carbohydrates 11.7 g; Sugar 6.1 g; Protein 5.9 g; Cholesterol 31 mg

Turkey Kale Bean Soup

Preparation Time: 10 minutes; Cooking Time: 8 hours; Serve: 8

Ingredients:
- 1 lb dry navy beans, rinsed and drained
- 2 cups kale, chopped
- 1 cup carrots, sliced
- 6 cups vegetable stock
- 1/2 cup red peppers, chopped

- 3/4 lb turkey meat
- 1/2 cup onion, chopped

Directions:
1. Add all ingredients except kale and red peppers into the cooking pot and stir well.
2. Cover instant pot aura with lid.
3. Select slow cook mode and cook on LOW for 8 hours.
4. Add kale and red peppers and stir well. Cover and let sit for 10 minutes.
5. Stir well and serve.

Nutritional Value (Amount per Serving):
Calories 288; Fat 3.1 g; Carbohydrates 39.7 g; Sugar 4.2 g; Protein 26.3 g; Cholesterol 32 mg

Healthy Tomato Spinach Soup

Preparation Time: 10 minutes; Cooking Time: 8 hours; Serve: 8

Ingredients:
- 10 oz baby spinach, washed
- 1 bay leaf
- 28 oz tomatoes, diced
- 4 cups vegetable broth
- 1 garlic clove, minced
- 1 large onion, chopped
- 2 celery ribs, chopped
- 2 medium carrots, chopped
- 1/2 tsp red pepper flakes, crushed
- 1 tsp dried oregano
- 1 tbsp dried basil

Directions:
1. Add all ingredients into the cooking pot and stir well.
2. Cover instant pot aura with lid.
3. Select slow cook mode and cook on LOW for 8 hours.
4. Stir well and serve.

Nutritional Value (Amount per Serving):
Calories 62; Fat 1.1 g; Carbohydrates 9.5 g; Sugar 4.8 g; Protein 4.8 g; Cholesterol 0 mg

Veggie Red Lentil Soup

Preparation Time: 10 minutes; Cooking Time: 8 hours; Serve: 8

Ingredients:
- 1 1/2 cups red lentils, rinsed and drained
- 2 celery stalks, chopped
- 1 bell pepper, chopped
- 4 carrots, peeled and chopped
- 6 1/2 cups vegetable stock
- 1/2 tsp oregano
- 1/2 tsp paprika
- 1 tsp parsley
- 1/2 onion, chopped
- 2 garlic cloves, minced
- 2 potatoes, peeled and chopped
- 4 kale leaves, chopped
- 1 tsp salt

Directions:
1. Add all ingredients into the cooking pot and stir well.
2. Cover instant pot aura with lid.
3. Select slow cook mode and cook on LOW for 8 hours.
4. Stir well and serve.

Nutritional Value (Amount per Serving):
Calories 208; Fat 0.6 g; Carbohydrates 39.5 g; Sugar 4.5 g; Protein 12.4 g; Cholesterol 0 mg

Creamy Asparagus Soup

Preparation Time: 10 minutes; Cooking Time: 8 hours; Serve: 4

Ingredients:
- 1 lb asparagus, ends trimmed and chopped
- 2 garlic cloves, minced
- 1 large onion, diced

- 1 tsp lemon juice
- 1/2 cup coconut yogurt
- 3 cups vegetable stock
- Pepper
- Salt

Directions:
1. Add all ingredients except coconut yogurt and lemon juice into the cooking pot and stir well.
2. Cover instant pot aura with lid.
3. Select slow cook mode and cook on LOW for 8 hours.
4. Puree the soup until smooth. Return soup into the cooking pot.
5. Stir in coconut yogurt and lemon juice.
6. Stir well and serve.

Nutritional Value (Amount per Serving):
Calories 69; Fat 1.1 g; Carbohydrates 12.2 g; Sugar 7.1 g; Protein 4.4 g; Cholesterol 0 mg

Broccoli Spinach Soup

Preparation Time: 10 minutes; Cooking Time: 4 hours 30 minutes; Serve: 6

Ingredients:
- 2 1/2 cups broccoli florets
- 5 oz baby spinach
- 1/2 tsp black pepper
- 4 1/2 cups vegetable broth
- 3 garlic cloves, minced
- 1 cup onion, chopped
- 1 1/2 tsp salt

Directions:
1. Add all ingredients except spinach into the cooking pot and stir well.
2. Cover instant pot aura with lid.
3. Select slow cook mode and cook on HIGH for 4 hours.
4. Add spinach and stir well, cook on LOW for 30 minutes more.
5. Transfer soup into the blender and blend until smooth.
6. Stir well and serve.

Nutritional Value (Amount per Serving):
Calories 58; Fat 1.3 g; Carbohydrates 6.5 g; Sugar 2.1 g; Protein 5.7 g; Cholesterol 0 mg

Sweet Potato Carrot Soup

Preparation Time: 10 minutes; Cooking Time: 8 hours; Serve: 2

Ingredients:
- 1 medium carrot, diced
- 1 onion, diced
- 1 lb sweet potatoes, peel and diced
- 3 cups of water
- 1/2 tbsp curry powder
- 1/2 tbsp ginger, grated
- 1/2 cinnamon stick
- Pepper
- Salt

Directions:
1. Add all ingredients into the cooking pot and stir well.
2. Cover instant pot aura with lid.
3. Select slow cook mode and cook on LOW for 8 hours. Remove cinnamon stick.
4. Puree the soup until smooth and serve.

Nutritional Value (Amount per Serving):
Calories 314; Fat 0.8 g; Carbohydrates 73.8 g; Sugar 5.1 g; Protein 4.7 g; Cholesterol 0 mg

Coconut Carrot Soup

Preparation Time: 10 minutes; Cooking Time: 8 hours; Serve: 6
Ingredients:

- 1 cup of coconut milk
- 3 cups vegetable broth
- 8 medium carrots, peeled and chopped
- 1 tsp curry powder
- 1 garlic clove, minced
- 1 onion, chopped
- 1/8 tsp allspice
- 1/4 tsp salt

Directions:
1. Add all ingredients except coconut milk into the cooking pot and stir well.
2. Cover instant pot aura with lid.
3. Select slow cook mode and cook on LOW for 8 hours.
4. Puree the soup until smooth, return soup into the cooking pot.
5. Stir in coconut milk and serve.

Nutritional Value (Amount per Serving):
Calories 154; Fat 10.3 g; Carbohydrates 12.8 g; Sugar 6.5 g; Protein 4.3 g; Cholesterol 0 mg

Coconut Salmon Stew

Preparation Time: 10 minutes; Cooking Time: 2 hours; Serve: 4
Ingredients:
- 8 oz wild-caught salmon
- 1/2 tsp coriander
- 1/2 cup water
- 14 oz coconut milk
- 1 tsp ginger, chopped
- 1 tbsp curry powder
- 1/2 small onion, diced
- 1/4 tsp pepper
- 1 1/2 tsp salt

Directions:
1. Add all ingredients into the cooking pot and stir well.
2. Cover instant pot aura with lid.
3. Select slow cook mode and cook on HIGH for 2 hours.
4. Stir well and serve.

Nutritional Value (Amount per Serving):
Calories 314; Fat 27.4 g; Carbohydrates 7.6 g; Sugar 3.7 g; Protein 13.6 g; Cholesterol 25 mg

Sweet Potato Soup

Preparation Time: 10 minutes; Cooking Time: 4 hours; Serve: 4
Ingredients:
- 2 lbs sweet potatoes, peeled and chopped
- 4 leeks, sliced
- 1/4 tsp pepper
- 1 tbsp ghee
- 1/2 tsp thyme
- 4 cups vegetable broth
- 1 1/2 tsp garlic salt

Directions:
1. Add all ingredients into the cooking pot and stir well.
2. Cover instant pot aura with lid.
3. Select slow cook mode and cook on LOW for 4 hours.
4. Puree the soup using a blender until smooth and creamy.
5. Stir well and serve.

Nutritional Value (Amount per Serving):
Calories 393; Fat 5.2 g; Carbohydrates 77.7 g; Sugar 5.6 g; Protein 9.9 g; Cholesterol 8 mg

Coconut Asparagus Soup

Preparation Time: 10 minutes; Cooking Time: 4 hours; Serve: 6
Ingredients:

- 1/2 lb asparagus, sliced into 1-inch pieces
- 1 cup of coconut milk
- 4 cups vegetable stock
- 1/2 lb mushrooms, sliced
- 2 tbsp olive oil
- 1/2 cup onion, chopped
- 1/4 tsp garlic salt

Directions:
1. Add all ingredients into the cooking pot and stir well.
2. Cover instant pot aura with lid.
3. Select slow cook mode and cook on LOW for 4 hours.
4. Stir well and serve.

Nutritional Value (Amount per Serving):
Calories 156; Fat 14.5 g; Carbohydrates 6.5 g; Sugar 3.6 g; Protein 3.3 g; Cholesterol 0 mg

Healthy & Creamy Asparagus Soup

Preparation Time: 10 minutes; Cooking Time: 8 hours; Serve: 8
Ingredients:
- 2 lbs asparagus, wash and trim
- 1 cup onion, chopped
- 1/2 cup coconut milk
- 5 cups of water
- Pepper
- Salt

Directions:
1. Add all ingredients except coconut milk into the cooking pot and stir well.
2. Cover instant pot aura with lid.
3. Select slow cook mode and cook on LOW for 8 hours.
4. Puree the soup until smooth, return soup into the cooking pot.
5. Stir in coconut milk and serve.

Nutritional Value (Amount per Serving):
Calories 63; Fat 3.7 g; Carbohydrates 6.6 g; Sugar 3.2 g; Protein 3 g; Cholesterol 0 mg

Ginger Broccoli Soup

Preparation Time: 10 minutes; Cooking Time: 3 hours; Serve: 6
Ingredients:
- 8 cups broccoli florets
- 2 tbsp ginger, chopped
- 4 cups leeks, chopped
- 2 tbsp olive oil
- 6 cups vegetable stock
- 1 tbsp olive oil
- 1 tsp turmeric
- 1/8 tsp black pepper
- 1 tsp salt

Directions:
1. Add all ingredients into the cooking pot and stir well.
2. Cover instant pot aura with lid.
3. Select slow cook mode and cook on LOW for 3 hours.
4. Puree the soup until smooth and serve.

Nutritional Value (Amount per Serving):
Calories 151; Fat 7.8 g; Carbohydrates 18.9 g; Sugar 5.1 g; Protein 4.9 g; Cholesterol 0 mg

Easy Cauliflower Leek Soup

Preparation Time: 10 minutes; Cooking Time: 8 hours; Serve: 2
Ingredients:
- 4 1/2 cups cauliflower florets
- 1 tbsp olive oil
- 2 cups leeks
- 2 cups vegetable stock
- 1 tsp salt

Directions:

1. Add all ingredients into the cooking pot and stir well.
2. Cover instant pot aura with lid.
3. Select slow cook mode and cook on LOW for 8 hours.
4. Puree the soup until smooth and serve.

Nutritional Value (Amount per Serving):
Calories 177; Fat 7.6 g; Carbohydrates 25.4 g; Sugar 9.6 g; Protein 6.2 g; Cholesterol 0 mg

Creamy Mushroom Soup

Preparation Time: 10 minutes; Cooking Time: 4 hours 30 minutes; Serve: 4

Ingredients:
- 8 oz mushrooms, washed and sliced
- 1 small onion, diced
- 1 cup heavy cream
- 4 cups chicken broth
- Pepper
- Salt

Directions:
1. Add all ingredients except heavy cream into the cooking pot and stir well.
2. Cover instant pot aura with lid.
3. Select slow cook mode and cook on LOW for 4 hours.
4. Puree the soup until smooth, return soup into the cooking pot.
5. Stir in heavy cream, cover and cook on LOW for 30 minutes more
6. Stir well and serve.

Nutritional Value (Amount per Serving):
Calories 161; Fat 12.7 g; Carbohydrates 5.3 g; Sugar 2.4 g; Protein 7.4 g; Cholesterol 41 mg

Squash Apple Soup

Preparation Time: 10 minutes; Cooking Time: 6 hours; Serve: 8

Ingredients:
- 1 apple, cored and diced
- 1 medium butternut squash, peeled, seeded and diced
- 1/2 cup can coconut milk
- 1/8 tsp ground cinnamon
- 1/8 tsp cayenne
- 2 garlic cloves, minced
- 2 cups vegetable stock
- 1/4 tsp black pepper
- 1 onion, diced
- 1 carrot, peeled and diced
- 1/2 Tsp salt

Directions:
1. Add all ingredients into the cooking pot and stir well.
2. Cover instant pot aura with lid.
3. Select slow cook mode and cook on LOW for 6 hours.
4. Puree the soup using a blender until smooth.
5. Stir well and serve.

Nutritional Value (Amount per Serving):
Calories 62; Fat 3.1 g; Carbohydrates 8.9 g; Sugar 4.4 g; Protein 0.9 g; Cholesterol 0 mg

Delicious Lamb Stew

Preparation Time: 10 minutes; Cooking Time: 8 hours; Serve: 2

Ingredients:
- 1/2 lb lean lamb, boneless and cubed
- 2 fresh thyme sprigs
- 1/4 tsp turmeric
- 1/4 cup green olives, sliced
- 2 tbsp lemon juice
- 1/2 onion, chopped
- 2 garlic cloves, minced
- 1/2 tsp black pepper
- 1/4 tsp salt

Directions:

1. Add all ingredients into the cooking pot and stir well.
2. Cover instant pot aura with lid.
3. Select slow cook mode and cook on LOW for 8 hours.
4. Stir well and serve.

Nutritional Value (Amount per Serving):
Calories 255; Fat 11.5 g; Carbohydrates 5.2 g; Sugar 1.6 g; Protein 31 g; Cholesterol 99 mg

Mushroom Beef Stew

Preparation Time: 10 minutes; Cooking Time: 8 hours; Serve: 8

Ingredients:
- 2 lbs stewing beef, cubed
- 4 oz can mushroom, sliced
- 1/2 cup water
- 1 packet dry onion soup mix
- 14 oz cream of mushroom soup
- 1/4 tsp black pepper
- 1/2 tsp salt

Directions:
1. Add all ingredients into the cooking pot and stir well.
2. Cover instant pot aura with lid.
3. Select slow cook mode and cook on LOW for 8 hours.
4. Stir well and serve.

Nutritional Value (Amount per Serving):
Calories 238; Fat 8.5 g; Carbohydrates 2.9 g; Sugar 0.4 g; Protein 35.2 g; Cholesterol 101 mg

Chapter 5: Poultry

Delicious Southwest Chicken

Preparation Time: 10 minutes; Cooking Time: 6 hours; Serve: 8
Ingredients:
- 4 chicken breasts, skinless & boneless
- 1 tsp cumin powder
- 1 tbsp chili powder
- 2 garlic cloves, minced
- 1 small onion, chopped
- 4 oz can green chilies, diced
- 15 oz can corn, drained
- 15 oz can black beans, drained & rinsed
- 1 cup of salsa
- 1 cup chicken broth
- 1/2 tsp salt

Directions:
1. Add all ingredients into the cooking pot and stir well.
2. Cover instant pot aura with lid.
3. Select slow cook mode and cook on LOW for 6 hours.
4. Remove chicken from pot and shred using a fork.
5. Return shredded chicken to the cooking pot and stir well.
6. Serve over cooked rice.

Nutritional Value (Amount per Serving):
Calories 256; Fat 6.6 g; Carbohydrates 23.9 g; Sugar 3.6 g; Protein 26.9 g; Cholesterol 65 mg

Flavors Peanut Butter Chicken

Preparation Time: 10 minutes; Cooking Time: 8 hours; Serve: 4
Ingredients:
- 3 lbs chicken breasts, bone-in & skinless
- 3 tbsp maple syrup
- 1/2 tbsp rice wine vinegar
- 1 tbsp coarse whole grain mustard
- 1 tbsp garlic, minced
- 2 tbsp chili garlic sauce
- 1/2 cup soy sauce
- 1/2 lime juice
- 1/4 cup peanut butter
- Pepper
- salt

Directions:
1. Season chicken with pepper and salt and place into the cooking pot.
2. Mix together remaining ingredients and pour over chicken in the cooking pot.
3. Cover instant pot aura with lid.
4. Select slow cook mode and cook on LOW for 8 hours.
5. Remove chicken from pot and shred using a fork.
6. Serve and enjoy.

Nutritional Value (Amount per Serving):
Calories 806; Fat 33.5 g; Carbohydrates 17.1 g; Sugar 11.1 g; Protein 104.6 g; Cholesterol 303 mg

Easy Salsa Chicken

Preparation Time: 10 minutes; Cooking Time: 3 hours; Serve: 4
Ingredients:
- 2 1/2 lbs chicken breasts, bone-in & skinless
- 1 1/2 cups salsa
- 3 tsp ranch seasoning
- Pepper
- Salt

Directions:
1. Add 1/2 cup salsa into the cooking pot then place chicken on top of salsa. Season with ranch seasoning, pepper, and salt.
2. Pour remaining salsa over chicken in the cooking pot.

3. Cover instant pot aura with lid.
4. Select slow cook mode and cook on HIGH for 3 hours.
5. Remove chicken from pot and shred using a fork.
6. Serve and enjoy.

Nutritional Value (Amount per Serving):
Calories 573; Fat 21.2 g; Carbohydrates 6.1 g; Sugar 3 g; Protein 83.5 g; Cholesterol 252 mg

Greek Lemon Chicken

Preparation Time: 10 minutes; Cooking Time: 6 hours; Serve: 4

Ingredients:
- 4 chicken breasts, skinless & boneless
- 3 tbsp parsley, chopped
- 1 cup chicken broth
- 1 tbsp lemon zest
- 1/4 cup lemon juice
- 2 tsp dried oregano
- 1 tbsp garlic, minced
- 1 tsp kosher salt

Directions:
1. Add all ingredients into the cooking pot and mix well.
2. Cover instant pot aura with lid.
3. Select slow cook mode and cook on LOW for 6 hours.
4. Serve and enjoy.

Nutritional Value (Amount per Serving):
Calories 296; Fat 11.3 g; Carbohydrates 1.7 g; Sugar 0.6 g; Protein 43.8 g; Cholesterol 130 mg

Easy Chicken Noodles

Preparation Time: 10 minutes; Cooking Time: 6 hours 30 minutes; Serve: 8

Ingredients:
- 4 chicken breasts, skinless & boneless
- 12 oz egg noodles
- 14.5 oz chicken broth
- 21 oz cream of chicken soup
- Pepper
- Salt

Directions:
1. Add chicken, broth, soup, pepper, and salt into the cooking pot and stir well.
2. Cover instant pot aura with lid.
3. Select slow cook mode and cook on HIGH for 6 hours.
4. Remove chicken from pot and shred using a fork, return shredded chicken to the pot and stir well.
5. Add noodles into the cooking pot and cook for 30 minutes more.
6. Stir well and serve.

Nutritional Value (Amount per Serving):
Calories 273; Fat 10.9 g; Carbohydrates 16.2 g; Sugar 0.7 g; Protein 25.9 g; Cholesterol 83 mg

Orange Chicken

Preparation Time: 10 minutes; Cooking Time: 7 hours; Serve: 6

Ingredients:
- 1 lb chicken breasts, skinless & boneless
- 2 tbsp soy sauce
- 1 cup sweet orange marmalade
- 1 cup BBQ sauce

Directions:
1. Add all ingredients into the cooking pot and stir well.
2. Cover instant pot aura with lid.
3. Select slow cook mode and cook on LOW for 7 hours.

4. Remove chicken from pot and shred using a fork, return shredded chicken to the pot and stir well.
5. Serve and enjoy.

Nutritional Value (Amount per Serving):
Calories 342; Fat 5.7 g; Carbohydrates 50.2 g; Sugar 43 g; Protein 22.2 g; Cholesterol 67 mg

Delicious BBQ Chicken

Preparation Time: 10 minutes; Cooking Time: 4 hours; Serve: 8
Ingredients:
- 3 lbs chicken breasts, skinless & boneless
- 2 tbsp brown sugar
- 1 tbsp Worcestershire sauce
- 1 tbsp olive oil
- 1/2 onion, grated
- 1 1/2 cups BBQ sauce

Directions:
1. Add all ingredients into the cooking pot and stir well.
2. Cover instant pot aura with lid.
3. Select slow cook mode and cook on HIGH for 4 hours.
4. Remove chicken from pot and shred using a fork, return shredded chicken to the pot and stir well.
5. Serve and enjoy.

Nutritional Value (Amount per Serving):
Calories 422; Fat 14.5 g; Carbohydrates 20.2 g; Sugar 15.1 g; Protein 49.3 g; Cholesterol 151 mg

Parmesan Chicken Rice

Preparation Time: 10 minutes; Cooking Time: 4 hours; Serve: 6
Ingredients:
- 4 chicken breasts, skinless & boneless
- 1/4 cup parmesan cheese, grated
- 1 cup of rice
- 1 3/4 cups milk
- 21 oz can cream of chicken soup
- Pepper
- Salt

Directions:
1. Season chicken with pepper and salt and place into the cooking pot.
2. Mix together rice, milk, and soup and pour over chicken and top with parmesan cheese.
3. Cover instant pot aura with lid.
4. Select slow cook mode and cook on HIGH for 4 hours.
5. Remove chicken from pot and chop, return chicken to the pot and stir well.
6. Serve and enjoy.

Nutritional Value (Amount per Serving):
Calories 453; Fat 16.7 g; Carbohydrates 35.6 g; Sugar 3.8 g; Protein 38.2 g; Cholesterol 107 mg

Queso Chicken Tacos

Preparation Time: 10 minutes; Cooking Time: 4 hours; Serve: 8
Ingredients:
- 2 lbs chicken breasts, boneless & skinless
- 1 1/2 cups Mexican cheese dip
- 10 oz can Rotel
- 1 oz taco seasoning

Directions:
1. Add all ingredients into the cooking pot and stir well.
2. Cover instant pot aura with lid.
3. Select slow cook mode and cook on LOW for 4-6 hours.

4. Remove chicken from pot and shred using a fork, return shredded chicken to the pot and stir well.
   5. Serve and enjoy.

Nutritional Value (Amount per Serving):
Calories 349; Fat 17.8 g; Carbohydrates 4.7 g; Sugar 0.9 g; Protein 39.5 g; Cholesterol 120 mg

Easy Mexican Chicken

Preparation Time: 10 minutes; Cooking Time: 6 hours; Serve: 6
Ingredients:
- 2 lbs chicken breasts, boneless & skinless
- 1/3 cup chicken stock
- 1 oz taco seasoning
- 2 cups salsa

Directions:
   1. Add all ingredients into the cooking pot and stir well.
   2. Cover instant pot aura with lid.
   3. Select slow cook mode and cook on LOW for 6 hours.
   4. Remove chicken from pot and shred using a fork, return shredded chicken to the pot and stir well.
   5. Serve and enjoy.

Nutritional Value (Amount per Serving):
Calories 321; Fat 11.9 g; Carbohydrates 6.2 g; Sugar 2.7 g; Protein 45.7 g; Cholesterol 136 mg

Mustard Mushroom Chicken

Preparation Time: 10 minutes; Cooking Time: 6 hours; Serve: 4
Ingredients:
- 4 chicken thighs, bone-in & skin-on
- 1 tsp garlic, minced
- 1 tsp grainy mustard
- 8 oz mushrooms, sliced
- 10.5 oz cream of mushroom soup
- Pepper
- Salt

Directions:
   1. Season chicken with pepper and salt and place into the cooking pot.
   2. Mix together remaining ingredients and pour over chicken.
   3. Cover instant pot aura with lid.
   4. Select slow cook mode and cook on LOW for 6 hours.
   5. Serve and enjoy.

Nutritional Value (Amount per Serving):
Calories 324; Fat 13.3 g; Carbohydrates 4.7 g; Sugar 1.5 g; Protein 44.8 g; Cholesterol 130 mg

Herb Chicken Breasts

Preparation Time: 10 minutes; Cooking Time: 5 hours; Serve: 6
Ingredients:
- 6 chicken breasts, boneless & skinless
- 1/3 cup dry white wine
- 1 garlic clove, crushed
- 1 tsp thyme, chopped
- 2 tsp fresh oregano, chopped
- Pepper
- Salt

Directions:
   1. Season chicken with pepper and salt and place into the cooking pot.
   2. Mix together remaining ingredients and pour over chicken.
   3. Cover instant pot aura with lid.
   4. Select slow cook mode and cook on LOW for 5 hours.

5. Serve and enjoy.

Nutritional Value (Amount per Serving):
Calories 291; Fat 10.9 g; Carbohydrates 1 g; Sugar 0.1 g; Protein 42.4 g; Cholesterol 130 mg

Balsamic Chicken

Preparation Time: 10 minutes; Cooking Time: 4 hours; Serve: 10

Ingredients:
- 4 chicken breasts, boneless & skinless
- 1/2 tsp thyme
- 1 tsp dried rosemary
- 1 tsp dried basil
- 1 tsp dried oregano
- 1 tbsp olive oil
- 1/2 cup balsamic vinegar
- 4 garlic cloves
- 1 onion, sliced
- 30 oz can tomatoes, diced
- Pepper
- Salt

Directions:
1. Season chicken with pepper and salt and place into the cooking pot.
2. Mix together remaining ingredients and pour over chicken.
3. Cover instant pot aura with lid.
4. Select slow cook mode and cook on HIGH for 4 hours.
5. Serve and enjoy.

Nutritional Value (Amount per Serving):
Calories 151; Fat 5.8 g; Carbohydrates 6.1 g; Sugar 3.4 g; Protein 17.9 g; Cholesterol 52 mg

Creamy Chicken Penne

Preparation Time: 10 minutes; Cooking Time: 6 hours; Serve: 6

Ingredients:
- 3 chicken breasts, boneless & skinless
- 1 lb penne pasta, cooked
- 2 cups cheddar cheese, shredded
- 1 cup sour cream
- 1/2 onion, diced
- 1 1/2 cups mushrooms, sliced
- 1/2 tsp dried thyme
- 1/2 cup chicken broth
- 21 oz can cream of chicken soup
- Pepper
- Salt

Directions:
1. Add chicken, soup, onions, mushrooms, thyme, pepper, and broth into the cooking pot and stir well.
2. Cover instant pot aura with lid.
3. Select slow cook mode and cook on LOW for 6 hours.
4. Remove chicken from pot and shred using a fork, return shredded chicken to the pot and stir well.
5. Stir in cheddar cheese, penne, and sour cream.
6. Serve and enjoy.

Nutritional Value (Amount per Serving):
Calories 690; Fat 33.6 g; Carbohydrates 52.2 g; Sugar 1.6 g; Protein 43.7 g; Cholesterol 185 mg

Tasty Chicken Fajita Pasta

Preparation Time: 10 minutes; Cooking Time: 6 hours; Serve: 6

Ingredients:
- 2 chicken breasts, skinless & boneless
- 2 cups cheddar cheese, shredded
- 16 oz penne pasta, cooked
- 2 cups chicken broth
- 10 oz can tomato, diced
- 2 tsp garlic, minced
- 1 bell peppers, diced
- 1/2 onion, diced

- 2 tbsp taco seasoning

Directions:
1. Add all ingredients except cheese and pasta into the cooking pot and stir well.
2. Cover instant pot aura with lid.
3. Select slow cook mode and cook on LOW for 6 hours.
4. Stir in cheese and pasta.
5. Serve and enjoy.

Nutritional Value (Amount per Serving):
Calories 620; Fat 25.2 g; Carbohydrates 56.2 g; Sugar 3.4 g; Protein 41.3 g; Cholesterol 157 mg

Moist & Juicy Chicken Breast

Preparation Time: 10 minutes; Cooking Time: 3 hours; Serve: 4

Ingredients:
- 4 chicken breasts, skinless and boneless
- 1/8 tsp paprika
- 1 tbsp butter
- 1/4 cup chicken broth
- 1/8 tsp onion powder
- 1/4 tsp garlic powder
- 1/2 tsp dried parsley
- 1/8 tsp pepper
- 1/2 tsp salt

Directions:
1. In a small bowl, mix together paprika, onion powder, garlic powder, parsley, pepper, and salt.
2. Rub chicken breasts with a spice mixture from both the sides.
3. Add broth and butter to the cooking pot and stir to combine.
4. Add chicken to the cooking pot.
5. Cover instant pot aura with lid.
6. Select slow cook mode and cook on LOW for 3 hours.
7. Serve and enjoy.

Nutritional Value (Amount per Serving):
Calories 307; Fat 13.8 g; Carbohydrates 0.4 g; Sugar 0.1 g; Protein 42.6 g; Cholesterol 138 mg

Asian Chicken

Preparation Time: 10 minutes; Cooking Time: 6 hours; Serve: 4

Ingredients:
- 4 chicken breasts, skinless and boneless
- 1/2 cup of soy sauce
- 1 tbsp ginger, minced
- 3 garlic cloves, chopped
- 1 onion, chopped
- 3 tbsp sesame seeds
- 1/3 cup rice vinegar
- 1/3 cup honey

Directions:
1. Add chicken into the cooking pot.
2. Add ginger, garlic, and onion on top of the chicken.
3. Add vinegar, honey, and soy sauce to the cooking pot. Season with pepper and salt.
4. Cover instant pot aura with lid.
5. Select slow cook mode and cook on LOW for 6 hours.
6. Shred chicken using a fork and stir well.
7. Serve and enjoy.

Nutritional Value (Amount per Serving):
Calories 451; Fat 14.3 g; Carbohydrates 31.6 g; Sugar 25 g; Protein 46.1 g; Cholesterol 130 mg

Flavorful Chicken Casserole

Preparation Time: 10 minutes; Cooking Time: 8 hours; Serve: 6
Ingredients:
- 4 chicken breasts, boneless & skinless
- 1 1/2 cups chicken stock
- 10.5 oz can cream of chicken soup
- 15 oz can corn kernels, drained
- 2 cups cheddar cheese, shredded
- 1 cup cooked rice
- 1 onion, chopped

Directions:
1. Add chicken into the cooking pot.
2. Add chopped onion over chicken.
3. In a bowl, stir together stock and soup and pour over the chicken.
4. Cover instant pot aura with lid.
5. Select slow cook mode and cook on LOW for 8 hours.
6. Remove chicken from cooking pot and shred using a fork.
7. Return shredded chicken to the cooking pot along with corn, cheese, and rice. Stir well.
8. Serve and enjoy.

Nutritional Value (Amount per Serving):
Calories 561; Fat 23.6 g; Carbohydrates 43.9 g; Sugar 3.6 g; Protein 43.2 g; Cholesterol 130 mg

Chicken Orzo

Preparation Time: 10 minutes; Cooking Time: 4 hours 30 minutes; Serve: 4
Ingredients:
- 1 lb chicken breasts, skinless and boneless, cut in half
- 3/4 cup whole wheat orzo
- 1 tsp Italian herbs
- 1 lemon juice
- 2 tbsp green onion, chopped
- 1/3 cup olives
- 1 lemon zest, grated
- 1 onion, sliced
- 1 cup chicken stock
- 1/2 cup bell pepper, diced
- 2 tomatoes, chopped

Directions:
1. Add all ingredients except olives and orzo into the cooking pot and stir well.
2. Cover instant pot aura with lid.
3. Select slow cook mode and cook on LOW for 4 hours.
4. Stir in olives and orzo and cook for 30 minutes more.
5. Serve and enjoy.

Nutritional Value (Amount per Serving):
Calories 333; Fat 10.6 g; Carbohydrates 22.3 g; Sugar 4.8 g; Protein 36.4 g; Cholesterol 101 mg

Garlic Herb Roasted Pepper Chicken

Preparation Time: 10 minutes; Cooking Time: 4 hours; Serve: 6
Ingredients:
- 2 lbs chicken thighs, skinless and boneless
- 1 cup roasted red peppers, chopped
- 1/2 cup chicken stock
- 1 cup olives
- 1 tsp rosemary
- 1 tsp dried thyme
- 1 tsp oregano
- 1 tbsp capers
- 3 garlic cloves, minced
- 1 onion, sliced
- 1 tbsp olive oil
- Pepper
- Salt

Directions:
1. Add all ingredients into the cooking pot and stir well.
2. Cover instant pot aura with lid.

3. Select slow cook mode and cook on LOW for 4 hours.
4. Stir well and serve.

Nutritional Value (Amount per Serving):
Calories 354; Fat 16.1 g; Carbohydrates 6 g; Sugar 2.2 g; Protein 44.7 g; Cholesterol 135 mg

Slow Cook Turkey Breast

Preparation Time: 10 minutes; Cooking Time: 4 hours 30 minutes; Serve: 6

Ingredients:
- 4 lbs turkey breast
- 1/2 fresh lemon juice
- 1/2 cup sun-dried tomatoes, chopped
- 1/2 cup olives, chopped
- 3 tbsp flour
- 3/4 cup chicken stock
- 4 garlic cloves, chopped
- 1 tsp dried oregano
- 1 onion, chopped
- 1/4 tsp pepper
- 1/2 tsp salt

Directions:
1. Add turkey breast, garlic, oregano, lemon juice, sun-dried tomatoes, olives, onion, pepper, and salt to the cooking pot.
2. Pour half stock over turkey.
3. Cover instant pot aura with lid.
4. Select slow cook mode and cook on LOW for 4 hours.
5. Whisk together remaining stock and flour and add into the cooking pot and stir well, cover, and cook on LOW for 30 minutes more.
6. Serve and enjoy.

Nutritional Value (Amount per Serving):
Calories 358; Fat 6.5 g; Carbohydrates 19.8 g; Sugar 12 g; Protein 52.7 g; Cholesterol 130 mg

Simple Chicken & Mushrooms

Preparation Time: 10 minutes; Cooking Time: 6 hours; Serve: 2

Ingredients:
- 2 chicken breasts, skinless and boneless
- 1 cup mushrooms, sliced
- 1/2 tsp thyme, dried
- 1 onion, sliced
- 1 cup chicken stock
- Pepper
- Salt

Directions:
1. Add all ingredients into the cooking pot and stir well.
2. Cover instant pot aura with lid.
3. Select slow cook mode and cook on LOW for 6 hours.
4. Stir well and serve.

Nutritional Value (Amount per Serving):
Calories 313; Fat 11.3 g; Carbohydrates 6.9 g; Sugar 3.3 g; Protein 44.3 g; Cholesterol 130 mg

Lemon Herb Chicken

Preparation Time: 10 minutes; Cooking Time: 4 hours; Serve: 4

Ingredients:
- 20 oz chicken breasts, skinless, boneless, and cut into pieces
- 3/4 cup chicken broth
- 1/2 tsp dried oregano
- 1 tsp dried parsley
- 2 tbsp olive oil
- 2 tbsp butter
- 1/2 cup fresh lemon juice
- 1/8 tsp dried thyme
- 1/4 tsp dried basil
- 3 tbsp rice flour
- 1 tsp salt

Directions:
1. In a bowl, toss chicken with rice flour.
2. Add butter and olive oil in a cooking pot and set instant pot aura on saute mode.
3. Add chicken to the cooking pot and cook until brown.
4. Add remaining ingredients on top of the chicken.
5. Cover instant pot aura with lid.
6. Select slow cook mode and cook on LOW for 4 hours.
7. Serve and enjoy.

Nutritional Value (Amount per Serving):
Calories 423; Fat 23.9 g; Carbohydrates 6.9 g; Sugar 0.8 g; Protein 42.7 g; Cholesterol 141 mg

Creamy Chicken Curry

Preparation Time: 10 minutes; Cooking Time: 6 hours; Serve: 6
Ingredients:
- 1 1/2 lbs chicken thighs, boneless
- 1/2 cup chicken broth
- 3 potatoes, peeled and cut into 1-inch pieces
- 15 oz can coconut milk
- 2 tbsp brown sugar
- 1/2 tsp red pepper, crushed
- 1/2 tsp coriander, crushed
- 2 tbsp curry powder
- 3 tbsp fresh ginger, chopped
- 1/2 tsp black pepper
- 1 tsp kosher salt

Directions:
1. Add all ingredients into the cooking pot and stir well.
2. Cover instant pot aura with lid.
3. Select slow cook mode and cook on LOW for 6 hours.
4. Stir well and serve.

Nutritional Value (Amount per Serving):
Calories 463; Fat 24.2 g; Carbohydrates 25.7 g; Sugar 4.8 g; Protein 37.1 g; Cholesterol 101 mg

Taco Chicken

Preparation Time: 10 minutes; Cooking Time: 6 hours; Serve: 8
Ingredients:
- 1 lb chicken breasts, skinless and boneless
- 2 tbsp taco seasoning
- 1 cup chicken broth

Directions:
1. Add all ingredients into the cooking pot and stir well.
2. Cover instant pot aura with lid.
3. Select slow cook mode and cook on LOW for 6 hours.
4. Remove chicken from pot and shred using a fork, return shredded chicken to the pot.
5. Stir well and serve.

Nutritional Value (Amount per Serving):
Calories 118; Fat 4.7 g; Carbohydrates 0.5 g; Sugar 0.1 g; Protein 17.3 g; Cholesterol 51 mg

Butter Chicken

Preparation Time: 10 minutes; Cooking Time: 5 hours; Serve: 5
Ingredients:
- 1 lb chicken thighs, boneless and skinless
- 1 lb chicken breasts, boneless and skinless
- 1 1/2 tbsp ginger paste
- 1 tbsp garam masala
- 1 tbsp curry powder
- 1/3 cup heavy whipping cream
- 1 1/2 tbsp butter
- 1/4 cup tomato paste

- 1/2 cup chicken broth
- 3/4 tsp kosher salt

Directions:
1. Cut chicken into the cooking pot.
2. pour remaining ingredients except whipping cream over chicken and stir well.
3. Cover instant pot aura with lid.
4. Select slow cook mode and cook on LOW for 5 hours.
5. Stir in cream and serve.

Nutritional Value (Amount per Serving):
Calories 427; Fat 20.3 g; Carbohydrates 4.7 g; Sugar 1.8 g; Protein 54.1 g; Cholesterol 182 mg

Spicy Chili Chicken

Preparation Time: 10 minutes; Cooking Time: 6 hours; Serve: 5
Ingredients:
- 1 lb chicken breasts, skinless and boneless
- 1 jalapeno pepper, chopped
- 1 poblano pepper, chopped
- 12 oz can green chilies
- 1/2 cup dried chives
- 1/2 tsp paprika
- 1/2 tsp dried sage
- 1/2 tsp cumin
- 1 tsp dried oregano
- 14 oz can tomato, diced
- 2 cups of water
- 1 tsp sea salt

Directions:
1. Add all ingredients into the cooking pot and stir well.
2. Cover instant pot aura with lid.
3. Select slow cook mode and cook on LOW for 6 hours.
4. Remove chicken from pot and shred using a fork, return shredded chicken to the pot.
5. Stir well and serve.

Nutritional Value (Amount per Serving):
Calories 212; Fat 7.1 g; Carbohydrates 8.9 g; Sugar 3.4 g; Protein 27.9 g; Cholesterol 81 mg

Pesto Chicken

Preparation Time: 10 minutes; Cooking Time: 7 hours; Serve: 2
Ingredients:
- 2 chicken breasts, skinless and boneless
- 2 cups cherry tomatoes, halved
- 2 tbsp basil pesto
- 2 cups zucchini, chopped
- 2 cups green beans, chopped

Directions:
1. Add all ingredients into the cooking pot and stir well.
2. Cover instant pot aura with lid.
3. Select slow cook mode and cook on LOW for 7 hours.
4. Stir well and serve.

Nutritional Value (Amount per Serving):
Calories 26; Fat 0.8 g; Carbohydrates 1.3 g; Sugar 0.6 g; Protein 3.4 g; Cholesterol 9 mg

Rosemary Turkey Breast

Preparation Time: 10 minutes; Cooking Time: 4 hours; Serve: 12
Ingredients:
- 6 lbs turkey breast, bone-in
- 4 fresh rosemary sprigs
- 1/2 cup water
- Pepper
- Salt

Directions:

1. Add all ingredients into the cooking pot and stir well.
2. Cover instant pot aura with lid.
3. Select slow cook mode and cook on LOW for 4 hours.
4. Serve and enjoy.

Nutritional Value (Amount per Serving):
Calories 237; Fat 3.8 g; Carbohydrates 9.8 g; Sugar 8 g; Protein 38.7 g; Cholesterol 98 mg

Garlic Olive Chicken

Preparation Time: 10 minutes; Cooking Time: 6 hours; Serve: 4
Ingredients:
- 2 1/2 lbs chicken legs
- 1 tbsp capers
- 5 garlic cloves, smashed
- 3 tbsp red wine vinegar
- 1 1/2 tsp dried oregano
- 1/3 cup white wine
- 1/4 cup fresh parsley, chopped
- 1/3 cup olives, pitted
- 1/2 cup prunes
- Pepper
- Salt

Directions:
1. Add all ingredients into the cooking pot and stir well.
2. Cover instant pot aura with lid.
3. Select slow cook mode and cook on LOW for 4 hours.
4. Serve and enjoy.

Nutritional Value (Amount per Serving):
Calories 630; Fat 22.4 g; Carbohydrates 16.9 g; Sugar 8.4 g; Protein 83 g; Cholesterol 252 mg

Delicious Chickpea Chicken

Preparation Time: 10 minutes; Cooking Time: 4 hours; Serve: 4
Ingredients:
- 2 lbs chicken thighs
- 1 tsp paprika
- 1 tbsp lemon juice
- 2 tbsp olive oil
- 1 tsp garlic, minced
- 3 cups grape tomatoes, sliced
- 14 oz can chickpeas, drained and rinsed
- 1 tsp chili powder
- 1 tsp curry powder
- 1 tsp cumin
- 1 tsp oregano
- 1 tsp coriander
- 1 lemon, sliced
- 1 tsp salt

Directions:
1. Add all ingredients into the cooking pot and stir well.
2. Cover instant pot aura with lid.
3. Select slow cook mode and cook on LOW for 4 hours.
4. Serve and enjoy.

Nutritional Value (Amount per Serving):
Calories 648; Fat 25.7 g; Carbohydrates 30.8 g; Sugar 4.1 g; Protein 72.3 g; Cholesterol 202 mg

Balsamic Chicken Breasts

Preparation Time: 10 minutes; Cooking Time: 6 hours; Serve: 6
Ingredients:
- 2 1/2 lbs chicken breasts, skinless and boneless
- 1 onion, sliced
- 1/2 tsp garlic powder
- 2 tsp Italian seasoning
- 1/2 cup chicken stock
- 1/2 cup balsamic vinegar
- 14 oz can tomato, drained and diced

- 1/4 tsp pepper
- 1/2 tsp salt

Directions:
1. Place chicken into the cooking pot.
2. In a small bowl, mix together garlic powder, Italian seasoning, pepper, and salt and sprinkle over chicken.
3. Pour remaining ingredients over chicken.
4. Cover instant pot aura with lid.
5. Select slow cook mode and cook on LOW for 6 hours.
6. Serve and enjoy.

Nutritional Value (Amount per Serving):
Calories 391; Fat 14.5 g; Carbohydrates 5.7 g; Sugar 3.4 g; Protein 55.6 g; Cholesterol 169 mg

Mediterranean Chicken

Preparation Time: 10 minutes; Cooking Time: 4 hours; Serve: 4

Ingredients:
- 4 chicken breasts, skinless and boneless
- 2 tbsp fresh lemon juice
- 1 cup roasted red peppers, chopped
- 1 cup olives
- 3 tsp Italian seasoning
- 2 tbsp capers
- 1 small onion, chopped
- 1 tbsp garlic, minced
- Pepper
- Salt

Directions:
1. Add all ingredients into the cooking pot and stir well.
2. Cover instant pot aura with lid.
3. Select slow cook mode and cook on LOW for 4 hours.
4. Stir well and serve.

Nutritional Value (Amount per Serving):
Calories 352; Fat 15.7 g; Carbohydrates 8 g; Sugar 3.3 g; Protein 43.4 g; Cholesterol 132 mg

Buffalo Chicken Drumsticks

Preparation Time: 10 minutes; Cooking Time: 4 hours; Serve: 6

Ingredients:
- 8 chicken drumsticks, skin removed
- 3 tbsp dried parsley
- 1/2 cup dry wine
- 1/2 cup hot sauce
- 3 garlic cloves, minced
- 1/4 cup olive oil

Directions:
1. Add all ingredients into the large zip-lock bag and place it in the fridge for 3 hours.
2. Pour marinated chicken into the cooking pot.
3. Cover instant pot aura with lid.
4. Select slow cook mode and cook on LOW for 4 hours.
5. Stir well and serve.

Nutritional Value (Amount per Serving):
Calories 197; Fat 12 g; Carbohydrates 1.5 g; Sugar 0.4 g; Protein 17.1 g; Cholesterol 54 mg

Caribbean Chicken

Preparation Time: 10 minutes; Cooking Time: 6 hours; Serve: 8

Ingredients:
- 3 lbs whole chicken
- 1 tsp cinnamon
- 1 tbsp allspice
- 1/3 cup fresh lime juice
- 1/2 tsp cayenne pepper
- 2 tsp kosher salt

Directions:
1. In a small bowl, mix together allspice, cinnamon, cayenne pepper, and kosher salt.
2. Rub spice mixture all over the chicken.
3. Place chicken into the cooking pot. Pour lime juice over the chicken.
4. Cover instant pot aura with lid.
5. Select slow cook mode and cook on LOW for 6 hours.
6. Slice and serve.

Nutritional Value (Amount per Serving):
Calories 327; Fat 12.7 g; Carbohydrates 1 g; Sugar 0.1 g; Protein 49.3 g; Cholesterol 151 mg

Caesar Chicken

Preparation Time: 10 minutes; Cooking Time: 8 hours; Serve: 4
Ingredients:
- 4 chicken breasts, skinless and boneless
- 3/4 cup creamy Caesar dressing
- 1/8 tsp black pepper
- 1/2 tsp dried parsley
- 1/4 cup fresh basil, chopped
- 1/8 tsp salt

Directions:
1. Place chicken into the cooking pot.
2. Add parsley, Caesar dressing, black pepper, and salt into the cooking pot.
3. Cover instant pot aura with lid.
4. Select slow cook mode and cook on LOW for 8 hours.
5. Remove chicken from pot and shred using a fork.
6. Garnish with basil and serve.

Nutritional Value (Amount per Serving):
Calories 428; Fat 24.3 g; Carbohydrates 4.6 g; Sugar 3 g; Protein 42.3 g; Cholesterol 137 mg

Onion Chicken

Preparation Time: 10 minutes; Cooking Time: 6 hours; Serve: 4
Ingredients:
- 2 lbs chicken
- 2 lbs onions, sliced
- 3 garlic cloves, minced
- 1 cup organic chicken broth
- 1 tsp thyme
- 1 tsp balsamic vinegar
- 2 tsp ghee, melted
- 1/4 tsp pepper
- 1/2 tsp salt

Directions:
1. Add half sliced onions into the cooking pot then place chicken on top of onions.
2. Add remaining onions on top of chicken.
3. In a small bowl, combine together remaining ingredients and pour on top of chicken.
4. Cover instant pot aura with lid.
5. Select slow cook mode and cook on LOW for 6 hours.
6. Serve and enjoy.

Nutritional Value (Amount per Serving):
Calories 466; Fat 9.6 g; Carbohydrates 22.4 g; Sugar 9.8 g; Protein 69.6 g; Cholesterol 180 mg

Lemon Pepper Chicken

Preparation Time: 10 minutes; Cooking Time: 6 hours; Serve: 4
Ingredients:
- 2 lbs chicken wings
- 1 tsp lemon zest
- 2 lemon juice
- 1 cup chicken broth

- 1 lemon, sliced
- 2 garlic cloves, minced
- 1 1/2 tsp black pepper

Directions:
1. Add all ingredients into the cooking pot and stir well.
2. Cover instant pot aura with lid.
3. Select slow cook mode and cook on LOW for 6 hours.
4. Stir well and serve.

Nutritional Value (Amount per Serving):
Calories 455; Fat 17.4 g; Carbohydrates 3.2 g; Sugar 1.1 g; Protein 67.4 g; Cholesterol 202 mg

Shredded Chicken

Preparation Time: 10 minutes; Cooking Time: 4 hours; Serve: 4
Ingredients:
- 1 lb chicken breasts, skinless and boneless
- 1/2 tsp ground cumin
- 1/8 tsp ground black pepper
- 1 cup harissa sauce
- 1/4 tsp garlic powder
- 1/2 tsp kosher salt

Directions:
1. Season chicken with garlic powder, cumin, pepper, and salt.
2. Place seasoned chicken into the cooking pot. Pour harissa sauce over the chicken.
3. Cover slow cooker with lid and cook on low for 4 hours.
4. Remove chicken from cooking pot and shred using a fork.
5. Serve and enjoy.

Nutritional Value (Amount per Serving):
Calories 1177; Fat 104.5 g; Carbohydrates 12.3 g; Sugar 12 g; Protein 32.9 g; Cholesterol 101 mg

Delicious Greek Chicken

Preparation Time: 10 minutes; Cooking Time: 8 hours; Serve: 8
Ingredients:
- 3 lbs chicken, cut into pieces
- 4 garlic cloves, minced
- 2 onions, quartered
- 6 medium potatoes, quartered
- 1 tbsp olive oil
- 3 tsp dried oregano
- 1/2 cup water
- 1/2 tsp black pepper
- 1 tsp salt

Directions:
1. Add potatoes into the cooking pot. Add garlic, onions, and chicken on top.
2. In a small bowl, mix together oregano, water, pepper, and salt. Pour over chicken.
3. Add olive oil
4. Cover instant pot aura with lid.
5. Select slow cook mode and cook on LOW for 8 hours.
6. Serve and enjoy.

Nutritional Value (Amount per Serving):
Calories 397; Fat 7.2 g; Carbohydrates 28.6 g; Sugar 3.1 g; Protein 52.4 g; Cholesterol 131 mg

Chicken Cacciatore

Preparation Time: 10 minutes; Cooking Time: 6 hours; Serve: 4
Ingredients:
- 6 chicken thighs, skin removed and bone-in
- 1 red pepper, sliced
- 28 oz tomatoes, chopped
- 1 cup chicken stock
- 1 cup dry red wine

- 4 garlic cloves, minced
- 1 cup mushrooms, sliced
- 1 onion, sliced
- Pepper
- Salt

Directions:
1. Add all ingredients into the cooking pot and stir well.
2. Cover instant pot aura with lid.
3. Select slow cook mode and cook on LOW for 6 hours.
4. Stir well and serve.

Nutritional Value (Amount per Serving):
Calories 532; Fat 17 g; Carbohydrates 15.9 g; Sugar 8.9 g; Protein 66.7 g; Cholesterol 195 mg

Ginger Garlic Broccoli Chicken

Preparation Time: 10 minutes; Cooking Time: 8 hours; Serve: 8

Ingredients:
- 4 chicken breast, skinless, boneless, and halves
- 1 garlic clove, chopped
- 1/4 cup white miso
- 2 cups chicken stock
- 1 lb broccoli florets
- 1 tbsp ginger, sliced

Directions:
1. Add all ingredients into the cooking pot and stir well.
2. Cover instant pot aura with lid.
3. Select slow cook mode and cook on LOW for 8 hours.
4. Stir well and serve.

Nutritional Value (Amount per Serving):
Calories 99; Fat 2.1 g; Carbohydrates 6.8 g; Sugar 1.7 g; Protein 13.4 g; Cholesterol 32 mg

Tasty Chicken Chili

Preparation Time: 10 minutes; Cooking Time: 6 hours; Serve: 4

Ingredients:
- 15 oz great northern beans, soaked overnight and drained
- 6 cups chicken stock
- 4 cups chicken, cooked and shredded
- 2 tsp ground cumin
- 2 cups salsa

Directions:
1. Add all ingredients into the cooking pot and stir well.
2. Cover instant pot aura with lid.
3. Select slow cook mode and cook on LOW for 6 hours.
4. Stir well and serve.

Nutritional Value (Amount per Serving):
Calories 625; Fat 6.7 g; Carbohydrates 76 g; Sugar 7.5 g; Protein 67 g; Cholesterol 108 mg

Balsamic Spinach Chicken

Preparation Time: 10 minutes; Cooking Time: 6 hours; Serve: 4

Ingredients:
- 3/4 lb chicken breasts, skinless, boneless and cut into strips
- 1 tbsp fresh parsley, minced
- 1 tbsp fresh oregano, minced
- 1/2 tsp black pepper
- 5 oz baby spinach
- 4 garlic cloves, minced
- 1/4 cup balsamic vinegar

Directions:
1. Add all ingredients except spinach into the cooking pot and stir well.
2. Cover instant pot aura with lid.

3. Select slow cook mode and cook on LOW for 6 hours.
4. Stir in spinach and serve.

Nutritional Value (Amount per Serving):
Calories 182; Fat 6.6 g; Carbohydrates 3.4 g; Sugar 0.3 g; Protein 26 g; Cholesterol 76 mg

Curried Chicken Thighs

Preparation Time: 10 minutes; Cooking Time: 4 hours; Serve: 4

Ingredients:
- 1 1/2 lbs chicken thighs
- 2 tbsp fresh ginger, minced
- 1 tsp cumin
- 1 tsp turmeric
- 1 tsp garam masala
- 1 cinnamon stick
- 2 bay leaves
- 1 medium onion, diced
- 1/4 cup fresh cilantro, chopped
- 2 tbsp tomato paste
- 14 oz can coconut milk
- 3 garlic cloves, minced
- 1 1/2 tsp salt

Directions:
1. Add all ingredients into the cooking pot and stir well.
2. Cover instant pot aura with lid.
3. Select slow cook mode and cook on LOW for 4 hours.
4. Shred the chicken using a fork.
5. Stir well and serve.

Nutritional Value (Amount per Serving):
Calories 555; Fat 34.2 g; Carbohydrates 10.8 g; Sugar 2.3 g; Protein 52.5 g; Cholesterol 151 mg

Healthy Cauliflower Chicken

Preparation Time: 10 minutes; Cooking Time: 6 hours; Serve: 4

Ingredients:
- 1 small cauliflower head, cut into florets
- 1 1/2 lbs chicken thighs, skinless, boneless and cut into halves
- 2 tbsp ginger, grated
- 2 tbsp tomato paste
- 28 oz can tomato, diced
- 1/4 cup raisins
- 1 onion, chopped
- 1 tbsp curry powder
- 1/2 tsp kosher salt

Directions:
1. Add all ingredients into the cooking pot and stir well.
2. Cover instant pot aura with lid.
3. Select slow cook mode and cook on LOW for 6 hours.
4. Stir well and serve.

Nutritional Value (Amount per Serving):
Calories 441; Fat 13.2 g; Carbohydrates 27.7 g; Sugar 16 g; Protein 53.7 g; Cholesterol 151 mg

Tomatillo Chicken

Preparation Time: 10 minutes; Cooking Time: 6 hours; Serve: 6

Ingredients:
- 6 chicken drumsticks, bone-in, and skin removed
- 1 1/2 cups tomatillo sauce
- 1 tbsp apple cider vinegar
- 1 tsp olive oil
- 1 tsp dried oregano
- Pepper
- Salt

Directions:
1. Add all ingredients into the cooking pot and stir well.

2. Cover instant pot aura with lid.
3. Select slow cook mode and cook on LOW for 6 hours.
4. Stir well and serve.

Nutritional Value (Amount per Serving):
Calories 95; Fat 3.4 g; Carbohydrates 2.1 g; Sugar 1 g; Protein 12.7 g; Cholesterol 40 mg

Mexican Chicken Thighs

Preparation Time: 10 minutes; Cooking Time: 5 hours; Serve: 4

Ingredients:
- 8 chicken thighs, bone-in, and skin-on
- 1 packet taco seasoning
- 1 cup chicken stock
- 1/4 tsp red pepper flakes
- 1/4 cup green onion, sliced

Directions:
1. Add stock and half taco seasoning into the cooking pot. Stir well.
2. Place chicken thighs to the cooking pot and season with remaining seasoning.
3. Cover instant pot aura with lid.
4. Select slow cook mode and cook on LOW for 5 hours.
5. Sprinkle with green onion and red pepper flakes.
6. Serve and enjoy.

Nutritional Value (Amount per Serving):
Calories 652; Fat 27 g; Carbohydrates 7.4 g; Sugar 0.3 g; Protein 89.9 g; Cholesterol 274 mg

Honey Dijon Mustard Chicken

Preparation Time: 10 minutes; Cooking Time: 8 hours; Serve: 4

Ingredients:
- 4 chicken thighs
- 1/4 cup Dijon mustard
- 2 tbsp honey
- 2 tbsp olive oil
- 1 tsp fresh rosemary, chopped
- Pepper
- Sea salt

Directions:
1. Place chicken in the cooking pot.
2. In a small bowl, mix together oil, mustard, honey, pepper, rosemary, and salt. Pour over chicken.
3. Cover instant pot aura with lid.
4. Select slow cook mode and cook on LOW for 8 hours.
5. Serve and enjoy.

Nutritional Value (Amount per Serving):
Calories 381; Fat 18.5 g; Carbohydrates 9.7 g; Sugar 8.8 g; Protein 43 g; Cholesterol 130 mg

Thai Chicken Wings

Preparation Time: 10 minutes; Cooking Time: 6 hours; Serve: 6

Ingredients:
- 3 lbs chicken wings
- 2 oz Thai basil, minced
- 8 oz green curry paste
- 1 tbsp coconut milk
- 1 tbsp fresh cilantro, minced
- 1 tbsp fresh ginger, minced

Directions:
1. Add chicken wings in the cooking pot.
2. In a bowl, whisk the coconut milk with cilantro, ginger, basil, and curry paste.
3. Pour coconut milk mixture over chicken wings.
4. Cover instant pot aura with lid.

5. Select slow cook mode and cook on LOW for 6 hours.
6. Serve and enjoy.

Nutritional Value (Amount per Serving):
Calories 537; Fat 23.8 g; Carbohydrates 10.5 g; Sugar 0.1 g; Protein 66.1 g; Cholesterol 202 mg

Chapter 6: Beef, Pork & Lamb

Delicious Beef Bean Sloppy Joes

Preparation Time: 10 minutes; Cooking Time: 7 hours; Serve: 8
Ingredients:
- 2 lbs ground beef
- 1 tsp chili powder
- 1 tbsp Worcestershire sauce
- 1/2 cup ketchup
- 8 oz can tomato sauce
- 28 oz can baked beans
- 2 garlic cloves, minced
- 1 small onion, chopped

Directions:
1. Set instant pot aura on sauté mode.
2. Add ground beef into the cooking pot and sauté until meat is no longer pink.
3. Add remaining ingredients and stir everything well.
4. Cover instant pot aura with lid.
5. Select slow cook mode and cook on LOW for 7 hours.
6. Stir well and serve.

Nutritional Value (Amount per Serving):
Calories 333; Fat 7.6 g; Carbohydrates 27.9 g; Sugar 13.3 g; Protein 39.9 g; Cholesterol 101 mg

Tasty Sriracha Pork Tenderloin

Preparation Time: 10 minutes; Cooking Time: 3 hours; Serve: 6
Ingredients:
- 2 1/2 lbs pork tenderloin
- 1 tsp dried oregano
- 1 tbsp garlic, minced
- 2 tbsp soy sauce
- 2 tbsp butter, melted
- 1/4 cup honey
- 1/4 cup sriracha
- Pepper
- Salt

Directions:
1. Season pork with pepper and salt and place into the cooking pot.
2. Mix together remaining ingredients and pour over pork tenderloin.
3. Cover instant pot aura with lid.
4. Select slow cook mode and cook on LOW for 3 hours.
5. Slice and serve.

Nutritional Value (Amount per Serving):
Calories 363; Fat 10.5 g; Carbohydrates 14.7 g; Sugar 11.7 g; Protein 50 g; Cholesterol 148 mg

Mediterranean Pork Chops

Preparation Time: 10 minutes; Cooking Time: 8 hours; Serve: 4
Ingredients:
- 4 pork chops, boneless
- 1 tsp dried basil
- 1 tsp dried oregano
- 1 tbsp poultry seasoning
- 1 tbsp garlic powder
- 1 tbsp paprika
- 2 garlic cloves, minced
- 1 cup chicken broth
- 1/4 cup olive oil
- Pepper
- Salt

Directions:
1. Add all ingredients except pork chops into the cooking pot and stir well.
2. Add pork chops into the cooking pot.
3. Cover instant pot aura with lid.
4. Select slow cook mode and cook on LOW for 8 hours.

5. Serve and enjoy.

Nutritional Value (Amount per Serving):
Calories 392; Fat 33.2 g; Carbohydrates 4.1 g; Sugar 0.9 g; Protein 20 g; Cholesterol 69 mg

Creamy Pork Chops

Preparation Time: 10 minutes; Cooking Time: 7 hours; Serve: 4

Ingredients:
- 1 lb pork chops
- 2 tbsp water
- 2 tbsp cornstarch
- 1 1/2 cups beef broth
- 10.5 oz can cream of chicken soup
- 1 envelope brown gravy mix
- 1/2 tsp pepper
- 1/2 tsp garlic powder
- 1 envelope ranch dressing mix

Directions:
1. Season pork chops with garlic powder, ranch dressing mix, and pepper.
2. Add broth, soup, and brown gravy mix into the cooking pot and stir well.
3. Add pork chops into the cooking pot.
4. Cover instant pot aura with lid.
5. Select slow cook mode and cook on LOW for 7 hours.
6. Remove pork chops from the cooking pot and place them on a plate.
7. In a small bowl, whisk together water and cornstarch and pour into the cooking pot and stir until the gravy thicken.
8. Pour gravy over pork chops and serve.

Nutritional Value (Amount per Serving):
Calories 488; Fat 33.6 g; Carbohydrates 14.1 g; Sugar 1.1 g; Protein 30 g; Cholesterol 104 mg

Onion Pork Chops

Preparation Time: 10 minutes; Cooking Time: 6 hours; Serve: 4

Ingredients:
- 2 lbs pork chops, boneless
- 1/3 cup butter, sliced
- 1 onion, sliced
- 1/8 tsp red pepper flakes
- 1/4 tsp garlic powder
- 2 tbsp brown sugar
- 1 tbsp apple cider vinegar
- 2 tbsp Worcestershire sauce
- 1/4 tsp pepper
- 1/4 tsp salt

Directions:
1. Add pork chops into the cooking pot.
2. Pour remaining ingredients over pork chops into the cooking pot.
3. Cover instant pot aura with lid.
4. Select slow cook mode and cook on LOW for 6 hours.
5. Serve and enjoy.

Nutritional Value (Amount per Serving):
Calories 899; Fat 71.8 g; Carbohydrates 8.8 g; Sugar 7.1 g; Protein 51.5 g; Cholesterol 236 mg

Delicious Sweet Pork Roast

Preparation Time: 10 minutes; Cooking Time: 8 hours; Serve: 6

Ingredients:
- 2 lbs pork roast, boneless
- 1 cup brown sugar
- 2 cups salsa

Directions:
1. Place pork roast into the cooking pot.
2. Mix together brown sugar and salsa and pour over pork roast in the cooking pot.

3. Cover instant pot aura with lid.
4. Select slow cook mode and cook on LOW for 8 hours.
5. Shred pork roast using the fork and serve.

Nutritional Value (Amount per Serving):
Calories 428; Fat 14.4 g; Carbohydrates 29.1 g; Sugar 26.1 g; Protein 44.5 g; Cholesterol 130 mg

Asian Pork Chops

Preparation Time: 10 minutes; Cooking Time: 7 hours; Serve: 6

Ingredients:
- 3 lbs pork chops, boneless
- 2 tbsp cornstarch
- 1 tsp black pepper
- 1 tsp garlic, minced
- 1 tbsp red chili paste
- 1/4 cup soy sauce
- 1/2 cup ketchup
- 1/2 cup brown sugar
- 1/2 tsp salt

Directions:
1. Add soy sauce, brown sugar ketchup, red chili paste, garlic, pepper, and salt into the cooking pot and stir well.
2. Add pork chops into the cooking pot.
3. Cover instant pot aura with lid.
4. Select slow cook mode and cook on LOW for 6 hours.
5. In a small bowl, mix together cornstarch and 2 tablespoons of water and pour into the cooking pot and stir well.
6. Cover again and cook on LOW for 1 hour more.
7. Serve and enjoy.

Nutritional Value (Amount per Serving):
Calories 817; Fat 56.9 g; Carbohydrates 21.5 g; Sugar 17.1 g; Protein 52.2 g; Cholesterol 196 mg

Sweet Applesauce Pork Chops

Preparation Time: 10 minutes; Cooking Time: 4 hours; Serve: 4

Ingredients:
- 3 pork chops, boneless
- 1 1/2 cups applesauce
- 1 tsp Worcestershire sauce
- 1/3 cup BBQ sauce
- 1 tsp garlic powder
- 1/4 tsp black pepper
- 2 tbsp brown sugar
- 2 tbsp butter
- 1/4 tsp salt

Directions:
1. Add butter into the cooking pot and set instant pot aura on sauté mode.
2. Add pork chops into the pot and cook until brown from both the sides.
3. Add remaining ingredients over pork chops in a cooking pot and stir well.
4. Cover instant pot aura with lid.
5. Select slow cook mode and cook on HIGH for 4 hours.
6. Stir well and serve.

Nutritional Value (Amount per Serving):
Calories 335; Fat 20.8 g; Carbohydrates 23.1 g; Sugar 19.5 g; Protein 13.8 g; Cholesterol 67 mg

Pork Chops with Potatoes

Preparation Time: 10 minutes; Cooking Time: 3 hours; Serve: 6

Ingredients:
- 6 pork chops, boneless
- 3 lbs potatoes, quartered
- 2 tbsp butter
- 2 tsp apple cider vinegar

- 2 tbsp ranch seasoning
- 1/2 cup olive oil

Directions:
1. Add pork chops into the cooking pot.
2. Mix together olive oil, ranch seasoning, and vinegar and pour over pork chops.
3. Add potatoes around the pork chops in the cooking pot. Top with butter.
4. Cover instant pot aura with lid.
5. Select slow cook mode and cook on HIGH for 3 hours.
6. Serve and enjoy.

Nutritional Value (Amount per Serving):
Calories 601; Fat 40.8 g; Carbohydrates 35.7 g; Sugar 2.6 g; Protein 21.8 g; Cholesterol 79 mg

Zesty Pulled Pork

Preparation Time: 10 minutes; Cooking Time: 8 hours; Serve: 6

Ingredients:
- 3 lbs pork shoulder
- 4 garlic cloves, cut into slivers
- 1 lime juice
- 1 tsp oregano
- 1/2 tsp cumin
- 1/2 tsp pepper
- 1 lime zest
- 1 tbsp salt

Directions:
1. Add garlic, lime juice, oregano, cumin, pepper, lime zest, and salt into the blender and blend until a smooth paste is formed.
2. Rub pork shoulder with marinade paste and place it in the refrigerator overnight.
3. Place the marinated pork shoulder into the cooking pot.
4. Cover instant pot aura with lid.
5. Select slow cook mode and cook on LOW for 8 hours.
6. Remove meat from cooking pot and shred using the fork.
7. Serve and enjoy.

Nutritional Value (Amount per Serving):
Calories 669; Fat 48.6 g; Carbohydrates 1.7 g; Sugar 0.2 g; Protein 53 g; Cholesterol 204 mg

Delicious Beef Fajitas

Preparation Time: 10 minutes; Cooking Time: 6 hours; Serve: 6

Ingredients:
- 2 lbs beef, sliced
- 1/4 cup beef broth
- 1 tbsp olive oil
- 2 tbsp fajita seasoning
- 15 oz can tomato, diced
- 1 onion, sliced
- 2 bell peppers, sliced

Directions:
1. Add all ingredients into the cooking pot and stir well.
2. Cover instant pot aura with lid.
3. Select slow cook mode and cook on LOW for 6 hours.
4. Stir well and serve.

Nutritional Value (Amount per Serving):
Calories 348; Fat 11.9 g; Carbohydrates 10.5 g; Sugar 5.2 g; Protein 47.3 g; Cholesterol 135 mg

BBQ Beef Ribs

Preparation Time: 10 minutes; Cooking Time: 8 hours; Serve: 6

Ingredients:
- 2 lbs beef back ribs
- 2 tbsp prepared mustard
- 1/2 cup vinegar
- 3/4 cup brown sugar

- 6 oz can tomato paste
- 1 cup ketchup
- 1 cup of water
- 1 tbsp salt

Directions:
1. Add beef ribs into the cooking pot.
2. Mix together the remaining ingredients and pour over beef ribs in the cooking pot.
3. Cover instant pot aura with lid.
4. Select slow cook mode and cook on LOW for 8 hours.
5. Stir well and serve.

Nutritional Value (Amount per Serving):
Calories 476; Fat 18.9 g; Carbohydrates 33.7 g; Sugar 30.3 g; Protein 42 g; Cholesterol 116 mg

Italian Beef Roast

Preparation Time: 10 minutes; Cooking Time: 6 hours; Serve: 6
Ingredients:
- 3 lbs beef chuck roast
- 15 oz tomato sauce
- 1 cup onion, diced
- 3 cups carrots, sliced
- 4 cups potatoes, sliced
- Pepper
- Salt

Directions:
1. Season beef roast with pepper and salt and place into the cooking pot.
2. Add potatoes, carrots, and onion around the roast in the cooking pot.
3. Pour tomato sauce over roast.
4. Cover instant pot aura with lid.
5. Select slow cook mode and cook on HIGH for 6 hours.
6. Shred the meat and serve.

Nutritional Value (Amount per Serving):
Calories 940; Fat 63.4 g; Carbohydrates 26.7 g; Sugar 7.7 g; Protein 62.6 g; Cholesterol 234 mg

Flavorful Sausage Casserole

Preparation Time: 10 minutes; Cooking Time: 6 hours 30 minutes; Serve: 6
Ingredients:
- 8 beef sausages
- 1 cup frozen peas
- 1 bay leaf
- 1 tsp dried thyme
- 1 carrot, diced
- 3 cups chicken stock
- 1 tbsp Worcestershire sauce
- 2 tbsp flour
- 2 garlic cloves, crushed
- 1 onion, chopped
- 2 tbsp butter

Directions:
1. Add sausage into the cooking pot and set instant pot aura on sauté mode.
2. Sauté sausage until brown. Remove sausage from pot and cut into the slices.
3. Add butter, garlic, and onion into the cooking pot and cook on sauté mode for 2 minutes.
4. Add flour and stir for 1 minute.
5. Add remaining ingredients into the cooking pot and stir well.
6. Cover instant pot aura with lid.
7. Select slow cook mode and cook on LOW for 6 hours.
8. Stir well and serve.

Nutritional Value (Amount per Serving):
Calories 228; Fat 17.3 g; Carbohydrates 10.8 g; Sugar 3.4 g; Protein 7.4 g; Cholesterol 36 mg

Beef Noodles

Preparation Time: 10 minutes; Cooking Time: 4 hours; Serve: 6
Ingredients:
- 1 1/2 lbs beef stew meat
- 1 onion, chopped
- 30 oz can tomato
- 12 oz egg noodles, cooked
- Pepper
- Salt

Directions:
1. Add meat, tomatoes, onion, pepper, and salt into the cooking pot and stir well.
2. Cover instant pot aura with lid.
3. Select slow cook mode and cook on HIGH for 4 hours.
4. Stir well and serve over cooked egg noodles.

Nutritional Value (Amount per Serving):
Calories 326; Fat 8.3 g; Carbohydrates 23.2 g; Sugar 5.8 g; Protein 38.5 g; Cholesterol 118 mg

Shredded Asian Beef

Preparation Time: 10 minutes; Cooking Time: 8 hours; Serve: 4
Ingredients:
- 2 lbs beef chuck roast
- 1 tsp ground ginger
- 1 tbsp sesame oil
- 2 tbsp honey
- 2 tbsp rice vinegar
- 1/3 cup soy sauce
- 1/3 cup hoisin sauce
- Pepper
- Salt

Directions:
1. Season meat with pepper and salt and place into the cooking pot.
2. Mix together remaining ingredients and pour over meat.
3. Cover instant pot aura with lid.
4. Select slow cook mode and cook on LOW for 8 hours.
5. Shred the meat using a fork and serve.

Nutritional Value (Amount per Serving):
Calories 950; Fat 67.3 g; Carbohydrates 20 g; Sugar 14.8 g; Protein 61.4 g; Cholesterol 234 mg

Garlic Beef Shanks

Preparation Time: 10 minutes; Cooking Time: 5 hours; Serve: 4
Ingredients:
- 2 lbs beef shanks
- 1/4 tsp pepper
- 1/2 tsp onion powder
- 1 tsp garlic powder
- 2 tbsp dried mix herbs
- 2 garlic cloves, minced
- 2 cups chicken broth
- 2 tsp salt

Directions:
1. Season meat with dried mix herbs, pepper, onion powder, garlic powder, and salt and place into the cooking pot.
2. Add garlic and broth on top of the meat.
3. Cover instant pot aura with lid.
4. Select slow cook mode and cook on HIGH for 5 hours.
5. Serve and enjoy.

Nutritional Value (Amount per Serving):
Calories 496; Fat 15.1 g; Carbohydrates 4.9 g; Sugar 0.9 g; Protein 79.6 g; Cholesterol 177 mg

Teriyaki Steak

Preparation Time: 10 minutes; Cooking Time: 8 hours; Serve: 6

Ingredients:
- 2 lbs rump steak, sliced
- 1/4 cup rice wine vinegar
- 1/4 cup beef stock
- 1/4 cup soy sauce
- 1/2 cup honey
- 2 tsp ginger garlic paste
- 1/4 tsp pepper

Directions:
1. Place steak into the cooking pot.
2. Mix together remaining ingredients and pour over steak.
3. Cover instant pot aura with lid.
4. Select slow cook mode and cook on LOW for 8 hours.
5. Serve and enjoy.

Nutritional Value (Amount per Serving):
Calories 378; Fat 9.4 g; Carbohydrates 25.2 g; Sugar 23.4 g; Protein 48.1 g; Cholesterol 0 mg

Delicious Beef Curry

Preparation Time: 10 minutes; Cooking Time: 8 hours 5 minutes; Serve: 6

Ingredients:
- 2 lb beef, cubed
- 1 cup beef stock
- 14 oz can tomato, crushed
- 2 tsp chili powder
- 2 tbsp tomato paste
- 1 onion, sliced

For the curry paste:
- 1 tbsp olive oil
- 1/4 cup vinegar
- 1/4 cup ground cumin
- 2 tsp mustard seeds
- 1/4 cup ground coriander
- 2 tsp turmeric
- 2 tsp garam masala
- 1/2 tsp cinnamon
- 2 tsp black pepper
- 2 tsp ginger, minced
- 3 tsp garlic, crushed

Directions:
1. Add all curry paste ingredients into the blender and blend until smooth.
2. Add curry paste into the cooking pot and set instant pot aura on sauté mode and sauté curry paste for 5 minutes.
3. Add remaining ingredients into the cooking pot and stir well.
4. Cover instant pot aura with lid.
5. Select slow cook mode and cook on LOW for 8 hours.
6. Stir well and serve.

Nutritional Value (Amount per Serving):
Calories 364; Fat 13.4 g; Carbohydrates 10.9 g; Sugar 4 g; Protein 48.8 g; Cholesterol 135 mg

Mushroom Beef Tips

Preparation Time: 10 minutes; Cooking Time: 6 hours; Serve: 6

Ingredients:
- 2 lbs beef sirloin tips, cut into 1-inch pieces
- 1 envelope onion soup mix
- 1/2 cup dry red wine
- 1 can cream of mushroom soup
- 8 oz mushrooms, sliced
- 1/8 tsp pepper

Directions:
1. Add all ingredients into the cooking pot and stir well.
2. Cover instant pot aura with lid.
3. Select slow cook mode and cook on LOW for 6 hours.
4. Stir well and serve.

Nutritional Value (Amount per Serving):
Calories 261; Fat 8.4 g; Carbohydrates 10.6 g; Sugar 1.8 g; Protein 33.5 g; Cholesterol 61 mg

Asian Lamb

Preparation Time: 10 minutes; Cooking Time: 4 hours; Serve: 6

Ingredients:
- 3 lbs lamb shoulder
- 1/4 cup rice wine vinegar
- 1 tbsp garlic, minced
- 1 tbsp olive oil
- 1/4 cup brown sugar
- 1/4 cup hoisin sauce
- 1/2 cup soy sauce

Directions:
1. Add oil into the cooking pot and set instant pot aura on sauté mode.
2. Add lamb shoulder into the cooking pot and sauté until brown from all the sides.
3. Mix remaining ingredients and pour over meat.
4. Cover instant pot aura with lid.
5. Select slow cook mode and cook on HIGH for 2 hours.
6. Turn lamb, cover, and cook on HIGH for 2 hours more.
7. Serve and enjoy.

Nutritional Value (Amount per Serving):
Calories 508; Fat 19.3 g; Carbohydrates 12.7 g; Sugar 9.1 g; Protein 65.5 g; Cholesterol 204 mg

Moroccan Lamb

Preparation Time: 10 minutes; Cooking Time: 4 hours; Serve: 8

Ingredients:
- 2 lbs lamb chops
- 1 cup beef stock
- 1/2 cup dried apricots, chopped
- 1 cup yogurt
- 2 tbsp flour
- 14 oz can tomato, crushed
- 14 oz can chickpeas, rinsed & drained
- 1 carrot, chopped
- 1 onion, sliced
- 1 tsp brown sugar
- 1 tsp turmeric
- 1 tsp cinnamon
- 1 tsp ground ginger
- 1 tsp ground coriander
- 1 tsp ground cumin
- 1 tsp salt

Directions:
1. In a bowl, mix together stock and spices.
2. Add lamb chops and remaining ingredients into the cooking pot.
3. Pour stock mixture over lamb chops.
4. Cover instant pot aura with lid.
5. Select slow cook mode and cook on HIGH for 4 hours.
6. Serve and enjoy.

Nutritional Value (Amount per Serving):
Calories 330; Fat 9.5 g; Carbohydrates 21.6 g; Sugar 6.1 g; Protein 37.5 g; Cholesterol 104 mg

Garlic & Rosemary Lamb

Preparation Time: 10 minutes; Cooking Time: 8 hours; Serve: 6

Ingredients:
- 2 lbs lamb shoulder
- 4 garlic cloves, sliced
- 3 sprigs of rosemary
- 1 onion, sliced
- Pepper
- Salt

Directions:
1. Place meat into the cooking pot.

2. Add remaining ingredients on top of meat in the cooking pot.
3. Cover instant pot aura with lid.
4. Select slow cook mode and cook on LOW for 8 hours.
5. Serve and enjoy.

Nutritional Value (Amount per Serving):
Calories 294; Fat 11.2 g; Carbohydrates 2.8 g; Sugar 0.8 g; Protein 42.8 g; Cholesterol 136 mg

Moroccan Lamb Stew

Preparation Time: 10 minutes; Cooking Time: 8 hours; Serve: 6
Ingredients:
- 2 lbs lamb shoulder, cut into chunks
- 2 tsp thyme
- 1/2 cup beef stock
- 14 oz can tomato, chopped
- 2 tbsp honey
- 2 garlic cloves, minced
- 1 onion, sliced
- 1 tbsp olive oil
- Pepper
- Salt

Directions:
1. Add all ingredients into the cooking pot and stir well.
2. Cover instant pot aura with lid.
3. Select slow cook mode and cook on LOW for 8 hours.
4. Stir well and serve.

Nutritional Value (Amount per Serving):
Calories 348; Fat 13.5 g; Carbohydrates 11.4 g; Sugar 8.8 g; Protein 43.6 g; Cholesterol 136 mg

Salsa Pork Chops

Preparation Time: 10 minutes; Cooking Time: 3 hours; Serve: 8
Ingredients:
- 8 pork chops, bone-in
- 3 tbsp olive oil
- 1 tsp garlic powder
- 1/2 tsp ground cumin
- 1/4 cup fresh lime juice
- 1/2 cup salsa
- Pepper
- Salt

Directions:
1. Add all ingredients into the cooking pot and stir well.
2. Cover instant pot aura with lid.
3. Select slow cook mode and cook on HIGH for 3 hours.
4. Serve and enjoy.

Nutritional Value (Amount per Serving):
Calories 307; Fat 25.2 g; Carbohydrates 1.5 g; Sugar 0.6 g; Protein 18.3 g; Cholesterol 69 mg

Curried Pork Chops

Preparation Time: 10 minutes; Cooking Time: 6 hours; Serve: 8
Ingredients:
- 2 lbs pork chops
- 1 tbsp dried rosemary
- 1/4 cup olive oil
- 1 tbsp ground cumin
- 1 tbsp fennel seeds
- 1 tbsp fresh chives, chopped
- 1 tbsp curry powder
- 1 tbsp dried thyme
- 1 tsp salt

Directions:
1. In a small bowl, mix cumin, rosemary, 2 tbsp oil, fennel seeds, chives, curry powder, thyme, and salt.
2. Rub cumin mixture over pork chops.

3. Place pork chops into the cooking pot.
4. Pour remaining olive oil over pork chops.
5. Cover instant pot aura with lid.
6. Select slow cook mode and cook on LOW for 6 hours.
7. Serve and enjoy.

Nutritional Value (Amount per Serving):
Calories 427; Fat 35 g; Carbohydrates 1.7 g; Sugar 0.1 g; Protein 25.9 g; Cholesterol 98 mg

Mexican Flank Steak

Preparation Time: 10 minutes; Cooking Time: 9 hours; Serve: 6
Ingredients:
- 1 1/2 lbs flank steak
- 2 bell pepper, sliced
- 1 1/2 tsp chili powder
- 15 oz salsa
- 3 garlic cloves, minced
- 1 onion, chopped
- 1/4 tsp pepper
- 1/2 tsp salt

Directions:
1. Add all ingredients into the large zip-lock bag, seal bag, and place in the fridge overnight.
2. Add marinated steak into the cooking pot.
3. Cover instant pot aura with lid.
4. Select slow cook mode and cook on LOW for 9 hours.
5. Slice and serve.

Nutritional Value (Amount per Serving):
Calories 264; Fat 9.8 g; Carbohydrates 10.1 g; Sugar 5 g; Protein 33.4 g; Cholesterol 62 mg

Braised Beef

Preparation Time: 10 minutes; Cooking Time: 8 hours; Serve: 6
Ingredients:
- 2 lbs beef chuck roast
- 1/4 cup balsamic vinegar
- 1 cup of water
- 1/4 cup all-purpose flour
- 1/4 cup dates, pitted and chopped
- 4 shallots, sliced
- 1 medium onion, sliced
- 1/4 tsp pepper
- 1/2 tsp salt

Directions:
1. Place meat into the cooking pot.
2. Mix together remaining ingredients and pour over meat.
3. Cover instant pot aura with lid.
4. Select slow cook mode and cook on LOW for 8 hours.
5. Serve and enjoy.

Nutritional Value (Amount per Serving):
Calories 603; Fat 42.2 g; Carbohydrates 12.5 g; Sugar 5.5 g; Protein 40.7 g; Cholesterol 156 mg

Artichoke Pepper Beef

Preparation Time: 10 minutes; Cooking Time: 6 hours; Serve: 6
Ingredients:
- 2 lbs stew beef, cut into 1-inch cubes
- 12 oz artichoke hearts, drained
- 1 onion, diced
- 2 cups marinara sauce
- 1 tsp dried basil
- 1 tsp dried oregano
- 12 oz roasted red peppers, drained and sliced

Directions:
1. Add all ingredients into the cooking pot and stir well.

2. Cover instant pot aura with lid.
3. Select slow cook mode and cook on LOW for 6 hours.
4. Stir well and serve.

Nutritional Value (Amount per Serving):
Calories 343; Fat 11.6 g; Carbohydrates 22.8 g; Sugar 11.2 g; Protein 37.3 g; Cholesterol 2 mg

Italian Beef Roast

Preparation Time: 10 minutes; Cooking Time: 6 hours; Serve: 6

Ingredients:
- 2 lbs chuck roast, boneless
- 2 tbsp balsamic vinegar
- 2 tsp herb de Provence
- 1/3 cup sun-dried tomatoes, chopped
- 8 garlic cloves, chopped
- 1/4 cup fresh parsley, chopped
- 1/4 cup olives, chopped
- 1/2 cup chicken stock

Directions:
1. Add all ingredients into the cooking pot and stir well.
2. Cover instant pot aura with lid.
3. Select slow cook mode and cook on LOW for 6 hours.
4. Remove meat from pot and shred using a fork.
5. Serve and enjoy.

Nutritional Value (Amount per Serving):
Calories 349; Fat 13.5 g; Carbohydrates 2.3 g; Sugar 0.4 g; Protein 51.1 g; Cholesterol 153 mg

Olive Feta Beef

Preparation Time: 10 minutes; Cooking Time: 6 hours; Serve: 6

Ingredients:
- 2 lbs beef stew meat, cut into half-inch pieces
- 1 cup olives, pitted and cut in half
- 30 oz can tomato, diced
- 1/2 cup feta cheese, crumbled
- 1/4 tsp pepper
- 12 tsp salt

Directions:
1. Add all ingredients into the cooking pot and stir well.
2. Cover instant pot aura with lid.
3. Select slow cook mode and cook on HIGH for 6 hours.
4. Serve and enjoy.

Nutritional Value (Amount per Serving):
Calories 370; Fat 14.5 g; Carbohydrates 9.2 g; Sugar 5.3 g; Protein 49.1 g; Cholesterol 146 mg

Olive Artichokes Beef

Preparation Time: 10 minutes; Cooking Time: 7 hours; Serve: 6

Ingredients:
- 2 lbs stew beef, cut into 1-inch cubes
- 1 tsp dried oregano
- 1/2 cup olives, pitted and chopped
- 14 oz can tomato, diced
- 15 oz can tomato sauce
- 32 oz chicken stock
- 1 bay leaf
- 1/2 tsp ground cumin
- 1 tsp dried basil
- 1 tsp dried parsley
- 3 garlic cloves, chopped
- 1 onion, diced
- 14 oz can artichoke hearts, drained and halved
- 1 tbsp olive oil

Directions:

1. Add the meat into the cooking pot then mix together the remaining ingredients and pour over the meat.
2. Cover instant pot aura with lid.
3. Select slow cook mode and cook on LOW for 7 hours.
4. Stir well and serve.

Nutritional Value (Amount per Serving):
Calories 322; Fat 13.2 g; Carbohydrates 14.2 g; Sugar 7.1 g; Protein 36.8 g; Cholesterol 0 mg

Sriracha Beef

Preparation Time: 10 minutes; Cooking Time: 4 hours; Serve: 6
Ingredients:
- 2 lbs beef chuck, sliced
- 1 tbsp sriracha sauce
- 1/3 cup parsley, chopped
- 2 tsp garlic powder
- 1 cup beef broth
- 1/2 medium onion, sliced
- 2 cups bell pepper, chopped
- 1 tsp black pepper
- 2 tsp salt

Directions:
1. Add the meat into the cooking pot then mix together the remaining ingredients and pour over the meat.
2. Cover instant pot aura with lid.
3. Select slow cook mode and cook on HIGH for 4 hours.
4. Stir well and serve.

Nutritional Value (Amount per Serving):
Calories 310; Fat 9.8 g; Carbohydrates 5.5 g; Sugar 3.1 g; Protein 47.5 g; Cholesterol 135 mg

Pork with Couscous

Preparation Time: 10 minutes; Cooking Time: 8 hours; Serve: 6
Ingredients:
- 2 lbs pork loin, boneless
- 1 cup couscous, cook according to packet instructions
- 2 tsp dried sage
- 1/2 tbsp garlic powder
- 1/2 tbsp paprika
- 3/4 cup chicken stock
- 2 tbsp olive oil
- 1 tsp basil
- 1 tsp oregano
- 1/4 tsp dried thyme
- 1/4 tsp dried rosemary

Directions:
1. Add the meat into the cooking pot then mix together the remaining ingredients except for couscous and pour over the meat.
2. Cover instant pot aura with lid.
3. Select slow cook mode and cook on LOW for 8 hours.
4. Remove meat from pot and shred using a fork.
5. Serve shredded meat with couscous.

Nutritional Value (Amount per Serving):
Calories 521; Fat 26.1 g; Carbohydrates 23.6 g; Sugar 0.3 g; Protein 45.3 g; Cholesterol 121 mg

Spicy Pork

Preparation Time: 10 minutes; Cooking Time: 8 hours; Serve: 7
Ingredients:
- 4 lbs pork shoulder, trimmed
- 2 lime juice
- 2 orange juices
- 2 onions, quartered
- 1 tbsp chili powder
- 1 tsp black pepper

- 4 garlic cloves, minced
- 2 tsp dried oregano
- 2 tsp ground cumin
- 2 tsp salt

Directions:
1. In a small bowl, mix together chili powder, pepper, oregano, cumin, and salt. Rub spice mixture over pork.
2. Place pork into the cooking pot.
3. Pour garlic, lime juice, orange juice, and onions over the pork.
4. Cover instant pot aura with lid.
5. Select slow cook mode and cook on LOW for 8 hours.
6. Remove pork from pot shred using a fork.
7. Return shredded pork to the pot and stir well.
8. Serve and enjoy.

Nutritional Value (Amount per Serving):
Calories 794; Fat 55.9 g; Carbohydrates 8.5 g; Sugar 3.7 g; Protein 61.3 g; Cholesterol 233 mg

Easy Pork Carnitas

Preparation Time: 10 minutes; Cooking Time: 8 hours; Serve: 8

Ingredients:
- 3 lbs pork roast
- 1 fresh lime juice
- 2 tbsp olive oil
- 2 tbsp fresh cilantro, chopped

Directions:
1. Add all ingredients into the cooking pot and stir well.
2. Cover instant pot aura with lid.
3. Select slow cook mode and cook on LOW for 8 hours.
4. Remove pork from pot shred using a fork.
5. Return shredded pork to the pot and stir well.
6. Serve and enjoy.

Nutritional Value (Amount per Serving):
Calories 384; Fat 19.5 g; Carbohydrates 0.5 g; Sugar 0.1 g; Protein 48.5 g; Cholesterol 146 mg

Orange Pork Carnitas

Preparation Time: 10 minutes; Cooking Time: 9 hours; Serve: 6

Ingredients:
- 3 lbs pork shoulder
- 3 tsp cumin
- 2 orange juices
- 2 tsp olive oil
- 2 tsp ground coriander
- 1/2 cup water
- 2 tsp salt

Directions:
1. Place the pork shoulder into the cooking pot.
2. Pour remaining ingredients over the pork shoulder.
3. Cover instant pot aura with lid.
4. Select slow cook mode and cook on LOW for 9 hours.
5. Remove meat from cooking pot and shred using a fork.
6. Serve and enjoy.

Nutritional Value (Amount per Serving):
Calories 693; Fat 50.4 g; Carbohydrates 3.4 g; Sugar 2.4 g; Protein 53.2 g; Cholesterol 204 mg

Grapefruit Pork Roast

Preparation Time: 10 minutes; Cooking Time: 8 hours; Serve: 6

Ingredients:

- 3 lbs pork shoulder roast, boneless and cut into 4 pieces
- 1/2 tbsp cumin
- 1 tbsp fresh oregano
- 2/3 cup grapefruit juice
- Pepper
- Salt

Directions:
1. Season meat with pepper and salt and place into the cooking pot.
2. Add cumin, oregano, and grapefruit juice into the blender and blend until smooth.
3. Pour blended mixture over meat.
4. Cover instant pot aura with lid.
5. Select slow cook mode and cook on LOW for 8 hours.
6. Remove meat from pot and shred using a fork.
7. Return shredded meat into the pot and stir well.
8. Serve and enjoy.

Nutritional Value (Amount per Serving):
Calories 594; Fat 46.4 g; Carbohydrates 2.8 g; Sugar 1.8 g; Protein 38.5 g; Cholesterol 161 mg

Garlic Tomatoes Chuck Roast

Preparation Time: 10 minutes; Cooking Time: 10 hours; Serve: 6
Ingredients:
- 2 lbs beef chuck roast
- 1/2 cup beef broth
- 1/4 cup sun-dried tomatoes, chopped
- 25 garlic cloves, peeled
- 1/4 cup olives, sliced
- 1 tsp dried Italian seasoning, crushed
- 2 tbsp balsamic vinegar

Directions:
1. Add the meat into the cooking pot then mix together the remaining ingredients except for couscous and pour over the meat.
2. Cover instant pot aura with lid.
3. Select slow cook mode and cook on LOW for 8 hours.
4. Remove meat from pot and shred using a fork.
5. Return shredded meat to the pot and stir well.

Nutritional Value (Amount per Serving):
Calories 582; Fat 43.1 g; Carbohydrates 5 g; Sugar 0.5 g; Protein 40.8 g; Cholesterol 156 mg

Stuffed Bell Peppers

Preparation Time: 10 minutes; Cooking Time: 4 hours; Serve: 4
Ingredients:
- 6 large eggs
- 4 oz green chilies, chopped
- 4 oz jack cheese, shredded
- 1/2 lb ground breakfast sausage
- 4 bell pepper, cut top and clean
- 1/8 tsp black pepper
- 1/4 tsp salt

Directions:
1. Brown sausage in a pan over medium heat. Drain excess grease.
2. Pour 1/2 cup water in the cooking pot.
3. In a bowl, whisk eggs until smooth. Stir green chilies, cheese, black pepper, and salt in eggs.
4. Spoon egg mixture and brown sausage into each bell pepper.
5. Place stuffed bell pepper in the cooking pot.
6. Cover instant pot aura with lid.
7. Select slow cook mode and cook on LOW for 4 hours.
8. Serve and enjoy.

Nutritional Value (Amount per Serving):
Calories 445; Fat 23.4 g; Carbohydrates 30.4 g; Sugar 18.2 g; Protein 29.7 g; Cholesterol 348 mg

Butter Beef

Preparation Time: 10 minutes; Cooking Time: 8 hours; Serve: 8

Ingredients:
- 3 lbs beef stew meat, cubed
- 1/2 cup butter
- 1 oz dry onion soup mix

Directions:
1. Place beef into the cooking pot and sprinkle with onion soup mix.
2. Add butter over the beef.
3. Cover instant pot aura with lid.
4. Select slow cook mode and cook on LOW for 8 hours.
5. Stir well and serve.

Nutritional Value (Amount per Serving):
Calories 428; Fat 22.1 g; Carbohydrates 2.3 g; Sugar 0.2 g; Protein 52 g; Cholesterol 183 mg

Poultry Seasoned Pork Chops

Preparation Time: 10 minutes; Cooking Time: 4 hours; Serve: 4

Ingredients:
- 4 pork chops
- 1 tbsp garlic powder
- 2 garlic cloves, minced
- 1 cup organic chicken broth
- 1 tsp dried basil
- 1 tsp dried oregano
- 1 tbsp poultry seasoning
- 1/4 cup olive oil
- Pepper
- Salt

Directions:
1. In a large bowl, whisk together oil, basil, oregano, poultry seasoning, garlic powder, garlic, and broth.
2. Pour bowl mixture into the cooking pot then place pork chops into the cooking pot.
3. Cover instant pot aura with lid.
4. Select slow cook mode and cook on HIGH for 4 hours.
5. Serve and enjoy.

Nutritional Value (Amount per Serving):
Calories 387; Fat 33 g; Carbohydrates 3.1 g; Sugar 0.8 g; Protein 19.8 g; Cholesterol 69 mg

Herb Lamb Chops

Preparation Time: 10 minutes; Cooking Time: 6 hours; Serve: 4

Ingredients:
- 8 lamb chops
- 2 garlic cloves, minced
- 1 tsp dried oregano
- 1 onion, sliced
- 1/2 tsp garlic powder
- 1/2 tsp dried thyme
- 1/8 tsp black pepper
- 1/4 tsp salt

Directions:
1. Place sliced onion into the cooking pot.
2. In a small bowl, combine together oregano, garlic powder, thyme, pepper, and salt.
3. Rub oregano mixture over the lamb chops and place over sliced onion. Add garlic on top of lamb chops.
4. Cover instant pot aura with lid.
5. Select slow cook mode and cook on LOW for 6 hours.
6. Serve and enjoy.

Nutritional Value (Amount per Serving):
Calories 225; Fat 8.3 g; Carbohydrates 3.7 g; Sugar 1.3 g; Protein 32.1 g; Cholesterol 101 mg

Delicious Beef Stroganoff

Preparation Time: 10 minutes; Cooking Time: 8 hours; Serve: 2

Ingredients:
- 1/2 lb beef stew meat
- 10 oz mushroom soup
- 1 medium onion, chopped
- 1/2 cup sour cream
- 2 oz mushrooms, sliced
- Pepper
- Salt

Directions:
1. Add all ingredients except cream into the cooking pot and stir well.
2. Cover instant pot aura with lid.
3. Select slow cook mode and cook on LOW for 8 hours.
4. Stir in cream and serve.

Nutritional Value (Amount per Serving):
Calories 482; Fat 27.6 g; Carbohydrates 18.1 g; Sugar 5 g; Protein 40 g; Cholesterol 127 mg

Taco Beef

Preparation Time: 10 minutes; Cooking Time: 6 hours; Serve: 12

Ingredients:
- 10 oz can tomato with green chilies
- 1 lb ground beef
- 1 envelope taco seasoning

Directions:
1. Add all ingredients into the cooking pot and stir well.
2. Cover instant pot aura with lid.
3. Select slow cook mode and cook on LOW for 6 hours.
4. Serve and enjoy.

Nutritional Value (Amount per Serving):
Calories 105; Fat 4.1 g; Carbohydrates 3.1 g; Sugar 0 g; Protein 13.4 g; Cholesterol 38 mg

Salsa Beef

Preparation Time: 10 minutes; Cooking Time: 6 hours; Serve: 6

Ingredients:
- 2 lbs beef stew meat, cut into 3/4-inch cubes
- 2 cups salsa
- 1/4 cup cilantro, chopped
- 1 garlic clove, minced
- 1 tbsp soy sauce, low sodium

Directions:
1. Add all ingredients into the cooking pot and stir well.
2. Cover instant pot aura with lid.
3. Select slow cook mode and cook on LOW for 6 hours.
4. Serve and enjoy.

Nutritional Value (Amount per Serving):
Calories 307; Fat 9.6 g; Carbohydrates 5.8 g; Sugar 0.8 g; Protein 2.7 g; Cholesterol 135 mg

Beef Ribs with Sauce

Preparation Time: 10 minutes; Cooking Time: 8 hours; Serve: 8

Ingredients:
- 2 lbs beef short ribs
- 3 oz cream cheese, softened
- 1 tsp garlic powder
- 2 cups mushrooms, sliced

- 1/2 cup chicken broth
- 1 tsp black pepper
- 1 tsp salt

Directions:
1. Add cream cheese, garlic powder, mushrooms, broth, pepper, and salt in the cooking pot and stir well.
2. Place beef ribs on the top of the cream cheese mixture in the cooking pot.
3. Cover instant pot aura with lid.
4. Select slow cook mode and cook on LOW for 8 hours.
5. Serve and enjoy.

Nutritional Value (Amount per Serving):
Calories 278; Fat 14.1 g; Carbohydrates 1.3 g; Sugar 0.5 g; Protein 34.5 g; Cholesterol 115 mg

Cheesy Taco Casserole

Preparation Time: 10 minutes; Cooking Time: 2 hours; Serve: 10
Ingredients:
- 1 lb ground beef
- 1/2 package taco seasoning
- 1 can tomatoes, diced
- 1 can black beans, drained
- 8 oz cheddar cheese, shredded
- 2 cups rice, cooked
- 1 cup of corn
- 1/2 onion, chopped

Directions:
1. Add the meat into the cooking pot and set instant pot aura on sauté mode and cook meat until brown.
2. Remove meat from the cooking pot.
3. Add in onions, corn, beans, tomatoes, and taco seasoning. Stir to combine and set aside.
4. Spread rice in the bottom of the cooking pot then layer with meat mixture and top with shredded cheese.
5. Cover instant pot aura with lid.
6. Select slow cook mode and cook on HIGH for 2 hours.
7. Serve and enjoy.

Nutritional Value (Amount per Serving):
Calories 414; Fat 12.1 g; Carbohydrates 47.4 g; Sugar 1.8 g; Protein 28 g; Cholesterol 67 mg

Shredded Chili Beef

Preparation Time: 10 minutes; Cooking Time: 8 hours; Serve: 6
Ingredients:
- 2 1/2 lbs beef chuck roast, trimmed
- 4 oz can green chilies, diced
- 7 oz can chipotle sauce
- 14 oz can tomato, diced
- 2 tbsp chili powder
- 1 tsp cumin
- 1 onion, sliced

Directions:
1. Add all ingredients into the cooking pot and stir well.
2. Cover instant pot aura with lid.
3. Select slow cook mode and cook on LOW for 8 hours.
4. Shred the meat using a fork and serve.

Nutritional Value (Amount per Serving):
Calories 754; Fat 54.8 g; Carbohydrates 11.9 g; Sugar 6.5 g; Protein 51.9 g; Cholesterol 195 mg

Garlic Chili Lime Shredded Beef

Preparation Time: 10 minutes; Cooking Time: 8 hours; Serve: 6
Ingredients:

- 2 lbs beef chuck roast
- 1 tsp chili powder
- 4 cups chicken stock
- 2 lime juice
- 3 garlic cloves, crushed
- 1 tsp salt

Directions:
1. Place meat into the bottom of the cooking pot.
2. Pour chicken stock over chuck roast. Season roast with chili powder, garlic, and salt.
3. Cover instant pot aura with lid.
4. Select slow cook mode and cook on LOW for 8 hours.
5. Shred chuck roast using a fork and pour lime juice over shredded meat.
6. Serve and enjoy.

Nutritional Value (Amount per Serving):
Calories 563; Fat 42.5 g; Carbohydrates 2.5 g; Sugar 0.8 g; Protein 40.2 g; Cholesterol 156 mg

Salsa Ground Beef

Preparation Time: 10 minutes; Cooking Time: 6 hours; Serve: 6
Ingredients:
- 1 lb ground beef
- 1 tsp paprika
- 1 1/2 cups salsa
- 1 tbsp molasses
- 1/2 tsp onion powder
- 1/2 tsp sea salt

Directions:
1. Add all ingredients into the cooking pot and stir well.
2. Cover instant pot aura with lid.
3. Select slow cook mode and cook on LOW for 6 hours.
4. Stir well and serve.

Nutritional Value (Amount per Serving):
Calories 169; Fat 4.9 g; Carbohydrates 6.9 g; Sugar 4 g; Protein 24 g; Cholesterol 68 mg

Pulled Beef

Preparation Time: 10 minutes; Cooking Time: 6 hours; Serve: 6
Ingredients:
- 3 lbs chuck roast, cut into 2-inch pieces
- 5 garlic cloves, diced
- 2 tbsp tomato paste
- 1 cup onion, diced
- 1 tbsp olive oil
- 1 cup chicken broth
- 1/2 cup salsa
- 1 tsp oregano
- 1 tsp cumin
- 1 tbsp chili powder
- 1 1/2 tsp sea salt

Directions:
1. Add all ingredients into the cooking pot and stir well.
2. Cover instant pot aura with lid.
3. Select slow cook mode and cook on LOW for 6 hours.
4. Serve and enjoy.

Nutritional Value (Amount per Serving):
Calories 544; Fat 21.8 g; Carbohydrates 6.1 g; Sugar 2.4 g; Protein 76.9 g; Cholesterol 229 mg

Asian Sirloin Steak

Preparation Time: 10 minutes; Cooking Time: 6 hours; Serve: 4
Ingredients:
- 1 lb sirloin steak, sliced
- 1 tbsp sesame oil
- 3 tbsp soy sauce
- 1 onion, sliced
- 1 cup mushrooms, sliced
- 1 green bell pepper, sliced

- 1/2 tsp red pepper flakes
- 1 tsp fresh ginger, grated
- 1 garlic cloves, minced

Directions:
1. Add steak, onion, mushrooms, and green bell pepper in the cooking pot.
2. In a small bowl, mix together the remaining ingredients and pour over top of meat and vegetables.
3. Cover instant pot aura with lid.
4. Select slow cook mode and cook on LOW for 6 hours.
5. Serve and enjoy.

Nutritional Value (Amount per Serving):
Calories 275; Fat 10.7 g; Carbohydrates 7 g; Sugar 3.2 g; Protein 36.4 g; Cholesterol 101 mg

Beef Bean Casserole

Preparation Time: 10 minutes; Cooking Time: 8 hours; Serve: 6
Ingredients:
- 1 lb ground beef, browned and drained
- 1 can tomatoes with juice
- 1 can cream of mushroom soup
- 1 lb potatoes, sliced
- 1 cup cheddar cheese, shredded
- 1 can red kidney beans, drained
- 1 cup corn, drained
- 1/4 cup onion, diced
- 1/2 tsp pepper
- 1 tsp salt

Directions:
1. Add all ingredients except cheese in the cooking pot and stir well.
2. Cover instant pot aura with lid.
3. Select slow cook mode and cook on LOW for 8 hours.
4. Top with shredded cheese and cover and cook for 30 minutes more.
5. Serve and enjoy.

Nutritional Value (Amount per Serving):
Calories 440; Fat 14.6 g; Carbohydrates 40.2 g; Sugar 3.8 g; Protein 37.6 g; Cholesterol 87 mg

Butter Steak Bites

Preparation Time: 10 minutes; Cooking Time: 8 hours; Serve: 4
Ingredients:
- 3 lbs round steak, cut into 1-inch cubes
- 1/2 cup chicken broth
- 1/2 tsp black pepper
- 4 tbsp butter, sliced
- 1 tsp garlic powder
- 1 tbsp onion, minced
- 1/2 tsp salt

Directions:
1. Place meat cubes in the cooking pot and pour broth over the meat.
2. Sprinkle with garlic powder, onion, pepper, and salt.
3. Place butter slices on top of the meat.
4. Cover instant pot aura with lid.
5. Select slow cook mode and cook on LOW for 8 hours.
6. Serve and enjoy.

Nutritional Value (Amount per Serving):
Calories 845; Fat 44.4 g; Carbohydrates 1 g; Sugar 0.4 g; Protein 103 g; Cholesterol 320 mg

Sweet & Sour Pork Tenderloin

Preparation Time: 10 minutes; Cooking Time: 6 hours; Serve: 4
Ingredients:

- 2 lbs lean pork tenderloin, cut into cubed
- 2 tbsp cornstarch
- 2 tomatoes, cut into sliced
- 1 small onion, sliced
- 1/4 cup apple cider vinegar
- 3 tbsp soy sauce
- 2 green bell peppers, cut into strips
- 1/4 cup brown sugar
- 1/4 tsp ground ginger

Directions:
1. Add all ingredients except bell pepper and tomatoes into the cooking pot and stir well.
2. Cover instant pot aura with lid.
3. Select slow cook mode and cook on LOW for 6 hours.
4. Stir in tomatoes and bell pepper.
5. Cover and cook on high for 10 minutes more
6. Stir well and serve over rice.

Nutritional Value (Amount per Serving):
Calories 421; Fat 8.3 g; Carbohydrates 22.2 g; Sugar 14.4 g; Protein 61.5 g; Cholesterol 166 mg

Orange Pork Roast

Preparation Time: 10 minutes; Cooking Time: 8 hours; Serve: 6

Ingredients:
- 4 lbs pork roast
- 1/4 cup orange marmalade
- 1/4 cup soy sauce
- 2 garlic cloves, minced
- 1 tbsp ketchup

Directions:
1. In a small bowl, mix together soy sauce, garlic, ketchup, and orange marmalade.
2. Brush soy sauce mixture all over pork roast.
3. Place pork roast in the cooking pot and pour the remaining sauce over pork roast.
4. Cover instant pot aura with lid.
5. Select slow cook mode and cook on LOW for 8 hours.
6. Slice and serve.

Nutritional Value (Amount per Serving):
Calories 668; Fat 28.5 g; Carbohydrates 10.6 g; Sugar 8.8 g; Protein 87 g; Cholesterol 260 mg

Hawaiian Pork

Preparation Time: 10 minutes; Cooking Time: 6 hours; Serve: 6

Ingredients:
- 4 lbs pork roast
- 4 tbsp liquid smoke
- 1 onion, sliced
- 3 garlic cloves, minced
- 3 tbsp soy sauce
- 1 tbsp sea salt

Directions:
1. Place onion in the bottom of the cooking pot.
2. In a small bowl, mix together garlic, soy sauce, liquid smoke, and sea salt.
3. Rub garlic mixture all over pork. Place pork in the cooking pot.
4. Cover instant pot aura with lid.
5. Select slow cook mode and cook on LOW for 6 hours.
6. Shred the pork using a fork and stir well.
7. Serve and enjoy.

Nutritional Value (Amount per Serving):
Calories 640; Fat 28.6 g; Carbohydrates 2.8 g; Sugar 0.9 g; Protein 87 g; Cholesterol 260 mg

Beef Heart

Preparation Time: 10 minutes; Cooking Time: 4 hours; Serve: 4

Ingredients:
- 1 lb beef heart, cut into cubes
- 1/4 tsp garlic powder
- 1/2 onion, sliced
- 1/2 tsp dried oregano
- 1/4 tsp pepper
- 1/2 tsp salt

Directions:
1. Add all ingredients into the cooking pot and stir well.
2. Cover instant pot aura with lid.
3. Select slow cook mode and cook on HIGH for 4 hours.
4. Stir well and serve.

Nutritional Value (Amount per Serving):
Calories 194; Fat 5.4 g; Carbohydrates 1.8 g; Sugar 0.6 g; Protein 32.5 g; Cholesterol 240 mg

Jalapeno Beef

Preparation Time: 10 minutes; Cooking Time: 8 hours; Serve: 8

Ingredients:
- 2 lbs beef chuck roast
- 1/2 cup Worcestershire sauce
- 1/2 cup beef broth
- 12 oz roasted red bell peppers, drained and chopped
- 4 jalapeno pepper, sliced
- 1 onion, sliced
- 1/2 tsp black pepper
- 1 tsp salt

Directions:
1. Add the meat into the cooking pot then mix together the remaining ingredients and pour over the meat.
2. Cover instant pot aura with lid.
3. Select slow cook mode and cook on LOW for 8 hours.
4. Remove meat from pot and shred using a fork.
5. Return shredded meat into the pot and stir well.
6. Serve and enjoy.

Nutritional Value (Amount per Serving):
Calories 488; Fat 34.5 g; Carbohydrates 6.6 g; Sugar 4.9 g; Protein 34.6 g; Cholesterol 132 mg

Spicy Green Chili Beef

Preparation Time: 10 minutes; Cooking Time: 8 hours; Serve: 8

Ingredients:
- 2 lbs beef chuck roast
- 1 tsp chili powder
- 4 fresh Anaheim Chile peppers, chopped
- 1 onion, sliced
- 1 tsp ground cumin
- 1 1/2 tsp salt

Directions:
1. Add the meat into the cooking pot then mix together the remaining ingredients and pour over the meat.
2. Cover instant pot aura with lid.
3. Select slow cook mode and cook on LOW for 8 hours.
4. Remove meat from pot and shred using a fork.
5. Return shredded meat into the pot and stir well.
6. Serve and enjoy.

Nutritional Value (Amount per Serving):
Calories 419; Fat 31.7 g; Carbohydrates 1.6 g; Sugar 0.6 g; Protein 29.9 g; Cholesterol 117 mg

Slow Cook Beef Brisket

Preparation Time: 10 minutes; Cooking Time: 8 hours; Serve: 8

Ingredients:
- 3 lbs beef brisket
- 2 tbsp garlic salt

For sauce:
- 1/2 tsp parsley
- 1/4 cup dried onion flakes
- 1/2 cup beef broth
- 28 oz tomatoes, diced
- 1/8 tsp pepper
- 1/8 tsp paprika
- 1/4 tsp onion powder

Directions:
1. Add the meat into the cooking pot then mix together the remaining ingredients and pour over the meat.
2. Cover instant pot aura with lid.
3. Select slow cook mode and cook on LOW for 8 hours.
4. Remove meat from pot and shred using a fork.
5. Return shredded meat into the pot and stir well.
6. Serve and enjoy.

Nutritional Value (Amount per Serving):
Calories 350; Fat 10.9 g; Carbohydrates 7 g; Sugar 3.8 g; Protein 53.3 g; Cholesterol 152 mg

Balsamic Lamb Chops

Preparation Time: 10 minutes; Cooking Time: 6 hours; Serve: 6

Ingredients:
- 3.5 lbs lamb chops, trimmed off
- 2 tbsp balsamic vinegar
- 4 garlic cloves, minced
- 1 large onion, sliced
- 1/2 tsp ground black pepper
- 2 tbsp rosemary
- 1/2 tsp salt

Directions:
1. Add onion into the cooking pot.
2. Place lamb chops on top of onions, then add rosemary, vinegar, garlic, pepper, and salt.
3. Cover instant pot aura with lid.
4. Select slow cook mode and cook on LOW for 6 hours.
5. Serve and enjoy.

Nutritional Value (Amount per Serving):
Calories 510; Fat 19.6 g; Carbohydrates 3.9 g; Sugar 1.1 g; Protein 74.8 g; Cholesterol 238 mg

Apple Butter Pork

Preparation Time: 10 minutes; Cooking Time: 6 hours; Serve: 6

Ingredients:
- 2 lbs pork tenderloin
- 1/2 tsp garlic powder
- 1 tbsp brown sugar
- 1 tbsp wholegrain mustard
- 1 tbsp apple cider vinegar
- 3/4 cup apple butter
- 1/2 tsp thyme
- 1 tsp paprika
- 1 tsp salt

Directions:
1. In a bowl, mix together brown sugar, thyme, garlic powder, paprika, and salt.
2. Rub brown sugar mixture all over pork tenderloin and place in the cooking pot.
3. Whisk together mustard, vinegar, apple cider, and apple butter. Pour over pork.
4. Cover instant pot aura with lid.
5. Select slow cook mode and cook on LOW for 6 hours.

6. Shred the meat using a fork and serve.

Nutritional Value (Amount per Serving):
Calories 287; Fat 5.6 g; Carbohydrates 17.1 g; Sugar 14 g; Protein 39.8 g; Cholesterol 110 mg

Creamy Mushroom Pork Chops

Preparation Time: 10 minutes; Cooking Time: 6 hours; Serve: 4

Ingredients:
- 4 pork chops, bone-in
- 1 can cream of mushroom soup
- 2 cups onion, chopped
- 1 tsp garlic, minced
- 16 oz mushrooms, sliced
- 1 can cream of chicken soup
- 1/2 tsp black pepper

Directions:
1. Add chopped onion into the cooking pot.
2. Place pork chops on top of onion in the cooking pot.
3. In a bowl, mix together the remaining ingredients and pour over pork chops.
4. Cover instant pot aura with lid.
5. Select slow cook mode and cook on LOW for 6 hours.
6. Serve over rice and enjoy.

Nutritional Value (Amount per Serving):
Calories 436; Fat 28.9 g; Carbohydrates 19.8 g; Sugar 5.9 g; Protein 25.2 g; Cholesterol 75 mg

Thyme Garlic Lamb Chops

Preparation Time: 10 minutes; Cooking Time: 6 hours; Serve: 2

Ingredients:
- 2 lamb shoulder chops, bone-in
- 1/2 cup red wine
- 1 cup beef broth
- 1/4 cup fresh thyme
- 1 tsp garlic paste
- Pepper
- Salt

Directions:
1. Add all ingredients into the cooking pot and stir well.
2. Cover instant pot aura with lid.
3. Select slow cook mode and cook on LOW for 6 hours.
4. Stir well and serve.

Nutritional Value (Amount per Serving):
Calories 237; Fat 7.1 g; Carbohydrates 6.4 g; Sugar 0.9 g; Protein 26.1 g; Cholesterol 75 mg

Apple Pork Loin

Preparation Time: 10 minutes; Cooking Time: 8 hours; Serve: 4

Ingredients:
- 1 1/2 lbs pork loin
- 3 apples, peeled, cored and chopped
- 1 cup apple cider
- 1 onion, sliced
- Pepper
- Salt

Directions:
1. Place pork in the cooking pot and top with sliced onion and apples.
2. Pour apple cider over pork onion and apple mixture.
3. Season with pepper and salt.
4. Cover instant pot aura with lid.
5. Select slow cook mode and cook on LOW for 8 hours.
6. Slice pork and serve.

Nutritional Value (Amount per Serving):

Calories 539; Fat 24.1 g; Carbohydrates 32.9 g; Sugar 25.3 g; Protein 47.3 g; Cholesterol 136 mg

Spicy Pork Chops

Preparation Time: 10 minutes; Cooking Time: 5 hours; Serve: 8
Ingredients:
- 4 lbs pork chops, boneless
- 1/4 cup cornstarch
- 1/2 cup brown sugar
- 1 tsp black pepper
- 1 tsp garlic, minced
- 1 tbsp red chili paste
- 1/4 cup soy sauce
- 1/2 cup ketchup
- 1/2 tsp kosher salt

Directions:
1. Add all ingredients except cornstarch and pork chop into the cooking pot and stir well.
2. Place pork chops in the cooking pot and stir well to coat.
3. Cover instant pot aura with lid.
4. Select slow cook mode and cook on LOW for 4 hours.
5. In a small bowl, whisk together little water and cornstarch and pour into the cooking pot.
6. Stir everything well and cook on low for 1 hour more.
7. Serve and enjoy.

Nutritional Value (Amount per Serving):
Calories 802; Fat 56.7 g; Carbohydrates 18 g; Sugar 12.9 g; Protein 51.9 g; Cholesterol 196 mg

Adobo Pulled Pork

Preparation Time: 10 minutes; Cooking Time: 8 hours; Serve: 4
Ingredients:
- 2 lbs pork
- 7 oz chipotle peppers in adobo sauce
- 1 can chicken broth
- 1 tbsp ground cumin
- 1 tbsp garlic, minced

Directions:
1. Add all ingredients into the cooking pot and stir well.
2. Cover instant pot aura with lid.
3. Select slow cook mode and cook on LOW for 8 hours.
4. Shred the meat using a fork.
5. Stir well and serve.

Nutritional Value (Amount per Serving):
Calories 381; Fat 11.1 g; Carbohydrates 3.9 g; Sugar 0.5 g; Protein 64.7 g; Cholesterol 175 mg

Delicious Curried Pork

Preparation Time: 10 minutes; Cooking Time: 8 hours; Serve: 6
Ingredients:
- 4 pork chops, boneless
- 1 tbsp curry powder
- 1 tbsp turmeric
- 8 oz baby carrots, peeled and chopped
- 1 tbsp fresh ginger, grated
- 4 garlic cloves, minced
- 1 small onion, chopped
- 1/2 cup chicken broth
- 1 tsp red pepper flakes
- 2 tsp cardamom
- 2 tsp cumin
- Pepper
- Sea salt

Directions:
1. Add all ingredients into the cooking pot and stir well.
2. Cover instant pot aura with lid.
3. Select slow cook mode and cook on LOW for 8 hours.

4. Shred the pork chops using a fork.
   5. Serve and enjoy.

Nutritional Value (Amount per Serving):
Calories 211; Fat 14 g; Carbohydrates 7.9 g; Sugar 2.5 g; Protein 13.4 g; Cholesterol 46 mg

Chili Cumin Pork

Preparation Time: 10 minutes; Cooking Time: 8 hours; Serve: 8

Ingredients:
- 3 lbs boneless pork, cubed
- 1 cup chicken broth
- 1 tsp oregano
- 1 tsp cumin
- 1 small onion, chopped
- 2 garlic cloves, minced
- 16 oz stewed tomatoes
- 4 oz green chilies, chopped
- 1 tbsp olive oil
- Pepper
- Salt

Directions:
1. Add all ingredients into the cooking pot and stir well.
2. Cover instant pot aura with lid.
3. Select slow cook mode and cook on LOW for 8 hours.
4. Serve and enjoy.

Nutritional Value (Amount per Serving):
Calories 325; Fat 8.9 g; Carbohydrates 13.5 g; Sugar 7.8 g; Protein 47.4 g; Cholesterol 124 mg

Orange Jalapeno Pork

Preparation Time: 10 minutes; Cooking Time: 8 hours; Serve: 6

Ingredients:
- 2 lbs pork shoulder, boneless and cut into 2 pieces
- 3 garlic cloves, minced
- 1 jalapeno pepper, halved
- 1 small onion, chopped
- 1 lime zest
- 1/4 cup lime juice
- 1/2 cup orange juice
- 1/4 cup vinegar
- 2 bay leaves
- 1/2 tsp paprika
- 1/2 tsp cumin
- 1 1/2 tsp dried oregano
- 1/2 tsp pepper
- 3/4 cup chicken broth
- 1 tsp salt

Directions:
1. Place pork roast into the cooking pot.
2. Add remaining ingredients into the cooking pot.
3. Cover instant pot aura with lid.
4. Select slow cook mode and cook on LOW for 8 hours.
5. Discard bay leaves. Shred the meat using a fork.
6. Serve and enjoy.

Nutritional Value (Amount per Serving):
Calories 469; Fat 32.7 g; Carbohydrates 5 g; Sugar 2.5 g; Protein 36.4 g; Cholesterol 136 mg

Beef Stew

Preparation Time: 10 minutes; Cooking Time: 8 hours; Serve: 4

Ingredients:
- 1 lb beef stew meat
- 1 tbsp curry powder
- 1 fresh jalapeno pepper, diced
- 1 tsp fresh ginger, chopped
- 2 garlic cloves, minced
- 1 tbsp vegetable oil
- 1 cup beef broth
- 1 onion, sliced

- 14 oz can tomato, diced
- Pepper
- Salt

Directions:
1. Add oil and meat into the cooking pot and set instant pot aura on sauté mode. Sauté meat until brown.
2. Pour remaining ingredients into the cooking pot.
3. Cover instant pot aura with lid.
4. Select slow cook mode and cook on LOW for 8 hours.
5. Serve and enjoy.

Nutritional Value (Amount per Serving):
Calories 293; Fat 11.1 g; Carbohydrates 9.8 g; Sugar 4.9 g; Protein 37.2 g; Cholesterol 101 mg

Asian Lamb Stew

Preparation Time: 10 minutes; Cooking Time: 4 hours; Serve: 4
Ingredients:
- 2 lbs lamb, boneless
- 2 tbsp vegetable oil
- 2 tsp ground cumin
- 2 tsp ground coriander
- 1 tsp ground turmeric
- 28 oz can tomato, crushed
- 1.5 tbsp maple syrup
- 2 medium onions, chopped
- 3 garlic cloves, chopped
- 1 tsp fresh ginger, grated
- 1 tsp dried mint
- 1 tsp garam masala
- 1 tsp red chili flakes
- 2 tsp salt

Directions:
1. Add oil, ginger, onion, and garlic into the cooking pot and set instant pot aura on sauté mode and sauté onion until softened.
2. Add lamb and sauté until browned.
3. Add remaining ingredients into the cooking and stir well.
4. Cover instant pot aura with lid.
5. Select slow cook mode and cook on HIGH for 4 hours.
6. Serve and enjoy.

Nutritional Value (Amount per Serving):
Calories 577; Fat 23.8 g; Carbohydrates 22.2 g; Sugar 13.6 g; Protein 66.5 g; Cholesterol 204 mg

Pork Chili

Preparation Time: 10 minutes; Cooking Time: 7 hours; Serve: 8
Ingredients:
- 2 lbs pork shoulder roast, boneless
- 8 oz can tomato sauce
- 15 oz can tomato, diced
- 15 oz can pinto beans, rinsed and drained
- 1 jalapeno pepper, diced
- 3 garlic cloves, minced
- 1 onion, diced
- 8 oz chicken broth
- 1 tsp cilantro, dried
- 1 tsp cumin
- 1 tsp chipotle chili powder
- 2 tsp chili powder

Directions:
1. Add all ingredients into the cooking pot and stir well.
2. Cover instant pot aura with lid.
3. Select slow cook mode and cook on LOW for 7 hours.
4. Remove pork roast from the cooking pot and shred with a fork.
5. Return pork roast into the cooking pot and mix well.
6. Serve warm and enjoy.

Nutritional Value (Amount per Serving):
Calories 370; Fat 24 g; Carbohydrates 14.9 g; Sugar 3.9 g; Protein 23.5 g; Cholesterol 80 mg

Beef Ragu

Preparation Time: 10 minutes; Cooking Time: 6 hours; Serve: 2

Ingredients:
- 1 lb chuck roast
- 1/2 tsp basil
- 1/2 tsp oregano
- 1 beef bouillon
- 1/2 tbsp garlic, minced
- 1/2 celery stalk, diced
- 1 small carrot, diced
- 1/4 cup red wine
- 1/4 cup water
- 3 oz tomato paste
- 14 oz can tomato, crushed
- 1/4 cup onion, diced
- 1/4 tsp black pepper
- 1/2 tsp salt

Directions:
1. Add all ingredients into the cooking pot and stir well.
2. Cover instant pot aura with lid.
3. Select slow cook mode and cook on LOW for 6 hours.
4. Shred the meat using a fork.
5. Stir well and serve over pasta.

Nutritional Value (Amount per Serving):
Calories 623; Fat 19.5 g; Carbohydrates 25 g; Sugar 14.8 g; Protein 79.8 g; Cholesterol 229 mg

Chapter 7: Fish & Seafood

Thai Shrimp Rice

Preparation Time: 10 minutes; Cooking Time: 3 hours 30 minutes; Serve: 6
Ingredients:
- 1 lb shrimp, peeled, deveined, & cooked
- 1/2 cup snow peas, cut into thin strips
- 2 cups white rice
- 1/4 cup raisins
- 1/4 cup flaked coconut
- 1 carrot, shredded
- 1 bell pepper, diced
- 1 onion, chopped
- 2 tbsp garlic, minced
- 2 lime juice
- 3/4 tsp cayenne
- 1 tsp cumin
- 1 tsp ground coriander
- 1 cup of water
- 28 oz chicken broth
- 1 tsp salt

Directions:
1. Add all ingredients except coconut, snow peas, and shrimp into the cooking pot and stir well.
2. Cover instant pot aura with lid.
3. Select slow cook mode and cook on LOW for 3 hours.
4. Stir in snow peas and shrimp, cover and cook on LOW for 30 minutes more.
5. Top with flaked coconut and serve.

Nutritional Value (Amount per Serving):
Calories 399; Fat 3.8 g; Carbohydrates 63.8 g; Sugar 7.4 g; Protein 25.8 g; Cholesterol 159 mg

Caribbean Shrimp

Preparation Time: 10 minutes; Cooking Time: 2 hours; Serve: 4
Ingredients:
- 12 oz frozen shrimp, thawed
- 2 cups cooked rice
- 1/2 cup tomatoes, diced
- 1 cup frozen peas, thawed
- 1/2 tsp dried oregano
- 1 tsp chili powder
- 1/2 tsp garlic powder
- 1/2 cup chicken broth

Directions:
1. Add shrimp, oregano, chili powder, garlic powder, and broth into the cooking pot and stir well.
2. Cover instant pot aura with lid.
3. Select slow cook mode and cook on LOW for 2 hours.
4. Stir in rice, tomatoes, and peas. Cover and let it sit for 10 minutes.
5. Stir well and serve.

Nutritional Value (Amount per Serving):
Calories 472; Fat 2.6 g; Carbohydrates 82.1 g; Sugar 2.8 g; Protein 27 g; Cholesterol 128 mg

Herb Lemon Cod

Preparation Time: 10 minutes; Cooking Time: 2 hours; Serve: 4
Ingredients:
- 4 cod fillets, frozen
- 1/4 cup water
- 1/2 lemon juice
- 2 tbsp herb de Provence

Directions:
1. Place fish fillets into the cooking pot.
2. Mix together the remaining ingredients and pour over fish fillets.
3. Cover instant pot aura with lid.

4. Select slow cook mode and cook on LOW for 2 hours.
5. Serve and enjoy.

Nutritional Value (Amount per Serving):
Calories 98; Fat 1.4 g; Carbohydrates 0.1 g; Sugar 0.1 g; Protein 20.9 g; Cholesterol 40 mg

White Fish Fillet with Tomatoes

Preparation Time: 10 minutes; Cooking Time: 2 hours; Serve: 4

Ingredients:
- 1 lb white fish fillets
- 1/3 cup chicken broth
- 1 tsp dried mix herbs
- 15 oz can tomato, diced
- 1 garlic cloves, minced
- 1 small onion, diced
- 1 bell pepper, diced
- 1/4 tsp black pepper
- 1/2 tsp salt

Directions:
1. Add tomatoes, broth, bell pepper, onion, and garlic into the cooking pot and stir well.
2. Add a fish fillet to the cooking pot and season with herbs, pepper, and salt.
3. Cover instant pot aura with lid.
4. Select slow cook mode and cook on LOW for 2 hours.
5. Serve and enjoy.

Nutritional Value (Amount per Serving):
Calories 241; Fat 8.7 g; Carbohydrates 10.2 g; Sugar 6 g; Protein 29.7 g; Cholesterol 87 mg

Coconut Fish Curry

Preparation Time: 10 minutes; Cooking Time: 2 hours; Serve: 3

Ingredients:
- 10 oz codfish fillets, cut into 2-inch cubes
- 1 1/2 cups broccoli florets
- 1 cup snow peas, sliced
- 14 oz coconut milk
- 1 stick lemongrass
- 1 1/2 tsp turmeric
- 1 red chili, chopped
- 1 tbsp ginger, chopped
- 2 garlic cloves, chopped

Directions:
1. Add all ingredients into the cooking pot and stir well.
2. Cover instant pot aura with lid.
3. Select slow cook mode and cook on LOW for 2 hours.
4. Serve and enjoy.

Nutritional Value (Amount per Serving):
Calories 457; Fat 32.9 g; Carbohydrates 17.3 g; Sugar 7.5 g; Protein 28 g; Cholesterol 52 mg

Louisiana Shrimp

Preparation Time: 10 minutes; Cooking Time: 1 hour 30 minutes; Serve: 4

Ingredients:
- 1 lb shrimp, deveined
- 1 tsp garlic, minced
- 1 tsp old bay seasoning
- 1 tbsp Worcestershire sauce
- 1 lemon juice
- 1/2 cup butter, sliced
- 1/2 tsp pepper
- 1/2 tsp salt

Directions:
1. Add all ingredients into the cooking pot and stir well.
2. Cover instant pot aura with lid.
3. Select slow cook mode and cook on HIGH for 1 1/2 hours.
4. Serve and enjoy.

Nutritional Value (Amount per Serving):
Calories 343; Fat 25 g; Carbohydrates 2.4 g; Sugar 0.3 g; Protein 26.2 g; Cholesterol 300 mg

Cajun Corn Shrimp

Preparation Time: 10 minutes; Cooking Time: 5 hours; Serve: 4

Ingredients:
- 12 oz shrimp, peeled & deveined
- 1/2 cup heavy cream
- 4 cups chicken broth
- 1 1/2 tsp Cajun seasoning
- 1/4 cup flour
- 1/2 lb baby potatoes, cut into chunks
- 16 oz frozen sweet corn
- Pepper
- Salt

Directions:
1. Add all ingredients except shrimp and cream into the cooking pot and stir well.
2. Cover instant pot aura with lid.
3. Select slow cook mode and cook on LOW for 4 hours.
4. Add shrimp and cream and stir well, cover, and cook on low for 1 hour.
5. Serve and enjoy.

Nutritional Value (Amount per Serving):
Calories 781; Fat 15.7 g; Carbohydrates 131.7 g; Sugar 20.7 g; Protein 46.8 g; Cholesterol 200 mg

BBQ Shrimp

Preparation Time: 10 minutes; Cooking Time: 1 hour; Serve: 4

Ingredients:
- 2 lbs shrimp, peeled & deveined
- 1 cup BBQ sauce
- 2 tsp garlic, minced
- 3 tbsp Worcestershire sauce
- 3 tbsp butter
- Pepper
- Salt

Directions:
1. Add all ingredients into the cooking pot and stir well.
2. Cover instant pot aura with lid.
3. Select slow cook mode and cook on LOW for 1 hour.
4. Serve and enjoy.

Nutritional Value (Amount per Serving):
Calories 453; Fat 12.7 g; Carbohydrates 28.8 g; Sugar 18.6 g; Protein 51.8 g; Cholesterol 501 mg

Delicious Shrimp Fajitas

Preparation Time: 10 minutes; Cooking Time: 5 hours 30 minutes; Serve: 4

Ingredients:
- 1 lb shrimp, deveined & peeled
- 1/2 tsp paprika
- 1 tsp taco seasoning
- 1/2 cup chicken broth
- 1 onion, sliced
- 1 tomato, quartered
- 2 red bell peppers, sliced
- 2 green bell peppers, sliced
- 1 tsp salt

Directions:
1. Add all ingredients except shrimp into the cooking pot and stir well.
2. Cover instant pot aura with lid.
3. Select slow cook mode and cook on LOW for 5 hours.
4. Add shrimp and stir well, cover, and cook on HIGH for 30 minutes more.
5. Stir well and serve.

Nutritional Value (Amount per Serving):

Calories 195; Fat 2.6 g; Carbohydrates 14.3 g; Sugar 7.7 g; Protein 28.3 g; Cholesterol 239 mg

Spicy Shrimp

Preparation Time: 10 minutes; Cooking Time: 50 minutes; Serve: 8

Ingredients:
- 2 lbs large shrimp, peeled and deveined
- 1 tbsp parsley, minced
- 1/4 tsp red pepper flakes, crushed
- 1 tsp paprika
- 5 garlic cloves, sliced
- 3/4 cup olive oil
- 1/4 tsp pepper
- 1 tsp kosher salt

Directions:
1. Add all ingredients except shrimp and parsley into the cooking pot and stir well.
2. Cover instant pot aura with lid.
3. Select slow cook mode and cook on HIGH for 30 minutes.
4. Add shrimp and stir well, Cover and cook on HIGH for 20 minutes.
5. Garnish with parsley and serve.

Nutritional Value (Amount per Serving):
Calories 257; Fat 19 g; Carbohydrates 2.9 g; Sugar 0.1 g; Protein 21.5 g; Cholesterol 162 mg

Healthy Lime Salmon

Preparation Time: 10 minutes; Cooking Time: 2 hours; Serve: 6

Ingredients:
- 1 1/2 lbs salmon fillets
- 2 tbsp fresh lime juice
- 2 tbsp fresh ginger, minced
- 1/2 onion, sliced
- 1/2 lime, sliced

Directions:
1. Place salmon fillets skin side down into the cooking pot.
2. Pour lime juice over salmon then sprinkle ginger on top.
3. Arrange onion and lime slices on top of salmon.
4. Cover instant pot aura with lid.
5. Select slow cook mode and cook on LOW for 2 hours.
6. Serve and enjoy.

Nutritional Value (Amount per Serving):
Calories 165; Fat 7.1 g; Carbohydrates 4 g; Sugar 0.8 g; Protein 22.4 g; Cholesterol 50 mg

Shrimp Pasta

Preparation Time: 10 minutes; Cooking Time: 1 hour 30 minutes; Serve: 4

Ingredients:
- 1 lb shrimp, peeled and deveined
- 1/4 cup fresh parsley, minced
- 1 cup wheat orzo pasta
- 1 tbsp butter
- 1/2 cup dry white wine
- 4 cups vegetable broth
- 2 tsp garlic, minced
- Pepper
- Salt

Directions:
1. Add all ingredients into the cooking pot and stir well.
2. Cover instant pot aura with lid.
3. Select slow cook mode and cook on LOW for 1 1/2 hours.
4. Stir well and serve.

Nutritional Value (Amount per Serving):
Calories 292; Fat 7.1 g; Carbohydrates 16.2 g; Sugar 2.5 g; Protein 33.4 g; Cholesterol 249 mg

Shrimp Scampi

Preparation Time: 10 minutes; Cooking Time: 1 hour 30 minutes; Serve: 6
Ingredients:
- 1 1/2 lbs shrimp
- 6 tbsp olive oil
- 1 1/2 cup beef broth
- 2 tbsp lemon juice
- 4 garlic cloves, minced
- Pepper and salt

Directions:
1. Add all ingredients into the cooking pot and stir well.
2. Cover instant pot aura with lid.
3. Select slow cook mode and cook on HIGH for 1 1/2 hours.
4. Stir well and serve.

Nutritional Value (Amount per Serving):
Calories 269; Fat 16.3 g; Carbohydrates 2.9 g; Sugar 0.4 g; Protein 27.2 g; Cholesterol 239 mg

Tasty Shrimp Curry

Preparation Time: 10 minutes; Cooking Time: 2 hours 15 minutes; Serve: 4
Ingredients:
- 1 lb shrimp
- 30 oz coconut milk
- 2 1/2 tsp lemon garlic seasoning
- 1 tbsp curry paste
- 15 oz water

Directions:
1. Add all ingredients except shrimp into the cooking pot and stir well.
2. Cover instant pot aura with lid.
3. Select slow cook mode and cook on HIGH for 2 hours.
4. Add shrimp into the cooking pot and stir well, cover, and cook on HIGH for 15 minutes more.
5. Stir well and serve.

Nutritional Value (Amount per Serving):
Calories 667; Fat 55.2 g; Carbohydrates 17.4 g; Sugar 7.8 g; Protein 30.9 g; Cholesterol 239 mg

Shrimp Fajita Soup

Preparation Time: 10 minutes; Cooking Time: 2 hours 10 minutes; Serve: 4
Ingredients:
- 1 lb shrimp
- 1 bell pepper, sliced
- 64 oz chicken stock
- 2 tbsp fajita seasoning
- 1 onion, sliced

Directions:
1. Add all ingredients except shrimp into the cooking pot and stir well.
2. Add shrimp and cook for 10 minutes more.
3. Stir well and serve.

Nutritional Value (Amount per Serving):
Calories 189; Fat 3.1 g; Carbohydrates 11.1 g; Sugar 4 g; Protein 27.7 g; Cholesterol 239 mg

Capers Salmon

Preparation Time: 10 minutes; Cooking Time: 2 hours; Serve: 2
Ingredients:
- 8 oz salmon
- 1 tbsp capers
- 1/3 cup water
- 2 tbsp lemon juice
- 1/4 tsp fresh rosemary, minced

Directions:

1. Place salmon into the cooking pot.
2. Pour lemon juice and water over salmon.
3. Sprinkle with rosemary and capers.
4. Cover instant pot aura with lid.
5. Select slow cook mode and cook on LOW for 2 hours.
6. Serve and enjoy.

Nutritional Value (Amount per Serving):
Calories 155; Fat 7.2 g; Carbohydrates 0.6 g; Sugar 0.3 g; Protein 22.2 g; Cholesterol 50 mg

Easy Cilantro Lime Salmon

Preparation Time: 10 minutes; Cooking Time: 2 hours; Serve: 4

Ingredients:
- 1 lb salmon fillets
- 3/4 cup fresh cilantro, chopped
- 1 tbsp olive oil
- 3 tbsp fresh lime juice
- 2 garlic cloves, chopped
- Pepper
- Salt

Directions:
1. Place salmon fillet into the cooking pot. Mix together remaining ingredients and pour over salmon.
2. Cover instant pot aura with lid.
3. Select slow cook mode and cook on HIGH for 2 hours.
4. Serve and enjoy.

Nutritional Value (Amount per Serving):
Calories 191; Fat 10.6 g; Carbohydrates 3.4 g; Sugar 0.6 g; Protein 22.3 g; Cholesterol 50 mg

Creamy Curried Shrimp

Preparation Time: 10 minutes; Cooking Time: 4 hours 10 minutes; Serve: 4

Ingredients:
- 2 cups shrimp, cooked
- 1 small onion, chopped
- 10 oz can cream of mushroom soup
- 1 cup sour cream
- 1 tsp curry powder

Directions:
1. Add all ingredients except cream into the cooking pot and stir well.
2. Cover instant pot aura with lid.
3. Select slow cook mode and cook on LOW for 4 hours.
4. Stir in cream and serve.

Nutritional Value (Amount per Serving):
Calories 219; Fat 14.1 g; Carbohydrates 10.4 g; Sugar 2.4 g; Protein 12.6 g; Cholesterol 117 mg

Herb Flounder Fillet

Preparation Time: 10 minutes; Cooking Time: 4 hours; Serve: 6

Ingredients:
- 2 lbs fresh flounder fillets
- 2 tbsp dried chives
- 2 tbsp lemon juice
- 3/4 cup chicken broth
- 4 tbsp fresh parsley, chopped
- 1 Tsp marjoram
- 2 tbsp dried onion, minced
- 1/2 tsp salt

Directions:
1. Season fish fillets with salt. Mix together lemon juice and broth. Stir in remaining ingredients.
2. Place rack into the cooking pot.

3. Place season fish fillet on the rack and pour lemon juice mixture over fish fillets.
4. Cover instant pot aura with lid.
5. Select slow cook mode and cook on HIGH for 4 hours.
6. Serve and enjoy.

Nutritional Value (Amount per Serving):
Calories 186; Fat 2.6 g; Carbohydrates 0.8 g; Sugar 0.4 g; Protein 37.3 g; Cholesterol 103 mg

Onion White Fish Fillet

Preparation Time: 10 minutes; Cooking Time: 4 hours; Serve: 6
Ingredients:
- 1 1/2 lbs white fish fillets
- 1 cup of water
- 2 tbsp butter, melted
- 2 lemons, divided
- 2 onions, sliced
- 4 whole peppercorns
- 1 bay leaf
- 2 Tsp salt

Directions:
1. Add all ingredients except fish fillets into the cooking pot and mix well.
2. Place fish fillets into the cooking pot.
3. Cover instant pot aura with lid.
4. Select slow cook mode and cook on HIGH for 4 hours.
5. Serve and enjoy.

Nutritional Value (Amount per Serving):
Calories 253; Fat 12.5 g; Carbohydrates 6 g; Sugar 2 g; Protein 28.4 g; Cholesterol 97 mg

Lemon Halibut

Preparation Time: 10 minutes; Cooking Time: 1 hour 30 minutes; Serve: 2
Ingredients:
- 12 oz halibut
- 1 tbsp fresh lemon juice
- 1 tbsp fresh dill
- 1 tbsp olive oil
- Pepper
- Salt

Directions:
1. Place halibut middle of foil and season with pepper and salt.
2. In a small bowl, whisk together dill, oil, and lemon juice.
3. Pour dill mixture over halibut. Wrap foil around the halibut.
4. Place foil packet into the cooking pot.
5. Cover instant pot aura with lid.
6. Select slow cook mode and cook on HIGH for 1 1/2 hour.
7. Serve and enjoy.

Nutritional Value (Amount per Serving):
Calories 472; Fat 37.3 g; Carbohydrates 1.1 g; Sugar 0.2 g; Protein 31.7 g; Cholesterol 100 mg

Garlicky Shrimp

Preparation Time: 10 minutes; Cooking Time: 1 hour; Serve: 8
Ingredients:
- 2 lbs large shrimp, peeled and deveined
- 1 tbsp parsley, minced
- 5 garlic cloves, sliced
- 1/4 Tsp red pepper flakes, crushed
- 1/4 Tsp black pepper
- 1 Tsp smoked paprika
- 3/4 cup olive oil
- 1 Tsp kosher salt

Directions:
1. Add all ingredients except shrimp and parsley into the cooking pot and stir well.

2. Cover instant pot aura with lid.
3. Select slow cook mode and cook on HIGH for 30 minutes.
4. Stir in shrimp, cover and cook on HIGH for 20 minutes.
5. Garnish with parsley and serve.

Nutritional Value (Amount per Serving):
Calories 257; Fat 19 g; Carbohydrates 2.9 g; Sugar 0.1 g; Protein 21.5 g; Cholesterol 162 mg

Hot Shrimp

Preparation Time: 10 minutes; Cooking Time: 1 hour; Serve: 6
Ingredients:
- 1 1/2 lbs large shrimp, unpeeled
- 1/2 cup butter
- 1 tsp Cajun seasoning
- 2 garlic cloves, minced
- 1 green onion, chopped
- 1 lemon juice
- 1 tbsp hot pepper sauce
- 1/4 cup Worcestershire sauce
- Pepper
- Salt

Directions:
1. Add all ingredients except shrimp and parsley into the cooking pot and stir well.
2. Cover instant pot aura with lid.
3. Select slow cook mode and cook on HIGH for 30 minutes.
4. Stir in shrimp, cover and cook on HIGH for 30 minutes.
5. Garnish with green onion and serve.

Nutritional Value (Amount per Serving):
Calories 241; Fat 15.4 g; Carbohydrates 4.7 g; Sugar 2.2 g; Protein 21.6 g; Cholesterol 203 mg

Easy Lemon Dill Salmon

Preparation Time: 10 minutes; Cooking Time: 2 hours; Serve: 2
Ingredients:
- 2 lbs salmon
- 2 garlic cloves, minced
- 1 lemon, sliced
- 1/4 cup fresh dill
- Pepper
- Salt

Directions:
1. Place salmon into the cooking pot. Season with fresh dill, garlic, pepper, and salt.
2. Arrange lemon slices over salmon.
3. Cover instant pot aura with lid.
4. Select slow cook mode and cook on HIGH for 2 hours.
5. Serve and enjoy.

Nutritional Value (Amount per Serving):
Calories 628; Fat 28.4 g; Carbohydrates 7.1 g; Sugar 0.8 g; Protein 89.7 g; Cholesterol 200 mg

Lemon Garlic Shrimp Curry

Preparation Time: 10 minutes; Cooking Time: 2 hours; Serve: 4
Ingredients:
- 1 lb shrimp, with shells
- 1/2 cup red curry sauce
- 15 oz water
- 30 oz coconut milk
- 1/4 cup cilantro
- 2 1/2 tsp lemon garlic seasoning

Directions:
1. Add all ingredients except shrimp into the cooking pot and stir well.
2. Cover instant pot aura with lid.
3. Select slow cook mode and cook on HIGH for 2 hours.
4. Add shrimp and stir well, cover, and cook for 15 minutes more.

5. Stir well and serve.

Nutritional Value (Amount per Serving):
Calories 650; Fat 53.7 g; Carbohydrates 16.9 g; Sugar 8.1 g; Protein 30.7 g; Cholesterol 239 mg

Shrimp Scallop Stew

Preparation Time: 10 minutes; Cooking Time: 4 hours 30 minutes; Serve: 6

Ingredients:
- 1 lb large shrimp
- 1/8 tsp cayenne pepper
- 1 lb scallops
- 1 medium onion, chopped
- 1 lb potatoes, cut into pieces
- 2 garlic cloves, minced
- 4 cups vegetable broth
- 1/4 tsp red chili flakes
- 1 tsp oregano, dried
- 1 tsp basil, dried
- 1 tsp thyme, dried
- 1 tbsp tomato paste
- 28 oz can tomato, crushed
- 1/4 tsp Pepper
- 1/2 tsp salt

Directions:
1. Add all ingredients except shrimp and scallop into the cooking pot and stir well.
2. Cover instant pot aura with lid.
3. Select slow cook mode and cook on LOW for 4 hours.
4. Add shrimp and scallops and stir well, cover, and cook for 30 minutes more.
5. Stir well and serve.

Nutritional Value (Amount per Serving):
Calories 246; Fat 1.7 g; Carbohydrates 25.3 g; Sugar 7 g; Protein 33 g; Cholesterol 133 mg

Salmon Curry

Preparation Time: 10 minutes; Cooking Time: 4 hours 20 minutes; Serve: 6

Ingredients:
- 6 salmon pieces
- 1 tsp cumin
- 1 tsp coriander
- 12 oz can tomato paste
- 1/2 cup chicken stock
- 2 cans of coconut milk
- 2 medium carrots, chopped
- 2 celery stalks, chopped
- 1 tsp turmeric powder
- 2 tsp hot paprika
- 1 tsp chili powder
- 2 tsp ginger, grated
- 4 garlic cloves, chopped
- 1 medium onion, chopped
- 1/2 tsp pepper
- 1/4 tsp salt

Directions:
1. Add all ingredients into the cooking pot and stir well.
2. Cover instant pot aura with lid.
3. Select slow cook mode and cook on LOW for 4 hours.
4. Stir well and serve.

Nutritional Value (Amount per Serving):
Calories 494; Fat 30.7 g; Carbohydrates 21.2 g; Sugar 11.7 g; Protein 39.7 g; Cholesterol 78 mg

Sweet & Spicy Pineapple Tuna

Preparation Time: 10 minutes; Cooking Time: 1 hour; Serve: 3

Ingredients:
- 6 oz can tuna, drained and flaked
- 2/3 cup can pineapple chunks, drained
- 1 1/2 tsp cornstarch
- 1/3 cup pineapple juice
- 2 tsp olive oil
- 1 onion, sliced
- 1 tbsp vinegar

- 1 tbsp sugar
- 1/2 bell pepper, cut into strips
- 1 tsp Tabasco sauce
- 1/8 tsp pepper

Directions:
1. Add oil, onion, and bell pepper into the cooking pot and set instant pot aura on sauté mode and sauté onion until softened.
2. Whisk together cornstarch and pineapple juice and pour over onion and bell pepper mixture.
3. Cook onion and bell pepper mixture until thickened. Stir well.
4. Add remaining ingredients into the cooking pot and stir well.
5. Cover instant pot aura with lid.
6. Select slow cook mode and cook on LOW for 1 hour.
7. Stir well and serve.

Nutritional Value (Amount per Serving):
Calories 181; Fat 3.7 g; Carbohydrates 21.4 g; Sugar 16.4 g; Protein 15.2 g; Cholesterol 17 mg

Shrimp Chicken Casserole

Preparation Time: 10 minutes; Cooking Time: 45 minutes; Serve: 10
Ingredients:
- 2 cups shrimp, cooked
- 4 cups rice, cooked
- 1 tbsp soy sauce
- 1/2 cup green pepper, chopped
- 1/2 cup milk
- 10 oz can cream of celery soup
- 2 cups of Chinese vegetables
- 1 cup chicken, cooked

Directions:
1. Add all ingredients into the cooking pot and stir well.
2. Cover instant pot aura with lid.
3. Select slow cook mode and cook on LOW for 45 minutes.
4. Stir well and serve.

Nutritional Value (Amount per Serving):
Calories 344; Fat 2.7 g; Carbohydrates 63.2 g; Sugar 1.2 g; Protein 14.5 g; Cholesterol 51 mg

Shrimp Chicken Mushroom Casserole

Preparation Time: 10 minutes; Cooking Time: 6 hours; Serve: 6
Ingredients:
- 2/3 cup slivered almonds
- 3 cups chicken breast, cooked and chopped
- 1 cup of water
- 3 cups chicken broth
- 2 tbsp butter, melted
- 8 green onions, chopped
- 12 oz frozen shrimp
- 1/3 cup soy sauce
- 4 oz can mushroom, sliced and drained
- 1 1/4 cup rice

Directions:
1. Add all ingredients into the cooking pot and stir well.
2. Cover instant pot aura with lid.
3. Select slow cook mode and cook on LOW for 6 hours.
4. Stir well and serve.

Nutritional Value (Amount per Serving):
Calories 398; Fat 12.5 g; Carbohydrates 37.5 g; Sugar 1.6 g; Protein 32.6 g; Cholesterol 131 mg

Healthy Seafood Pasta

Preparation Time: 10 minutes; Cooking Time: 1 hour; Serve: 6
Ingredients:

- 1 lb shrimp, cooked and peeled
- 3 cups Monterey jack cheese, shredded
- 2 cups sour cream
- Linguine, cooked
- 1/2 lb scallops, cooked
- 1/2 lb crabmeat
- 2 tbsp butter, melted
- 1/8 tsp pepper

Directions:
1. Add sour cream, butter, and cheese in the cooking pot and stir well.
2. Add remaining ingredients and stir to well.
3. Cover instant pot aura with lid.
4. Select slow cook mode and cook on LOW for 1 hour.
5. Serve over cooked linguine and enjoy it.

Nutritional Value (Amount per Serving):
Calories 629; Fat 39.3 g; Carbohydrates 23.1 g; Sugar 2.8 g; Protein 45.1 g; Cholesterol 289 mg

Lemon White Fish Fillet

Preparation Time: 10 minutes; Cooking Time: 3 hours; Serve: 4
Ingredients:
- 1 1/2 lbs white fish fillets
- 1 tbsp lemon juice
- 1 tsp Worcestershire sauce
- 3 tbsp butter, melted
- 2 tbsp Dijon mustard

Directions:
1. Place fish fillets in the cooking pot.
2. In a small bowl, mix together the remaining ingredients and pour over fish fillets.
3. Cover instant pot aura with lid.
4. Select slow cook mode and cook on LOW for 3 hours.
5. Serve and enjoy.

Nutritional Value (Amount per Serving):
Calories 376; Fat 21.8 g; Carbohydrates 0.8 g; Sugar 0.4 g; Protein 42.1 g; Cholesterol 154 mg

Clam Chowder

Preparation Time: 10 minutes; Cooking Time: 3 hours; Serve: 4
Ingredients:
- 6.5 oz can clam, undrained and minced
- 1 1/2 cups half and half
- 15 oz clam chowder
- 1/4 cup cooking sherry
- 1/4 cup butter

Directions:
1. Add all ingredients into the cooking pot and stir well.
2. Cover instant pot aura with lid.
3. Select slow cook mode and cook on LOW for 3 hours.
4. Stir well and serve.

Nutritional Value (Amount per Serving):
Calories 360; Fat 25 g; Carbohydrates 25.9 g; Sugar 3 g; Protein 6.6 g; Cholesterol 70 mg

Salmon Vegetable Chowder

Preparation Time: 10 minutes; Cooking Time: 4 hours; Serve: 8
Ingredients:
- 1/2 cup instant potatoes
- 16 oz can salmon
- 2 tbsp parsley, chopped
- 1/2 cup onion, diced
- 1 cup celery, diced
- 1 1/2 cups potatoes, cubed
- 2 tbsp carrots, shredded
- 2 tbsp bell peppers, chopped
- 2 tsp fresh lemon juice
- 4 cups of milk

- 1/4 tsp black pepper
- 1/2 tsp salt
- Water

Directions:
1. Add potatoes, parsley, onions, celery, pepper, and salt into the cooking pot.
2. Pour water over vegetables to cover the vegetables.
3. Cover instant pot aura with lid.
4. Select slow cook mode and cook on HIGH for 3 hours.
5. Add salmon, instant potatoes, carrots, bell peppers, milk, and lemon juice. Stir well.
6. Cover instant pot aura with lid.
7. Select slow cook mode and cook on HIGH for 1 hour.
8. Serve and enjoy.

Nutritional Value (Amount per Serving):
Calories 212; Fat 6.1 g; Carbohydrates 22.2 g; Sugar 7.9 g; Protein 17.1 g; Cholesterol 41 mg

Cod Curry

Preparation Time: 10 minutes; Cooking Time: 2 hours; Serve: 4

Ingredients:
- 1 lb cod fish fillet
- 1 tbsp curry powder
- 3 tbsp red curry paste
- 15 oz can coconut milk
- 12 oz bag julienned carrots
- 1 red bell pepper, sliced
- 1 tsp garlic powder
- 1 tsp ground ginger
- Pepper
- Salt

Directions:
1. Add all ingredients into the cooking pot and stir well.
2. Cover instant pot aura with lid.
3. Select slow cook mode and cook on LOW for 2 hours.
4. Serve over rice and enjoy.

Nutritional Value (Amount per Serving):
Calories 392; Fat 27.4 g; Carbohydrates 9.3 g; Sugar 1.7 g; Protein 28.7 g; Cholesterol 62 mg

Shrimp Curry

Preparation Time: 10 minutes; Cooking Time: 2 hours 15 minutes; Serve: 4

Ingredients:
- 1 lb shrimp, with shells
- 1/2 cup red curry sauce
- 15 oz water
- 30 oz coconut milk

Directions:
1. Add all ingredients except shrimp into the cooking pot and stir well.
2. Cover instant pot aura with lid.
3. Select slow cook mode and cook on HIGH for 2 hours.
4. Add shrimp and stir well, cover, and cook for 15 minutes more.
5. Stir well and serve.

Nutritional Value (Amount per Serving):
Calories 634; Fat 53.4 g; Carbohydrates 14.4 g; Sugar 7.5 g; Protein 30.7 g; Cholesterol 239 mg

Delicious Fish Tacos

Preparation Time: 10 minutes; Cooking Time: 4 hours; Serve: 6

Ingredients:
- 6 white fish fillets, frozen
- 1/2 tsp garlic, minced
- 1 can Rotel, drained
- 2 tbsp lime juice
- 1 1/2 tbsp dried cilantro
- Salt

Directions:
1. Add all ingredients into the cooking pot and stir well.
2. Cover instant pot aura with lid.
3. Select slow cook mode and cook on LOW for 4 hours.
4. Flake fish with a fork.
5. Serve into taco shells.

Nutritional Value (Amount per Serving):
Calories 304; Fat 11.8 g; Carbohydrates 8.3 g; Sugar 0.6 g; Protein 38.9 g; Cholesterol 119 mg

Lime Salmon

Preparation Time: 10 minutes; Cooking Time: 2 hours 40 minutes; Serve: 4

Ingredients:
- 1 lb salmon fillets
- 3 garlic cloves, chopped
- 1 tbsp olive oil
- 2 tbsp lime juice
- 1/4 tsp kosher salt

Directions:
1. Place salmon fillet skin side down in the cooking pot.
2. Mix together remaining ingredients and pour over salmon.
3. Cover instant pot aura with lid.
4. Select slow cook mode and cook on LOW for 2 1/2 hours.
5. Serve and enjoy.

Nutritional Value (Amount per Serving):
Calories 189; Fat 10.5 g; Carbohydrates 2.6 g; Sugar 0.4 g; Protein 22.2 g; Cholesterol 50 mg

Delicious Fish Gratin

Preparation Time: 10 minutes; Cooking Time: 1 hour 40 minutes; Serve: 6

Ingredients:
- 3 lbs frozen white fish fillets
- 1/4 tbsp ground nutmeg
- 1/2 tbsp dry mustard
- 1 cup cheddar cheese, shredded
- 1 1/2 tsp lemon juice
- 1 1/4 cup milk
- 3 tbsp flour
- 6 tbsp butter
- 1 1/2 tsp salt

Directions:
1. Add butter into the cooking pot and set instant pot aura on sauté mode.
2. Add flour, nutmeg, mustard, salt, and flour and stir until smooth. Slowly stir in milk and cook until thickens.
3. Add cheese and lemon juice. Stir well and cook until cheese melted.
4. Place fish fillets into the cooking pot.
5. Cover instant pot aura with lid.
6. Select slow cook mode and cook on HIGH for 1 1/2 hour.
7. Serve hot and enjoy.

Nutritional Value (Amount per Serving):
Calories 414; Fat 19.9 g; Carbohydrates 6.2 g; Sugar 2.6 g; Protein 53.4 g; Cholesterol 54 mg

Mango Shrimp Rice

Preparation Time: 10 minutes; Cooking Time: 1 hour; Serve: 2

Ingredients:
- 4 oz frozen shrimp, peeled and deveined
- 1/2 tsp jerk seasoning
- 1/2 cup can mango with juice, diced
- 1 cup instant rice
- 1 cup of coconut milk

Directions:
1. Add all ingredients into the cooking pot and stir well.
2. Cover instant pot aura with lid.
3. Select slow cook mode and cook on HIGH for 1 hour.
4. Stir well and serve.

Nutritional Value (Amount per Serving):
Calories 706; Fat 30.2 g; Carbohydrates 88.9 g; Sugar 11.9 g; Protein 20.9 g; Cholesterol 85 mg

Lemon Orange White Fish Fillets

Preparation Time: 10 minutes; Cooking Time: 1 hour 40 minutes; Serve: 4

Ingredients:
- 1 1/2 lbs fish fillets
- 5 tbsp parsley, chopped
- 1 medium onion, chopped
- 2 tsp orange rind, grated
- 2 tsp lemon rind, grated
- 4 tsp olive oil
- Pepper
- Salt

Directions:
1. Season fish fillets with pepper and salt and place into the cooking pot.
2. Drizzle fish fillets with olive oil.
3. Pour remaining ingredients over fish fillets.
4. Cover instant pot aura with lid.
5. Select slow cook mode and cook on LOW for 1 1/2 hour.
6. Serve and enjoy.

Nutritional Value (Amount per Serving):
Calories 449; Fat 25.7 g; Carbohydrates 32.2 g; Sugar 1.3 g; Protein 25.4 g; Cholesterol 58 mg

Garlic Butter Salmon

Preparation Time: 10 minutes; Cooking Time: 2 hours; Serve: 2

Ingredients:
- 2 salmon fillets
- 1 tbsp butter, melted
- 1/8 tsp black pepper
- 2 garlic cloves, minced
- 1/2 tsp parsley, minced
- 1/2 tbsp lime juice

Directions:
1. Take one aluminum foil sheet and place salmon in the middle of the sheet.
2. In a small bowl, mix together butter, pepper, garlic, parsley, and lime juice.
3. Brush butter mixture over salmon fillets.
4. Wrap foil around the salmon fillets and place them into the cooking pot.
5. Cover instant pot aura with lid.
6. Select slow cook mode and cook on HIGH for 2 hours.
7. Serve and enjoy.

Nutritional Value (Amount per Serving):
Calories 294; Fat 16.8 g; Carbohydrates 2 g; Sugar 0.2 g; Protein 34.8 g; Cholesterol 94 mg

Tasty Seafood Fondue

Preparation Time: 10 minutes; Cooking Time: 1 hour; Serve: 8

Ingredients:
- 1/4 cup scallops, cooked and chopped
- 1/2 cup crabmeat, cooked and chopped
- 1/2 cup shrimp, cooked and chopped
- 1 cup lobster chunked, cooked
- 2 cups cheddar cheese, grated
- 2 cans condensed cream of celery soup
- 1/4 tsp cayenne pepper
- 1/4 tsp paprika

Directions:
1. Add all ingredients into the cooking pot and stir well.
2. Cover instant pot aura with lid.
3. Select slow cook mode and cook on HIGH for 1 hour.
4. Serve and enjoy.

Nutritional Value (Amount per Serving):
Calories 199; Fat 12.9 g; Carbohydrates 9.2 g; Sugar 2.3 g; Protein 11.6 g; Cholesterol 52 mg

Lemon Dill White Fish Fillet

Preparation Time: 10 minutes; Cooking Time: 1 hour 40 minutes; Serve: 2
Ingredients:
- 12 oz white fish fillets
- 1 1/2 tsp dried dill
- 1 tbsp lemon juice
- 1 tbsp butter, melted
- Pepper
- Salt

Directions:
1. Place fish fillets on the center of the foil piece.
2. In a small bowl, mix together butter, dill, lemon juice, pepper, and salt.
3. Brush fish fillets with butter mixture.
4. Wrap foil around the halibut and place it into the cooking pot.
5. Cover instant pot aura with lid.
6. Select slow cook mode and cook on HIGH for 1 1/2 hour.
7. Serve and enjoy.

Nutritional Value (Amount per Serving):
Calories 347; Fat 18.6 g; Carbohydrates 0.6 g; Sugar 0.2 g; Protein 41.9 g; Cholesterol 146 mg

Marinara Shrimp

Preparation Time: 10 minutes; Cooking Time: 6 hours 20 minutes; Serve: 4
Ingredients:
- 1 lb shelled shrimp, cooked
- 1 can tomatoes, peeled and chopped
- 1/4 tsp pepper
- 1 tsp oregano
- 6 oz can tomato paste
- 1 garlic clove, minced
- 2 tbsp parsley, minced
- 1/2 tsp basil
- 1/2 tsp salt

Directions:
1. Add all ingredients except shrimp into the cooking pot and stir well.
2. Cover instant pot aura with lid.
3. Select slow cook mode and cook on LOW for 6 hours.
4. Stir in shrimp. Cover and cook on HIGH for 10 minutes more.
5. Serve and enjoy.

Nutritional Value (Amount per Serving):
Calories 153; Fat 1.7 g; Carbohydrates 10.5 g; Sugar 6.4 g; Protein 26.4 g; Cholesterol 147 mg

Shrimp Casserole

Preparation Time: 10 minutes; Cooking Time: 8 hours; Serve: 6
Ingredients:
- 1 1/2 lbs frozen shrimp, peeled and deveined
- 1 can Rotel
- 1 can cream of chicken soup
- 1 can cream of celery soup
- 1 cup chicken broth
- 2 cups rice, uncooked
- 1 tsp dried parsley
- 1 tbsp garlic powder
- 1 yellow bell pepper, chopped

- 1 red bell pepper, chopped
- 1 onion, chopped
- 1 tsp pepper
- 1 tsp salt

Directions:
1. Add all ingredients into the cooking pot and stir well.
2. Cover instant pot aura with lid.
3. Select slow cook mode and cook on LOW for 8 hours.
4. Stir well and serve.

Nutritional Value (Amount per Serving):
Calories 495; Fat 8.2 g; Carbohydrates 70.7 g; Sugar 4.6 g; Protein 32.3 g; Cholesterol 180 mg

Asian Salmon

Preparation Time: 10 minutes; Cooking Time: 1 hour; Serve: 6

Ingredients:
- 6 salmon fillets
- 1/8 cup lime juice
- 1/2 cup maple syrup
- 1 tsp ginger, minced
- 2 tsp garlic, crushed
- 1/4 cup soy sauce

Directions:
1. Place salmon fillets in the cooking pot.
2. In a bowl, mix together the remaining ingredients and pour over salmon fillets.
3. Cover instant pot aura with lid.
4. Select slow cook mode and cook on HIGH for 1 hour.
5. Serve and enjoy.

Nutritional Value (Amount per Serving):
Calories 312; Fat 11.1 g; Carbohydrates 19 g; Sugar 15.8 g; Protein 35.3 g; Cholesterol 78 mg

BBQ Shrimp

Preparation Time: 10 minutes; Cooking Time: 1 hour; Serve: 6

Ingredients:
- 1 1/2 lbs large shrimp, unpeeled, rinsed and drained
- 1/4 cup Worcestershire sauce
- 1/2 cup butter, cut into pieces
- 1 tsp Old bay seasoning
- 2 garlic cloves, minced
- 1 lemon juice
- 1 tbsp hot sauce
- Pepper
- Salt

Directions:
1. Add all ingredients except shrimp into the cooking pot and stir well.
2. Cover instant pot aura with lid.
3. Select slow cook mode and cook on HIGH for 30 minutes.
4. Add shrimp, cover pot, and cook on HIGH for 30 minutes more.
5. Stir well and serve.

Nutritional Value (Amount per Serving):
Calories 240; Fat 15.4 g; Carbohydrates 4.6 g; Sugar 2.2 g; Protein 21.6 g; Cholesterol 203 mg

Shrimp Grits

Preparation Time: 10 minutes; Cooking Time: 3 hours 40 minutes; Serve: 8

Ingredients:
- 2 lbs raw shrimp
- 1 cup cheddar cheese, shredded
- 1 tsp dried thyme
- 1 tbsp onion powder
- 1 tbsp garlic powder
- 1 1/2 cups grits
- 6 cups chicken broth
- 1/2 tsp hot sauce
- 1/2 cup parmesan cheese, grated
- 4 oz cream cheese

- Pepper
- Salt

Directions:
1. Add all ingredients except shrimp into the cooking pot and stir well.
2. Cover instant pot aura with lid.
3. Select slow cook mode and cook on LOW for 3 hours.
4. Add shrimp and stir well, cover, and cook on LOW for 30 minutes more.
5. Stir well and serve.

Nutritional Value (Amount per Serving):
Calories 322; Fat 14.4 g; Carbohydrates 9.2 g; Sugar 1.8 g; Protein 37.1 g; Cholesterol 274 mg

Honey Salmon

Preparation Time: 10 minutes; Cooking Time: 1 hour; Serve: 6

Ingredients:
- 6 salmon fillets
- 1 tbsp ginger garlic paste
- 1/4 cup soy sauce
- 2 tbsp lime juice
- 1/4 cup honey

Directions:
1. Place salmon fillets in the cooking pot.
2. In a bowl, mix together the remaining ingredients and pour over salmon.
3. Cover instant pot aura with lid.
4. Select slow cook mode and cook on HIGH for 1 hour.
5. Serve and enjoy.

Nutritional Value (Amount per Serving):
Calories 292; Fat 11.2 g; Carbohydrates 14.2 g; Sugar 12 g; Protein 35.5 g; Cholesterol 78 mg

Chapter 8: Snacks & Appetizers

Chili Cheese Dip

Preparation Time: 10 minutes; Cooking Time: 3 hours; Serve: 12
Ingredients:
- 1 lb ground beef
- 4 oz cream cheese, cubed & softened
- 2 1/2 cups cheddar cheese, shredded
- 1 tsp cumin
- 1 1/2 tsp chili powder
- 1 1/2 tsp garlic powder
- 4 oz can green chilies, chopped
- 1 cup chicken broth
- 1 1/2 cup salsa
- 15 oz can chili beans
- 3 tbsp all-purpose flour
- 1 small onion, chopped

Directions:
1. Set instant pot aura on sauté mode.
2. Add ground beef and onion into the cooking pot and sauté until meat is no longer pink.
3. Add flour and stir well to combine.
4. Add remaining ingredients and stir everything well.
5. Cover instant pot aura with lid.
6. Select slow cook mode and cook on LOW for 3 hours.
7. Stir well and serve.

Nutritional Value (Amount per Serving):
Calories 584; Fat 16.3 g; Carbohydrates 53.1 g; Sugar 17.1 g; Protein 41.4 g; Cholesterol 69 mg

Perfect Hamburger Dip

Preparation Time: 10 minutes; Cooking Time: 2 hours; Serve: 16
Ingredients:
- 2 lbs Velveeta subbed
- 1 lb sausage
- 1 lb hamburger
- 16 oz jar salsa
- 10.5 oz can cream of mushroom soup

Directions:
1. Add sausage and hamburger into the cooking pot and set instant pot aura on sauté mode.
2. Sauté sausage and hamburger until cooked through.
3. Add remaining ingredients into the cooking pot and stir well.
4. Cover instant pot aura with lid.
5. Select slow cook mode and cook on LOW for 2 hours.
6. Stir well and serve with tortilla chips.

Nutritional Value (Amount per Serving):
Calories 335; Fat 13 g; Carbohydrates 32.5 g; Sugar 4.8 g; Protein 20.3 g; Cholesterol 54 mg

Easy Queso Dip

Preparation Time: 10 minutes; Cooking Time: 2 hours; Serve: 12
Ingredients:
- 1 lb white American cheese
- 4 oz can green chilies
- 1 tbsp butter
- 1/2 cup milk

Directions:
1. Add all ingredients into the cooking pot and stir well.
2. Cover instant pot aura with lid.
3. Select slow cook mode and cook on LOW for 2 hours.
4. Stir well and serve.

Nutritional Value (Amount per Serving):
Calories 164; Fat 13.4 g; Carbohydrates 3.6 g; Sugar 13.2 g; Protein 7.2 g; Cholesterol 37 mg

Spicy Chili Queso Dip

Preparation Time: 10 minutes; Cooking Time: 2 hours; Serve: 10
Ingredients:
- 32 oz Velveeta cheese, chop into chunks
- 1/2 tsp cayenne pepper
- 2 tbsp cumin
- 2 tbsp paprika
- 3 tbsp chili powder
- 6 tbsp lime juice
- 2 cups of milk
- 30 oz can no bean chili

Directions:
1. Add all ingredients into the cooking pot and stir well.
2. Cover instant pot aura with lid.
3. Select slow cook mode and cook on LOW for 2 hours. Stir halfway through.
4. Stir well and serve.

Nutritional Value (Amount per Serving):
Calories 401; Fat 26 g; Carbohydrates 27 g; Sugar 10.4 g; Protein 23.5 g; Cholesterol 83 mg

Creamy Corn Dip

Preparation Time: 10 minutes; Cooking Time: 2 hours; Serve: 8
Ingredients:
- 30 oz can corn, drained
- 4 bacon slices, cooked and crumbled
- 1/2 tsp chili powder
- 2 green onions, sliced
- 1 jalapeno pepper, minced
- 1 cup pepper jack cheese, shredded
- 1/2 cup mayonnaise
- 8 oz cream cheese, softened

Directions:
1. Add all ingredients into the cooking pot and stir well.
2. Cover instant pot aura with lid.
3. Select slow cook mode and cook on LOW for 2 hours.
4. Top with bacon and serve.

Nutritional Value (Amount per Serving):
Calories 345; Fat 23.8 g; Carbohydrates 24.9 g; Sugar 4.4 g; Protein 11.8 g; Cholesterol 59 mg

Flavorful Pizza Dip

Preparation Time: 10 minutes; Cooking Time: 2 hours; Serve: 6
Ingredients:
- 16 oz cream cheese
- 16 oz mozzarella cheese, shredded
- 1 tsp garlic powder
- 3/4 cup Marinara sauce
- 1/2 cup fresh basil, chopped
- 10 oz pepperoni
- Pepper
- Salt

Directions:
1. Add all ingredients into the cooking pot and stir well.
2. Cover instant pot aura with lid.
3. Select slow cook mode and cook on HIGH for 2 hours. Stir after every 30 minutes.
4. Stir well and serve.

Nutritional Value (Amount per Serving):
Calories 740; Fat 61.3 g; Carbohydrates 9.4 g; Sugar 3 g; Protein 38.5 g; Cholesterol 173 mg

Mexican Quinoa Dip

Preparation Time: 10 minutes; Cooking Time: 3 hours; Serve: 12
Ingredients:
- 1 cup quinoa, uncooked
- 2 cups salsa

- 2 cups corn kernels
- 2 cups vegetable broth
- 1/2 tsp paprika
- 1/2 tsp ground cumin
- 1/2 tsp black pepper
- 1 tsp oregano
- 1 tsp garlic, minced
- 1 tbsp lime juice
- 1 1/2 tbsp chili powder
- 1 cup bell pepper, chopped
- 1 cup black beans
- 1/4 tsp salt

Directions:
1. Add all ingredients into the cooking pot and stir well.
2. Cover instant pot aura with lid.
3. Select slow cook mode and cook on HIGH for 3 hours.
4. Stir well and serve.

Nutritional Value (Amount per Serving):
Calories 156; Fat 1.9 g; Carbohydrates 28.7 g; Sugar 3.3 g; Protein 8.1 g; Cholesterol 0 mg

Buffalo Chicken Dip

Preparation Time: 10 minutes; Cooking Time: 3 hours; Serve: 8
Ingredients:
- 1 lb chicken breasts, sliced
- 1/2 cup cheddar cheese, shredded
- 8 oz cream cheese, softened
- 1 tbsp ranch seasoning
- 1/4 cup buffalo wing sauce
- 1/4 cup chicken broth

Directions:
1. Add chicken, ranch seasoning, buffalo sauce, and broth into the cooking pot.
2. Cover instant pot aura with lid.
3. Select slow cook mode and cook on HIGH for 3 hours.
4. Remove chicken from pot and shred using a fork, return shredded chicken to the pot and stir well.
5. Add cream cheese and cheddar cheese and stir well and cook for 30 minutes more.
6. Serve and enjoy.

Nutritional Value (Amount per Serving):
Calories 240; Fat 16.5 g; Carbohydrates 0.9 g; Sugar 0.1 g; Protein 20.5 g; Cholesterol 89 mg

Perfect Sausage Dip

Preparation Time: 10 minutes; Cooking Time: 1 hour 30 minutes; Serve: 6
Ingredients:
- 12 oz sausage, cooked
- 1/2 tsp onion powder
- 1 tsp garlic, minced
- 24 oz cream cheese
- 10 oz Rotel
- 1/2 tsp salt

Directions:
1. Add all ingredients into the cooking pot and stir well.
2. Cover instant pot aura with lid.
3. Select slow cook mode and cook on HIGH for 1 1/2 hours.
4. Stir well and serve.

Nutritional Value (Amount per Serving):
Calories 767; Fat 56.5 g; Carbohydrates 38.8 g; Sugar 2 g; Protein 25.5 g; Cholesterol 172 mg

Crab Dip

Preparation Time: 10 minutes; Cooking Time: 2 hours; Serve: 4
Ingredients:
- 1 lb lump crab meat
- 2 cups mozzarella cheese, shredded
- 1/2 tsp ground mustard
- 2 tbsp Worcestershire sauce

- 1/4 cup lemon juice
- 1 garlic clove, minced
- 1 jalapeno pepper, minced
- 1 bell pepper, diced
- 4 oz cream cheese, softened

Directions:
1. Add all ingredients into the cooking pot and stir well.
2. Cover instant pot aura with lid.
3. Select slow cook mode and cook on HIGH for 2 hours.
4. Stir well and serve.

Nutritional Value (Amount per Serving):
Calories 246; Fat 21.9 g; Carbohydrates 7.8 g; Sugar 3.5 g; Protein 23.2 g; Cholesterol 103 mg

Cheesy Artichoke Dip

Preparation Time: 10 minutes; Cooking Time: 2 hours; Serve: 6
Ingredients:
- 14 oz can artichokes, drained & chopped
- 1 lb spinach, stems removed
- 1/4 tsp black pepper
- 1 garlic cloves, minced
- 1/4 cup parmesan cheese, grated
- 1/2 lb cream cheese, cubed
- 1 cup mozzarella cheese, shredded

Directions:
1. Add all ingredients into the cooking pot and stir well.
2. Cover instant pot aura with lid.
3. Select slow cook mode and cook on HIGH for 2 hours.
4. Stir well and serve.

Nutritional Value (Amount per Serving):
Calories 230; Fat 16.6 g; Carbohydrates 12.4 g; Sugar 1.1 g; Protein 11.4 g; Cholesterol 51 mg

Artichoke Crab Dip

Preparation Time: 10 minutes; Cooking Time: 2 hours 30 minutes; Serve: 6
Ingredients:
- 16 oz can lump crab meat, drained
- 8 oz cream cheese
- 14 oz can artichoke hearts, drained & chopped
- 1/3 cup sour cream
- 2/3 cup parmesan cheese, shredded
- 2 tsp Worcestershire sauce
- 2 tbsp lemon juice
- 1/2 tsp Italian seasoning
- 1/2 tsp black pepper
- 1 1/2 tsp old bay seasoning
- 2 tsp garlic, minced
- 1/2 tsp kosher salt

Directions:
1. Add all ingredients into the cooking pot and stir well.
2. Cover instant pot aura with lid.
3. Select slow cook mode and cook on HIGH for 1 1/2 hours.
4. Stir well and serve.

Nutritional Value (Amount per Serving):
Calories 332; Fat 22.3 g; Carbohydrates 6.8 g; Sugar 1.1 g; Protein 27.2 g; Cholesterol 128 mg

Corn Jalapeno Popper Dip

Preparation Time: 10 minutes; Cooking Time: 2 hours; Serve: 8
Ingredients:
- 2 jalapeno peppers, seeded & diced
- 45 oz can fire-roasted corn, drained
- 1/2 lb bacon, cooked & chopped
- 8 oz cream cheese, cubed
- 1 cup Mexican cheese blend, shredded
- 1/2 cup sour cream

- Pepper
- Salt

Directions:
1. Add all ingredients except cream cheese and bacon into the cooking pot and stir well.
2. Add cream cheese on top of corn mixture into the cooking pot.
3. Cover instant pot aura with lid.
4. Select slow cook mode and cook on LOW for 2 hours.
5. Top with bacon and serve.

Nutritional Value (Amount per Serving):
Calories 481; Fat 26.3 g; Carbohydrates 41.7 g; Sugar 5 g; Protein 23.2 g; Cholesterol 70 mg

Southwest Spicy Artichoke Dip

Preparation Time: 10 minutes; Cooking Time: 2 hours; Serve: 25

Ingredients:
- 1/2 cup pepper jack cheese, shredded
- 1/2 bell pepper, chopped
- 4.5 oz can green chilies, chopped
- 8 oz cream cheese, cubed
- 9 oz frozen spinach, thawed & squeezed
- 14 oz artichoke hearts, drained & chopped

Directions:
1. Add all ingredients except pepper jack cheese into the cooking pot and stir well.
2. Cover instant pot aura with lid.
3. Select slow cook mode and cook on LOW for 2 hours.
4. Add pepper jack cheese and stir well.
5. Serve and enjoy.

Nutritional Value (Amount per Serving):
Calories 52; Fat 4 g; Carbohydrates 2.7 g; Sugar 0.3 g; Protein 2.1 g; Cholesterol 12 mg

Slow Cook Salsa

Preparation Time: 10 minutes; Cooking Time: 4 hours; Serve: 8

Ingredients:
- 7 cups tomatoes, chopped
- 4 jalapeno peppers, chopped
- 1 green bell pepper, chopped
- 1 red bell pepper, chopped
- 2 onions, chopped
- 1 tbsp fresh sage, chopped
- 3 tbsp fresh basil, chopped
- 1 tbsp fresh cilantro, chopped
- 1 tsp ground coriander
- 1/4 cup apple cider vinegar
- 1 tsp salt

Directions:
1. Add all ingredients except sage, basil, and cilantro into the cooking pot and stir well.
2. Cover instant pot aura with lid.
3. Select slow cook mode and cook on LOW for 4 hours.
4. Add sage, basil, and cilantro into the cooking pot and stir well.
5. Transfer salsa mixture into the food processor and process until getting the desired consistency.
6. Serve and enjoy.

Nutritional Value (Amount per Serving):
Calories 54; Fat 0.6 g; Carbohydrates 11.7 g; Sugar 7.1 g; Protein 2.2 g; Cholesterol 0 mg

Baked Jalapeno Poppers

Preparation Time: 10 minutes; Cooking Time: 20 minutes; Serve: 20

Ingredients:

- 10 jalapeno peppers, sliced in half & scoop out insides
- 1 tsp cumin
- 1 tsp garlic powder
- 1 tsp chili powder
- 8 oz cheddar cheese, shredded
- 8 oz cream cheese, softened
- Pepper
- salt

Directions:
1. In a bowl, mix together cream cheese, cheddar cheese, chili powder, garlic powder, cumin, pepper, and salt.
2. Stuff cream cheese mixture into each jalapeno half.
3. Place stuff jalapeno half into the cooking pot.
4. Cover instant pot aura with lid.
5. Select bake mode then set the temperature to 350 F and timer for 20 minutes.
6. Serve and enjoy.

Nutritional Value (Amount per Serving):
Calories 90; Fat 7.9 g; Carbohydrates 1.2 g; Sugar 0.4 g; Protein 3.8 g; Cholesterol 24 mg

Delicious Bean Dip

Preparation Time: 10 minutes; Cooking Time: 1 hour 30 minutes; Serve: 16
Ingredients:
- 16 oz can refried beans
- 1/3 cup salsa
- 1 cup sour cream
- 4.5 oz can green chilies
- 1 1/4 cups Mexican cheese
- 1 tsp chili powder
- 1 tsp cumin
- 1/2 tsp onion powder
- 1/2 tsp garlic powder
- 1 lime juice
- Pepper
- Salt

Directions:
1. Add all ingredients into the cooking pot and stir well.
2. Cover instant pot aura with lid.
3. Select slow cook mode and cook on HIGH for 1 1/2 hours.
4. Stir well and serve.

Nutritional Value (Amount per Serving):
Calories 128; Fat 9.4 g; Carbohydrates 6.9 g; Sugar 0.4 g; Protein 6.2 g; Cholesterol 25 mg

Perfect Cheesy Bean Dip

Preparation Time: 10 minutes; Cooking Time: 4 hours; Serve: 12
Ingredients:
- 16 oz can refried beans
- 8 oz cheddar cheese, shredded
- 1 1/2 tsp garlic powder
- 1 1/2 tsp onion powder
- 2 tbsp taco seasoning mix
- 1 cup sour cream
- 8 oz cream cheese

Directions:
1. Add refried beans, garlic powder, onion powder, taco seasoning, sour cream, and half cream cheese into the cooking pot and stir well.
2. Add remaining cream cheese and cheddar cheese on top of the refried bean mixture.
3. Cover instant pot aura with lid.
4. Select slow cook mode and cook on LOW for 4 hours.
5. Stir well and serve.

Nutritional Value (Amount per Serving):
Calories 225; Fat 17.4 g; Carbohydrates 8.7 g; Sugar 0.5 g; Protein 8.9 g; Cholesterol 52 mg

Salsa Queso Dip

Preparation Time: 10 minutes; Cooking Time: 1 hour 30 minutes; Serve: 6

Ingredients:
- 8 oz cream cheese
- 1 jalapeno pepper, diced
- 1/2 cup salsa verde
- 4 oz American cheese
- 8 oz pepper jack cheese
- 4 oz cheddar cheese
- 3/4 cup milk

Directions:
1. Add all ingredients into the cooking pot and stir well.
2. Cover instant pot aura with lid.
3. Select slow cook mode and cook on HIGH for 1 1/2 hours. Stir mixture after 1 hour.
4. Stir well and serve.

Nutritional Value (Amount per Serving):
Calories 463; Fat 38.6 g; Carbohydrates 5.2 g; Sugar 3.3 g; Protein 19.2 g; Cholesterol 131 mg

Pinto Bean Dip

Preparation Time: 10 minutes; Cooking Time: 2 hours; Serve: 10

Ingredients:
- 15 oz can pinto beans, drained
- 1 oz ranch dressing mix
- 3 cups cheddar cheese, shredded
- 16 oz sour cream
- 16 oz can refried beans

Directions:
1. Add pinto beans, ranch dressing mix, 1 cup cheddar cheese, sour cream, and refried beans into the cooking pot and stir well.
2. Sprinkle remaining cheese on top of the dip mixture.
3. Cover instant pot aura with lid.
4. Select slow cook mode and cook on HIGH for 2 hours.
5. Stir well and serve.

Nutritional Value (Amount per Serving):
Calories 314; Fat 21.7 g; Carbohydrates 16 g; Sugar 0.5 g; Protein 14.5 g; Cholesterol 59 mg

Broccoli Dip

Preparation Time: 10 minutes; Cooking Time: 1 hour; Serve: 24

Ingredients:
- 2 cups cheddar cheese, shredded
- 1/2 cup parmesan cheese, grated
- 2 cups frozen broccoli, chopped
- 8 oz ranch dip
- 4 tbsp bell pepper, chopped

Directions:
1. Add all ingredients into the cooking pot and stir well.
2. Cover instant pot aura with lid.
3. Select slow cook mode and cook on LOW for 1 hour.
4. Stir well and serve.

Nutritional Value (Amount per Serving):
Calories 92; Fat 7.8 g; Carbohydrates 2.8 g; Sugar 1.5 g; Protein 3.9 g; Cholesterol 15 mg

Texas Dip

Preparation Time: 10 minutes; Cooking Time: 6 hours; Serve: 8

Ingredients:
- 1 1/2 cups Velveeta cheese, cubed
- 4 oz can green chilies, diced
- 1 onion, chopped
- 2 cups fresh tomatoes, diced

Directions:
1. Add all ingredients into the cooking pot and stir well.
2. Cover instant pot aura with lid.
3. Select slow cook mode and cook on LOW for 6 hours.
4. Stir well and serve.

Nutritional Value (Amount per Serving):
Calories 72; Fat 4.3 g; Carbohydrates 5.8 g; Sugar 3.1 g; Protein 4.1 g; Cholesterol 14 mg

Nacho Dip

Preparation Time: 10 minutes; Cooking Time: 2 hours; Serve: 8

Ingredients:
- 8 oz cream cheese, cut into chunks
- 1 cup cheddar cheese, shredded
- 1/4 cup milk
- 1/2 cup salsa

Directions:
1. Add all ingredients into the cooking pot and stir well.
2. Cover instant pot aura with lid.
3. Select slow cook mode and cook on LOW for 2 hours.
4. Stir well and serve.

Nutritional Value (Amount per Serving):
Calories 164; Fat 14.8 g; Carbohydrates 2.3 g; Sugar 1 g; Protein 6.2 g; Cholesterol 47 mg

Cheesy Onion Dip

Preparation Time: 10 minutes; Cooking Time: 4 hours 30 minutes; Serve: 12

Ingredients:
- 4 onions, sliced
- 1/2 cup mozzarella cheese
- 8 oz sour cream
- 2 tbsp olive oil
- 2 tbsp butter
- Pepper
- Salt

Directions:
1. Add oil, butter, and onions into the cooking pot and stir well.
2. Cover instant pot aura with lid.
3. Select slow cook mode and cook on HIGH for 4 hours.
4. Transfer onion mixture to the blender with sour cream, pepper, and salt and blend until creamy.
5. Return onion dip into the cooking pot.
6. Add mozzarella cheese and stir well.
7. Cover instant pot aura with lid.
8. Select slow cook mode and cook on LOW for 30 minutes.
9. Stir well and serve.

Nutritional Value (Amount per Serving):
Calories 95; Fat 8.5 g; Carbohydrates 4.3 g; Sugar 1.6 g; Protein 1.4 g; Cholesterol 14 mg

Italian Tomato Dip

Preparation Time: 10 minutes; Cooking Time: 1 hour; Serve: 20

Ingredients:
- 1/4 cup sun-dried tomatoes
- 1 tbsp mayonnaise
- 8 oz cream cheese
- 3 garlic cloves
- 1/4 tsp white pepper
- 1 tsp pine nuts, toasted
- 3/4 oz fresh basil

Directions:

1. Add all ingredients into the blender and blend until smooth.
2. Pour blended mixture into the cooking pot.
3. Cover instant pot aura with lid.
4. Select slow cook mode and cook on LOW for 1 hour.
5. Stir well and serve.

Nutritional Value (Amount per Serving):
Calories 45; Fat 4.3 g; Carbohydrates 0.8 g; Sugar 0.1 g; Protein 1 g; Cholesterol 13 mg

Crab Shrimp Dip

Preparation Time: 10 minutes; Cooking Time: 2 hours; Serve: 10

Ingredients:
- 6 oz can crab meat, drained
- 1 cup shrimp, drained
- 8 oz package cream cheese
- 1/2 cup almonds, chopped
- 1 Tsp horseradish
- 6 tbsp onion, chopped

Directions:
1. Add all ingredients into the cooking pot and stir well.
2. Cover instant pot aura with lid.
3. Select slow cook mode and cook on LOW for 2 hours.
4. Stir well and serve.

Nutritional Value (Amount per Serving):
Calories 128; Fat 10.4 g; Carbohydrates 58 g; Sugar 0.9 g; Protein 6.8 g; Cholesterol 58 mg

Walnut Crab Dip

Preparation Time: 10 minutes; Cooking Time: 3 hours; Serve: 24

Ingredients:
- 8 oz imitation crab strands, dried
- 8 oz cream cheese
- 1/4 cup walnuts, chopped
- 1 tsp hot sauce
- 2 tbsp onion, chopped
- 1 tsp paprika

Directions:
1. Add all ingredients except walnuts and paprika into the blender and blend well.
2. Pour blended mixture into the cooking pot and stir well.
3. Top with chopped walnuts and sprinkle with paprika.
4. Cover instant pot aura with lid.
5. Select slow cook mode and cook on LOW for 3 hours.
6. Serve and enjoy.

Nutritional Value (Amount per Serving):
Calories 53; Fat 4.2 g; Carbohydrates 2.4 g; Sugar 0.6 g; Protein 1.8 g; Cholesterol 12 mg

Navy Bean Dip

Preparation Time: 10 minutes; Cooking Time: 2 hours; Serve: 4

Ingredients:
- 15 oz can navy beans, drained
- 1/2 fresh lemon juice
- 2 garlic clove, minced
- 1 tbsp olive oil
- 1/2 tsp thyme
- 1/4 tsp salt

Directions:
1. Add all ingredients into the cooking pot and stir well.
2. Cover instant pot aura with lid.
3. Select slow cook mode and cook on LOW for 2 hours.
4. Mash the bean mixture until smooth.
5. Serve with tortilla chips and enjoy.

Nutritional Value (Amount per Serving):
Calories 327; Fat 6.6 g; Carbohydrates 57 g; Sugar 0.1 g; Protein 26.7 g; Cholesterol 0 mg

Classic Salsa

Preparation Time: 10 minutes; Cooking Time: 2 hours; Serve: 6

Ingredients:
- 3 large tomatoes, chopped
- 1 tbsp vinegar
- 1 garlic clove, minced
- 1 bell pepper, chopped
- 1 small onion, chopped
- 1/4 cup fresh cilantro, chopped
- 1/4 tsp pepper
- 1/2 tsp cumin
- 1 tsp salt

Directions:
1. Add all ingredients into the cooking pot and mix well.
2. Cover instant pot aura with lid.
3. Select slow cook mode and cook on LOW for 2 hours.
4. Stir well and serve.

Nutritional Value (Amount per Serving):
Calories 30; Fat 0.3 g; Carbohydrates 6.5 g; Sugar 3.9 g; Protein 1.2 g; Cholesterol 0 mg

Mexican Dip

Preparation Time: 10 minutes; Cooking Time: 1 hour; Serve: 6

Ingredients:
- 1 cup tomatoes with green chilies
- 8 oz Velveeta cheese, cut into cube
- 1 tsp taco seasoning

Directions:
1. Add cheese into the cooking pot.
2. Select slow cook mode and cook on LOW for 30 minutes. Stir occasionally.
3. Add taco seasoning and tomatoes with green chilies and stir well.
4. Cover instant pot aura with lid.
5. Select slow cook mode and cook on LOW for 30 minutes.
6. Stir well and serve.

Nutritional Value (Amount per Serving):
Calories 176; Fat 11.6 g; Carbohydrates 9.9 g; Sugar 2.7 g; Protein 10.5 g; Cholesterol 36 mg

Chapter 9: Desserts

Delicious Apple Crisp

Preparation Time: 10 minutes; Cooking Time: 3 hours; Serve: 8
Ingredients:
- 2 lbs apples, peeled & sliced
- 1/2 cup butter
- 1/4 tsp ground nutmeg
- 1/2 tsp ground cinnamon
- 2/3 cup brown sugar
- 2/3 cup flour
- 2/3 cup old-fashioned oats

Directions:
1. Add sliced apples into the cooking pot.
2. In a mixing bowl, mix together flour, nutmeg, cinnamon, sugar, and oats.
3. Add butter into the flour mixture and mix until mixture is crumbly.
4. Sprinkle flour mixture over sliced apples.
5. Cover instant pot aura with lid.
6. Select slow cook mode and cook on HIGH for 2-3 hours.
7. Top with vanilla ice-cream and serve.

Nutritional Value (Amount per Serving):
Calories 251; Fat 12.1 g; Carbohydrates 33.5 g; Sugar 11.9 g; Protein 2.1 g; Cholesterol 31 mg

Easy Peach Cobbler Cake

Preparation Time: 10 minutes; Cooking Time: 45 minutes; Serve: 8
Ingredients:
- 3/4 cup butter, cut into pieces
- 1 oz yellow cake mix
- 20 oz can pineapples, crushed
- 21 oz can peach pie filling

Directions:
1. Pour crushed pineapples and peach pie filling into the cooking pot and spread evenly.
2. Sprinkle cake mix on top of pineapple mixture then places butter pieces on top of the cake mix.
3. Cover instant pot aura with lid.
4. Select Bake mode and set the temperature to 350 F and time for 45 minutes.
5. Serve with vanilla ice cream.

Nutritional Value (Amount per Serving):
Calories 175; Fat 2.3 g; Carbohydrates 38.5 g; Sugar 21.1 g; Protein 1.2 g; Cholesterol 0 mg

Strawberry Dump Cake

Preparation Time: 10 minutes; Cooking Time: 40 minutes; Serve: 12
Ingredients:
- 16 oz box cake mix
- 20 oz can pineapple, crushed
- 2 1/2 cups strawberries, frozen, thawed, & sliced

Directions:
1. Add strawberries into the cooking pot and spread evenly.
2. Mix together cake mix and crushed pineapple and pour over sliced strawberries and spread evenly.
3. Cover instant pot aura with lid.
4. Select Bake mode and set the temperature to 350 F and time for 40 minutes.
5. Serve and enjoy.

Nutritional Value (Amount per Serving):
Calories 175; Fat 2.3 g; Carbohydrates 38.5 g; Sugar 21.1 g; Protein 1.2 g; Cholesterol 0 mg

Baked Apples

Preparation Time: 10 minutes; Cooking Time: 30 minutes; Serve: 6

Ingredients:
- 4 apples, sliced
- 1/2 tsp cinnamon
- 1 tbsp butter, melted

Directions:
1. Toss sliced apples with butter and cinnamon and place them into the cooking pot.
2. Cover instant pot aura with lid.
3. Select Bake mode and set the temperature to 375 F and time for 30 minutes.
4. Serve and enjoy.

Nutritional Value (Amount per Serving):
Calories 95; Fat 2.2 g; Carbohydrates 20.7 g; Sugar 15.5 g; Protein 0.4 g; Cholesterol 5 mg

Baked Peaches

Preparation Time: 10 minutes; Cooking Time: 10 minutes; Serve: 6

Ingredients:
- 3 ripe peaches, slice in half & remove the pit
- 1/4 tsp cinnamon
- 2 tbsp brown sugar
- 1 tbsp butter

Directions:
1. Mix together butter, brown sugar, and cinnamon and place in the middle of each peach piece.
2. Place peaches in the cooking pot.
3. Cover instant pot aura with lid.
4. Select Bake mode and set the temperature to 375 F and time for 10 minutes.
5. Serve and enjoy.

Nutritional Value (Amount per Serving):
Calories 58; Fat 2.1 g; Carbohydrates 10 g; Sugar 9.9 g; Protein 0.7 g; Cholesterol 5 mg

Delicious Peach Crisp

Preparation Time: 10 minutes; Cooking Time: 45 minutes; Serve: 8

Ingredients:
- 8 cups can peach, sliced
- 1/2 cup butter, cubed
- 1/2 cup brown sugar
- 1/2 cup all-purpose flour
- 1 1/2 cups rolled oats
- 2 tbsp cornstarch
- 1/2 cup sugar

Directions:
1. Add peaches, cornstarch, and sugar into the cooking pot and stir well.
2. Mix together butter, brown sugar, flour, and oats and sprinkle over peaches.
3. Cover instant pot aura with lid.
4. Select Bake mode and set the temperature to 350 F and time for 30-45 minutes.
5. Serve with ice cream

Nutritional Value (Amount per Serving):
Calories 477; Fat 12.6 g; Carbohydrates 87.6 g; Sugar 67.5 g; Protein 3 g; Cholesterol 31 mg

Gingerbread Pudding Cake

Preparation Time: 10 minutes; Cooking Time: 2 hours 30 minutes; Serve: 6

Ingredients:
- 1 egg
- 1 1/4 cups whole wheat flour
- 1/8 tsp ground nutmeg
- 1/2 tsp ground ginger

- 1/2 tsp ground cinnamon
- 3/4 tsp baking soda
- 1 cup of water
- 1/2 cup molasses
- 1 tsp vanilla
- 1/4 cup sugar
- 1/4 cup butter, softened
- 1/4 tsp salt

Directions:
1. In a bowl, beat sugar and butter until combined. Add egg and beat until combined.
2. Add water, molasses, and vanilla and beat until well combined.
3. Add flour, nutmeg, ginger, cinnamon, baking soda, and salt and stir until combined.
4. Pour batter into the cooking pot.
5. Cover instant pot aura with lid.
6. Select slow cook mode and cook on HIGH for 2 1/2 hours.
7. Serve with vanilla ice-cream.

Nutritional Value (Amount per Serving):
Calories 287; Fat 8.7 g; Carbohydrates 49.1 g; Sugar 23.8 g; Protein 3.7 g; Cholesterol 48 mg

Healthy Blueberry Cobbler

Preparation Time: 10 minutes; Cooking Time: 2 hours 30 minutes; Serve: 6

Ingredients:
- 2 1/4 cups all-purpose flour
- 4 cups blueberries
- 8 tbsp butter, melted
- 1 tsp cinnamon
- 1 tbsp cornstarch
- 3 1/2 tsp baking powder
- 1 1/4 cups sugar
- 1 tsp salt

Directions:
1. Add blueberries into the cooking pot.
2. Mix together flour, cinnamon, cornstarch, baking powder, sugar, and salt and sprinkle over blueberries evenly.
3. Pour melted butter over flour mixture evenly.
4. Cover instant pot aura with lid.
5. Select slow cook mode and cook on LOW for 2 1/2 hours.
6. Serve with vanilla ice-cream.

Nutritional Value (Amount per Serving):
Calories 527; Fat 16.2 g; Carbohydrates 94.3 g; Sugar 51.4 g; Protein 5.8 g; Cholesterol 41 mg

Easy Peach Cobbler

Preparation Time: 10 minutes; Cooking Time: 3 hours; Serve: 6

Ingredients:
- 1/2 cup butter, cut into pieces
- 1 box cake mix
- 30 oz can sliced peaches in syrup

Directions:
1. Add sliced peaches with syrup into the cooking pot.
2. Sprinkle cake mix on top of sliced peaches.
3. Spread butter pieces on top of the cake mix.
4. Cover instant pot aura with lid.
5. Select slow cook mode and cook on HIGH for 3 hours.
6. Serve with vanilla ice-cream.

Nutritional Value (Amount per Serving):
Calories 601; Fat 24.9 g; Carbohydrates 87.9 g; Sugar 66.2 g; Protein 5.3 g; Cholesterol 41 mg

Peach Compote

Preparation Time: 10 minutes; Cooking Time: 2 hours; Serve: 8

Ingredients:
- 8 ripe peaches, peeled & sliced
- 1 tsp vanilla
- 1 tsp cinnamon
- 1/4 cup butter, cut into pieces
- 1/2 cup brown sugar
- 1/2 cup sugar

Directions:
1. Add peaches, vanilla, cinnamon, brown sugar, and sugar into the cooking pot and stir well.
2. Spread butter pieces on top of the peach mixture.
3. Cover instant pot aura with lid.
4. Select slow cook mode and cook on LOW for 2 hours.
5. Serve with vanilla ice-cream.

Nutritional Value (Amount per Serving):
Calories 193; Fat 6.2 g; Carbohydrates 35.7 g; Sugar 35.4 g; Protein 1.5 g; Cholesterol 15 mg

Cinnamon Apples

Preparation Time: 10 minutes; Cooking Time: 2 hours; Serve: 5

Ingredients:
- 5 apples, peeled and sliced
- 1 1/4 tsp ground cinnamon
- 1 tbsp cornstarch
- 2 tbsp maple syrup
- 2/3 cup apple cider

Directions:
1. In a bowl, mix together apple cider, cinnamon, cornstarch, maple syrup, and 1/4 cup water.
2. Add apples into the cooking pot the pour apple cider mixture over apples.
3. Cover instant pot aura with lid.
4. Select slow cook mode and cook on LOW for 2 hours. Stir after 1 hour.
5. Stir well and serve.

Nutritional Value (Amount per Serving):
Calories 160; Fat 0.5 g; Carbohydrates 42 g; Sugar 31.6 g; Protein 0.6 g; Cholesterol 0 mg

Choco Rice Pudding

Preparation Time: 10 minutes; Cooking Time: 2 hours 30 minutes; Serve: 8

Ingredients:
- 2 cups sticky rice, rinsed & drained
- 1/2 cup chocolate chips
- 1/2 cup brown sugar
- 14 oz coconut milk
- 12 oz can evaporate milk
- 3 cups of water
- 1/2 cup cocoa powder

Directions:
1. Add rice, water, and cocoa powder into the cooking pot and stir well.
2. Cover instant pot aura with lid.
3. Select slow cook mode and cook on HIGH for 2 hours.
4. Add remaining ingredients and stir everything well, cover, and cook for 30 minutes more.
5. Serve and enjoy.

Nutritional Value (Amount per Serving):
Calories 327; Fat 19.4 g; Carbohydrates 36.4 g; Sugar 16 g; Protein 6.7 g; Cholesterol 15 mg

Chocolate Fudge

Preparation Time: 10 minutes; Cooking Time: 1 hour; Serve: 30

Ingredients:
- 3 cups chocolate chips
- 1 tbsp butter

- 1 tsp vanilla
- 14 oz sweetened condensed milk

Directions:
1. Add all ingredients into the cooking pot and stir well.
2. Select slow cook mode and cook on LOW for 1 hour. Stir after every 15 minutes.
3. Once done pour into the greased tin. Place in the fridge for 2 hours or until set.
4. Cut into pieces and serve.

Nutritional Value (Amount per Serving):
Calories 136; Fat 6.5 g; Carbohydrates 17.2 g; Sugar 15.9 g; Protein 2.3 g; Cholesterol 9 mg

Chocolate Brownies

Preparation Time: 10 minutes; Cooking Time: 2 hours 30 minutes; Serve: 8
Ingredients:
- 3 eggs
- 1 cup butter, melted
- 1 cup peanut butter chips
- 1 tsp vanilla
- 1/3 cup all-purpose flour
- 2/3 cup unsweetened cocoa powder
- 1/3 cup brown sugar
- 1 1/4 cup sugar
- 1/2 tsp salt

Directions:
1. Line instant pot aura cooking pot with parchment paper.
2. In a mixing bowl, beat butter, sugar, brown sugar, cocoa powder, flour, eggs, vanilla, and salt until smooth.
3. Add peanut butter chips in the batter and fold well.
4. Pour batter into the cooking pot.
5. Cover instant pot aura with lid.
6. Select slow cook mode and cook on LOW for 2 1/2 hours.
7. Slice and serve.

Nutritional Value (Amount per Serving):
Calories 544; Fat 33.7 g; Carbohydrates 63.3 g; Sugar 55.5 g; Protein 4.3 g; Cholesterol 122 mg

Tasty Cherry Cobbler

Preparation Time: 10 minutes; Cooking Time: 2 hours; Serve: 6
Ingredients:
- 1/2 cup butter, cut into pieces
- 1 box cake mix
- 30 oz can cherry pie filling

Directions:
1. Add cherry pie filling into the cooking pot then sprinkle cake mix over cherry pie filling evenly.
2. Spread butter pieces on top of the cake mix.
3. Cover instant pot aura with lid.
4. Select slow cook mode and cook on HIGH for 2 hours.
5. Serve and enjoy.

Nutritional Value (Amount per Serving):
Calories 671; Fat 25 g; Carbohydrates 107.8 g; Sugar 47.6 g; Protein 4.6 g; Cholesterol 41 mg

Pineapple Cherry Dump Cake

Preparation Time: 10 minutes; Cooking Time: 3 hours; Serve: 6
Ingredients:
- 15 oz can pineapple, crushed
- 3/4 cup pecans, chopped
- 1 1/2 stick butter, cubed
- 1 box cake mix
- 15 oz can cherry pie filling

Directions:
1. Add cherry pie filling and crushed pineapple into the cooking pot and stir well.
2. Sprinkle cake mix over cherry pie filling mixture evenly.
3. Spread butter pieces and pecans on top of cake mix.
4. Cover instant pot aura with lid.
5. Select slow cook mode and cook on HIGH for 3 hours.
6. Serve and enjoy.

Nutritional Value (Amount per Serving):
Calories 794; Fat 42.7 g; Carbohydrates 99.5 g; Sugar 55.2 g; Protein 6.2 g; Cholesterol 61 mg

White Chocolate Fudge

Preparation Time: 10 minutes; Cooking Time: 1 hour; Serve: 12
Ingredients:
- 2 cups white chocolate, chopped
- 1/2 cup white chocolate chips
- 1/4 cup heavy whipping cream
- 1/3 cup honey
- 1 tsp vanilla

Directions:
1. Add honey, heavy whipping cream, and white chocolate into the cooking pot and stir well.
2. Cover instant pot aura with lid.
3. Select slow cook mode and cook on HIGH for 1 hour.
4. Add white chocolate chips to the cooking pot and stir until white chocolate melts. Stir in vanilla.
5. Pour melted chocolate into the parchment-lined baking dish and place it in the fridge until set.
6. Cut into squares and serve.

Nutritional Value (Amount per Serving):
Calories 229; Fat 12.3 g; Carbohydrates 28.8 g; Sugar 28.7 g; Protein 2.2 g; Cholesterol 11 mg

Applesauce

Preparation Time: 10 minutes; Cooking Time: 8 hours; Serve: 6
Ingredients:
- 10 medium apples, peeled, cored and sliced
- 1/4 cup sugar
- 1/4 cup water
- 1 tsp ground cinnamon

Directions:
1. Add all ingredients into the cooking pot and stir well.
2. Cover instant pot aura with lid.
3. Select slow cook mode and cook on LOW for 8 hours.
4. Transfer apple mixture into the blender and blend until smooth.
5. Serve and enjoy.

Nutritional Value (Amount per Serving):
Calories 226; Fat 0.7 g; Carbohydrates 60 g; Sugar 47 g; Protein 1 g; Cholesterol 0 mg

Delicious Bread Pudding

Preparation Time: 10 minutes; Cooking Time: 4 hours; Serve: 8
Ingredients:
- 5 eggs
- 8 cups of bread cubes
- 1 tbsp vanilla
- 4 cups of milk
- 3/4 cup maple syrup
- 1 tbsp cinnamon

Directions:

1. In a large bowl, whisk together eggs, sugar, cinnamon, vanilla, and milk.
2. Add bread cubes into the cooking pot.
3. Pour egg mixture on top of bread cubes and let sit for 15 minutes.
4. Cover instant pot aura with lid.
5. Select slow cook mode and cook on LOW for 4 hours.
6. Serve and enjoy.

Nutritional Value (Amount per Serving):
Calories 254; Fat 9.3 g; Carbohydrates 32.9 g; Sugar 23.5 g; Protein 10.5 g; Cholesterol 122 mg

Rice Pudding

Preparation Time: 10 minutes; Cooking Time: 4 hours; Serve: 6
Ingredients:
- 3/4 cup long-grain rice
- 3/4 cup sugar
- 3 cups of milk
- 1/2 tsp cinnamon
- 1 tsp vanilla
- 2 tbsp butter
- 1/4 tsp salt

Directions:
1. Add all ingredients into the cooking pot and stir well.
2. Cover instant pot aura with lid.
3. Select slow cook mode and cook on LOW for 4 hours.
4. Stir well and serve.

Nutritional Value (Amount per Serving):
Calories 276; Fat 6.5 g; Carbohydrates 49.7 g; Sugar 30.6 g; Protein 5.7 g; Cholesterol 49.7 mg

Tapioca Pudding

Preparation Time: 10 minutes; Cooking Time: 4 hours; Serve: 4
Ingredients:
- 1 egg, beaten
- 4 cups of milk
- 1/2 cup sugar
- 1 tsp vanilla
- 1/2 cup tapioca pearls
- 1/8 tsp salt

Directions:
1. Add all ingredients into the cooking pot and stir well.
2. Cover instant pot aura with lid.
3. Select slow cook mode and cook on LOW for 4 hours.
4. Stir well and serve.

Nutritional Value (Amount per Serving):
Calories 280; Fat 6.1 g; Carbohydrates 48.5 g; Sugar 36.2 g; Protein 9.4 g; Cholesterol 61 mg

Pecan Caramel Rice Pudding

Preparation Time: 10 minutes; Cooking Time: 4 hours; Serve: 8
Ingredients:
- 3/4 cup white rice, long grain
- 1 cup caramel sauce
- 1 cup pecans, toasted and chopped
- 3 tbsp butter, cut into cubes
- 1 tsp vanilla
- 3 cups of milk
- 1/2 tsp salt

Directions:
1. Add rice, milk, and caramel sauce into the cooking pot and stir well to combine.
2. Cover instant pot aura with lid.
3. Select slow cook mode and cook on LOW for 4 hours.
4. Stir in vanilla, butter, and salt.

5. Top with pecans and serve.

Nutritional Value (Amount per Serving):
Calories 322; Fat 13.5 g; Carbohydrates 46.9 g; Sugar 4.6 g; Protein 6 g; Cholesterol 19 mg

Pineapple Tapioca

Preparation Time: 10 minutes; Cooking Time: 3 hours; Serve: 6

Ingredients:
- 15 oz can pineapple, crushed and undrained
- 2 1/2 cups pineapple juice
- 2 1/2 cups water
- 3/4 cup sugar
- 1/2 cup tapioca pearl

Directions:
1. Add all ingredients except pineapple into the cooking pot and stir well.
2. Cover instant pot aura with lid.
3. Select slow cook mode and cook on HIGH for 3 hours.
4. Stir in pineapple.
5. Serve chilled and enjoy.

Nutritional Value (Amount per Serving):
Calories 237; Fat 0.2 g; Carbohydrates 60.8 g; Sugar 46.1 g; Protein 0.7 g; Cholesterol 0 mg

Brown Rice Pudding

Preparation Time: 10 minutes; Cooking Time: 4 hours; Serve: 6

Ingredients:
- 2 cups brown rice
- 5 cups of milk
- 1 cinnamon stick
- 3 tbsp chia seeds
- 1/2 cup raisins

Directions:
1. Add all ingredients into the cooking pot and stir well.
2. Cover instant pot aura with lid.
3. Select slow cook mode and cook on LOW for 4 hours.
4. Stir well and serve.

Nutritional Value (Amount per Serving):
Calories 380; Fat 6.7 g; Carbohydrates 69.2 g; Sugar 16.3 g; Protein 12.2 g; Cholesterol 17 mg

Coconut Rice Pudding

Preparation Time: 10 minutes; Cooking Time: 4 hours; Serve: 8

Ingredients:
- 2/3 cup brown rice
- 14 oz coconut milk
- 1/4 cup coconut palm sugar
- 1 tsp cinnamon
- 1 tsp vanilla extract
- 2/3 cup raisins
- 1 2/3 cup almond milk

Directions:
1. Add all ingredients except raisins and vanilla into the cooking pot and stir well.
2. Cover instant pot aura with lid.
3. Select slow cook mode and cook on LOW for 4 hours.
4. Add raisins and vanilla and stir well.
5. Serve warm and enjoy.

Nutritional Value (Amount per Serving):
Calories 347; Fat 24.7 g; Carbohydrates 33.4 g; Sugar 15.1 g; Protein 3.9 g; Cholesterol 0 mg

Chia Strawberry Jam

Preparation Time: 10 minutes; Cooking Time: 2 hours; Serve: 6

Ingredients:
- 1 lb strawberries, sliced
- 2 tsp chia seeds
- 1/4 tsp lemon juice
- 3 dates, pitted and chopped
- 1/4 cup fresh basil, chopped

Directions:
1. Add all ingredients into the cooking pot and stir well.
2. Cover instant pot aura with lid.
3. Select slow cook mode and cook on LOW for 2 hours.
4. Transfer strawberry mixture into the blender and blend until get the desired consistency.
5. Serve and enjoy.

Nutritional Value (Amount per Serving):
Calories 52; Fat 1.3 g; Carbohydrates 10.4 g; Sugar 6.3 g; Protein 1.2 g; Cholesterol 0 mg

Maple Pears

Preparation Time: 10 minutes; Cooking Time: 4 hours; Serve: 4

Ingredients:
- 4 ripe pears, peel, core, and cut the bottom
- 1/4 cup maple syrup
- 2 cups orange juice
- 1 tbsp ginger, sliced
- 1 cinnamon stick
- 5 cardamom pods

Directions:
1. Place pears into the cooking pot.
2. Mix together the remaining ingredients and pour over pears into the cooking pot.
3. Cover instant pot aura with lid.
4. Select slow cook mode and cook on LOW for 4 hours.
5. Serve warm and enjoy.

Nutritional Value (Amount per Serving):
Calories 242; Fat 0.8 g; Carbohydrates 61.1 g; Sugar 42.6 g; Protein 2 g; Cholesterol 0 mg

Cinnamon Coconut Rice Pudding

Preparation Time: 10 minutes; Cooking Time: 6 hours; Serve: 8

Ingredients:
- 1 cup rice, rinsed and uncooked
- 4 cups of coconut milk
- 2 cups coconut cream
- 1 tsp ground cinnamon
- 1 tsp vanilla

Directions:
1. Add all ingredients into the cooking pot and stir well.
2. Cover instant pot aura with lid.
3. Select slow cook mode and cook on LOW for 6 hours.
4. Stir well and serve.

Nutritional Value (Amount per Serving):
Calories 501; Fat 43.1 g; Carbohydrates 28.8 g; Sugar 6.1 g; Protein 5.8 g; Cholesterol 0 mg

Fruit Compote

Preparation Time: 10 minutes; Cooking Time: 6 hours; Serve: 8

Ingredients:
- 10 Cherries
- 4 tbsp raisins
- 10 oz plums, dried
- 10 oz apricots, dried

- 30 oz can peach, un-drained and sliced
- 10 oz can oranges, un-drained

Directions:
1. Add all ingredients into the cooking pot and stir well.
2. Cover instant pot aura with lid.
3. Select slow cook mode and cook on LOW for 6 hours.
4. Stir well and serve.

Nutritional Value (Amount per Serving):
Calories 254; Fat 0.7 g; Carbohydrates 64.3 g; Sugar 28.7 g; Protein 2.5 g; Cholesterol 0 mg

Pumpkin Pie Pudding

Preparation Time: 10 minutes; Cooking Time: 6 hours; Serve: 8

Ingredients:
- 2 eggs, beaten
- 2 tbsp butter, melted
- 1/2 cup biscuit mix
- 3/4 cup sugar
- 12 oz milk
- 15 oz can pumpkin
- 1 1/2 tsp vanilla extract
- 2 tsp pumpkin pie spice

Directions:
1. Add all ingredients into the cooking pot and mix well.
2. Cover instant pot aura with lid.
3. Select slow cook mode and cook on LOW for 6 hours.
4. Serve with ice-cream and enjoy it.

Nutritional Value (Amount per Serving):
Calories 185; Fat 6.1 g; Carbohydrates 30.1 g; Sugar 23.5 g; Protein 4 g; Cholesterol 52 mg

Chocolate Almond Fudge

Preparation Time: 10 minutes; Cooking Time: 6 hours; Serve: 30

Ingredients:
- 8 oz chocolate chips
- 1/2 cup milk
- 2 tbsp almonds, sliced
- 2 tbsp swerve
- 1 tbsp butter, melted

Directions:
1. Add chocolate chips, milk, butter, and swerve into the cooking pot and stir well.
2. Cover instant pot aura with lid.
3. Select slow cook mode and cook on LOW for 2 hours.
4. Add almonds and stir fudge until smooth.
5. Pour fudge mixture into the greased baking dish and spread evenly.
6. Place baking dish in the refrigerator until the fudge set.
7. Cut into squares and serve.

Nutritional Value (Amount per Serving):
Calories 49; Fat 2.9 g; Carbohydrates 4.9 g; Sugar 4.1 g; Protein 0.8 g; Cholesterol 3 mg

Delicious Chocolate Cake

Preparation Time: 10 minutes; Cooking Time: 2 hours 30 minutes; Serve: 10

Ingredients:
- 3 large eggs
- 1 ½ tsp baking powder
- 3 tbsp whey protein powder
- 1/2 cup cocoa powder
- 1/2 tsp vanilla
- 2/3 cup almond milk
- 6 tbsp butter, melted
- 1/2 cup Swerve
- 1 cup almond flour
- Pinch of salt

Directions:

1. Line instant pot aura cooking pot with parchment paper.
2. In a mixing bowl, whisk together almond flour, baking powder, protein powder, cocoa powder, swerve, and salt.
3. Stir in eggs, vanilla, almond milk, and butter until well combined.
4. Cover instant pot aura with lid.
5. Select slow cook mode and cook on LOW for 2 1/2 hours.
6. Serve and enjoy.

Nutritional Value (Amount per Serving):
Calories 166; Fat 18.9 g; Carbohydrates 7.4 g; Sugar 1.5 g; Protein 12.2 g; Cholesterol 93 mg

Fudge Brownies

Preparation Time: 10 minutes; Cooking Time: 3 hours; Serve: 12

Ingredients:
- 2 large eggs
- 1 cup of sugar
- 10 oz chocolate chips
- 1/2 cup butter
- 1/4 tsp ground cinnamon
- 1 cup flour
- 1 tsp vanilla
- Pinch of salt

Directions:
1. Melt chocolate chips and butter in a small saucepan over low heat. Stir until smooth and remove the saucepan from heat.
2. Stir in sugar and eggs, mix until well combined.
3. Add vanilla and salt. Add cinnamon and flour and mix until well combined.
4. Add remaining chocolate chips and fold well.
5. Line instant pot aura cooking pot with parchment paper.
6. Pour batter into the cooking pot.
7. Cover instant pot aura with lid.
8. Select slow cook mode and cook on LOW for 3 hours.
9. Let it cool completely. Slice and serve.

Nutritional Value (Amount per Serving):
Calories 308; Fat 15.6 g; Carbohydrates 38.8 g; Sugar 29 g; Protein 4 g; Cholesterol 57 mg

Hot Chocolate

Preparation Time: 10 minutes; Cooking Time: 2 hours; Serve: 6

Ingredients:
- 2 cups chocolate chips
- 6 cups of milk
- 1 tsp vanilla
- 14 oz condensed milk
- 1 1/2 cups whipping cream

Directions:
1. Add all ingredients into the cooking pot and stir well.
2. Cover instant pot aura with lid.
3. Select slow cook mode and cook on LOW for 2 hours.
4. Stir well and serve.

Nutritional Value (Amount per Serving):
Calories 724; Fat 36.6 g; Carbohydrates 82.2 g; Sugar 76 g; Protein 18.2 g; Cholesterol 89 mg

Apple Walnut Cake

Preparation Time: 10 minutes; Cooking Time: 4 hours; Serve: 10

Ingredients:
- 18 oz yellow cake mix
- 21 oz can apple pie filling
- 1/3 cup walnuts, chopped
- 1/2 cup butter, melted

Directions:
1. Place apple pie filling into the Crockpot.
2. In a bowl, mix together butter and cake mix and spoon over apple pie filling. Top with walnuts.
3. Cover instant pot aura with lid.
4. Select slow cook mode and cook on LOW for 4 hours.
5. Serve and enjoy.

Nutritional Value (Amount per Serving):
Calories 387; Fat 17.7 g; Carbohydrates 55.8 g; Sugar 30.4 g; Protein 3.4 g; Cholesterol 25 mg

Walnut Peanut Butter Cake

Preparation Time: 10 minutes; Cooking Time: 2 hours 30 minutes; Serve: 10
Ingredients:
- 2 eggs
- 1/2 cup water
- 2 cups chocolate cake mix
- 1/2 cup walnuts, chopped
- 6 tbsp peanut butter

Directions:
1. Add all ingredients into the large bowl and beat for 2 minutes.
2. Line instant pot aura cooking pot with parchment paper.
3. Pour batter into the cooking pot.
4. Cover instant pot aura with lid.
5. Select slow cook mode and cook on HIGH for 2 1/2 hours.
6. Cut into pieces and serve.

Nutritional Value (Amount per Serving):
Calories 236; Fat 14.1 g; Carbohydrates 24.5 g; Sugar 12.5 g; Protein 6.8 g; Cholesterol 33 mg

Butter Cake

Preparation Time: 10 minutes; Cooking Time: 30 minutes; Serve: 8
Ingredients:
- 1 egg, beaten
- 1 cup all-purpose flour
- 1/2 tsp vanilla extract
- 3/4 cup sugar
- 1/2 cup butter, softened

Directions:
1. Line instant pot aura cooking pot with parchment paper.
2. In a mixing bowl, mix together sugar and butter.
3. Add egg, flour, and vanilla and mix until combined.
4. Pour batter into the cooking pot.
5. Cover instant pot aura with lid.
6. Select bake mode then set the temperature to 350 F and timer for 30 minutes.
7. Slice and serve.

Nutritional Value (Amount per Serving):
Calories 238; Fat 12.2 g; Carbohydrates 30.8 g; Sugar 18.9 g; Protein 2.4 g; Cholesterol 51 mg

Cocoa Almond Butter Brownies

Preparation Time: 10 minutes; Cooking Time: 20 minutes; Serve: 4
Ingredients:
- 1/2 cup almond butter, melted
- 1 cup bananas, overripe
- 1 scoop protein powder
- 2 tbsp cocoa powder

Directions:
1. Line instant pot aura cooking pot with parchment paper.

2. Add all ingredients into the blender and blend until smooth.
3. Pour batter into the cooking pot.
4. Cover instant pot aura with lid.
5. Select bake mode then set the temperature to 350 F and timer for 20 minutes.
6. Slice and serve.

Nutritional Value (Amount per Serving):
Calories 82; Fat 2.1 g; Carbohydrates 11.4 g; Sugar 5 g; Protein 6.9 g; Cholesterol 16 mg

Banana Brownies

Preparation Time: 10 minutes; Cooking Time: 20 minutes; Serve: 12
Ingredients:
- 1 egg
- 2 bananas, mashed
- 1 tsp vanilla
- 1/2 cup sugar
- 4 oz white chocolate
- 1 cup all-purpose flour
- 1/4 cup butter
- 1/4 tsp salt

Directions:
1. Line instant pot aura cooking pot with parchment paper.
2. Add butter and white chocolate in a microwave-safe bowl and microwave for 30 seconds. Stir until melted.
3. Stir in sugar. Add mashed bananas, eggs, vanilla, and salt and mix until combined. Add flour and stir to combine.
4. Pour batter into the cooking pot.
5. Cover instant pot aura with lid.
6. Select bake mode then set the temperature to 350 F and timer for 20 minutes.
7. Slice and serve.

Nutritional Value (Amount per Serving):
Calories 178; Fat 7.4 g; Carbohydrates 26.4 g; Sugar 16.4 g; Protein 2.3 g; Cholesterol 26 mg

Moist Yogurt Cake

Preparation Time: 10 minutes; Cooking Time: 35 minutes; Serve: 12
Ingredients:
- 2 eggs
- 7 oz all-purpose flour
- 2 tsp baking powder
- 8.5 oz yogurt
- 4 tbsp oil
- 7 oz sugar

Directions:
1. Line instant pot aura cooking pot with parchment paper.
2. In a large bowl, add yogurt, oil, eggs, sugar, flour, and baking powder and mix until smooth.
3. Pour batter into the cooking pot.
4. Cover instant pot aura with lid.
5. Select bake mode then set the temperature to 350 F and timer for 35 minutes.
6. Slice and serve.

Nutritional Value (Amount per Serving):
Calories 188; Fat 5.7 g; Carbohydrates 31 g; Sugar 18.1 g; Protein 3.8 g; Cholesterol 28 mg

Chapter 10: 30-Day Meal Plan

Day 1
Breakfast-Perfect Cranberry Eggnog Oatmeal
Lunch- Rosemary Turkey Breast
Dinner- Salsa Pork Chops
Day 2
Breakfast- Broccoli Ham Casserole
Lunch- Capers Salmon
Dinner- Moroccan Lamb
Day 3
Breakfast- Easy Brown Sugar Oatmeal
Lunch- Pesto Chicken
Dinner- Cheesy Cauliflower Casserole
Day 4
Breakfast- Perfect Breakfast Potatoes
Lunch- Spicy Chili Chicken
Dinner-Asian Lamb
Day 5
Breakfast- Healthy Strawberry Oatmeal
Lunch- Vegetable Farro
Dinner- Mushroom Beef Tips
Day 6
Breakfast- Delicious Breakfast Burrito
Lunch- Rich & Creamy Mac and Cheese
Dinner-Teriyaki Steak
Day 7
Breakfast- Pumpkin Pie Oatmeal
Lunch- Broccoli Rice Casserole
Dinner- Simple Chicken & Mushrooms
Day 8
Breakfast- Apple Cranberry Oatmeal
Lunch- Slow Cook Turkey Breast
Dinner- Garlic Beef Shanks
Day 9
Breakfast- Cinnamon Roll Casserole
Lunch- Cauliflower Lentil Sweet Potato Curry
Dinner- Beef Noodles
Day 10
Breakfast- Apple Cinnamon Steel Cut Oatmeal
Lunch- Garlic Herb Roasted Pepper Chicken
Dinner- Shrimp Pasta
Day 11
Breakfast- Cranberry Apple French Toast
Lunch- Quinoa Coconut Curry
Dinner- Chicken Orzo
Day 12
Breakfast- Hearty Pumpkin Spice Oatmeal
Lunch- Flavorful Chicken Casserole
Dinner- Flavorful Sausage Casserole
Day 13
Breakfast- Hash Brown Breakfast Casserole
Lunch- Easy Vegan Gumbo
Dinner- Delicious Beef Fajitas
Day 14
Breakfast- Healthy Banana Nut Oatmeal
Lunch- Asian Chicken
Dinner- Healthy Lime Salmon
Day 15
Breakfast- Steel Cut Peach Oatmeal
Lunch- Moist & Juicy Chicken Breast
Dinner- Pork Chops with Potatoes
Day 16
Breakfast- Healthy Apple Pie Amaranth Porridge
Lunch- Tasty Chicken Fajita Pasta
Dinner- Spicy Shrimp
Day 17
Breakfast- Breakfast Tater Tot Egg Bake
Lunch- Creamy Chicken Penne

Dinner- Lentil Chickpea Pumpkin Curry
Day 18
Breakfast- Cauliflower Hash Browns Casserole
Lunch- Healthy Split Pea Curry
Dinner- Balsamic Chicken
Day 19
Breakfast- Carrot Cake Oatmeal
Lunch- Cajun Corn Shrimp
Dinner- Herb Chicken Breasts
Day 20
Breakfast- Peach Breakfast Oatmeal
Lunch- Asian Vegetarian Tikka Masala
Dinner- Mustard Mushroom Chicken
Day 21
Breakfast- Cheesy Potatoes
Lunch- Louisiana Shrimp
Dinner- Easy Mexican Chicken
Day 22
Breakfast- Breakfast Bread Pudding
Lunch- Parmesan Chicken Rice
Dinner- Sweet Applesauce Pork Chops
Day 23
Breakfast- Rice Raisins Pudding
Lunch- Delicious Thai Pineapple Curry
Dinner- Orange Chicken
Day 24
Breakfast- Healthy Whole Grain Porridge

Lunch- Coconut Fish Curry
Dinner- Asian Pork Chops
Day 25
Breakfast- Sweet Berry Oatmeal
Lunch- Easy Chicken Noodles
Dinner- Delicious Sweet Pork Roast
Day 26
Breakfast- Flavorful Millet Porridge
Lunch- White Fish Fillet with Tomatoes
Dinner- Onion Pork Chops
Day 27
Breakfast- Cinnamon Apple Barley
Lunch- Greek Lemon Chicken
Dinner- Creamy Pork Chops
Day 28
Breakfast- Feta Spinach Quiche
Lunch- Herb Lemon Cod
Dinner- Easy Salsa Chicken
Day 29
Breakfast- Healthy Breakfast Casserole
Lunch- Flavors Peanut Butter Chicken
Dinner- Caribbean Shrimp
Day 30
Breakfast- Spinach Pepper Omelet
Lunch- Thai Shrimp Rice
Dinner- Mediterranean Pork Chops

Conclusion

In this cookbook, we have used one of the advanced cooking appliances known as Instant pot Aura multi-cooker. It runs on advanced microprocessor technology. It is one of the smart cooking appliances full fill your daily cooking needs. Instant pot Aura is not a pressure cooker it uses as a slow cooker and also used as a multi-cooker. It performs different appliance operations in a single pot like it bakes your favorite cake and cookies, roast your favorite chicken, steam rice and multigrain, sauté food, make yogurt, and reheat your food. Slow cooking is one of the healthiest methods of cooking delicious and tasty food.

The book contains different types of healthy, nutritious, and delicious recipes from breakfast to desserts. All the recipes written in this book are unique and well tasted in instant pot aura multi-cooker. The recipes are written in a simple and easily understandable form. All the recipes are given its exact preparation and cooking time, at the end of each recipe exact nutritional values are given.

Printed in Great Britain
by Amazon